SERIOUS PLAY

Creativity and Innovation in Social Work

SERIOUS PLAY

Creativity and Innovation in Social Work

Harold H. Weissman, Editor/Senior Author

National Association of Social Workers, Inc., Silver Spring, MD 20910

Richard L. Edwards, ACSW, *President*
Mark G. Battle, ACSW, *Executive Director*

Library of Congress Cataloging-in-Publication Data

Serious play.

"Developed out of two conferences on innovation sponsored by the doctoral program of Hunter College School of Social Work."—Pref.
Includes index.
1. Social service—United States. 2. Creative ability. I. Weissman, Harold H. II. Hunter College. School of Social Work. III. Title: Creativity and innovation in social work. IV. Title: Innovation in social work.
HV91.S35 1990   361.3'2   89-35206
ISBN 0-87101-171-9

Printed in the United States of America

Cover and interior design by Michael David Brown, Inc.

3

To
Judith Weissman
and
Michael Weissman
age 3
Our Most Creative Endeavor

Mother: Michael can count, but I don't think he understands the concept of numbers.

Father: Oh, that's easy to teach.

Father: Michael, would you rather have two ice cream cones, or one ice cream cone?

Michael: Two ice cream cones.

Father: Would you rather have three ice cream cones or two ice cream cones?

Michael: Two ice cream cones.

Father: Michael, are you sure you would rather have two ice cream cones than three ice cream cones?

Michael: Yeah, you can only hold two ice cream cones.

Contents

Preface

This book developed from two conferences on innovation sponsored by the Doctoral Program of the Hunter College School of Social Work. Originally, our idea was to publish a set of proceedings, but as the planning committee mulled over the material the focus of interest shifted from substantive innovations to the process of innovation itself.

Why did this shift occur? It occurred because, as the only one who read all of the articles, I felt that some of the innovations reported on were not as interesting or important to the field as the processes through which these innovations evolved. Since I had to do most of the work, the others on the committee acquiesced to my view and to the recruitment of additional papers.

Although it is symbolically apt for a book on innovation to undergo a process of innovation, the book will have to be judged on its merits. Change in and of itself is no virtue, as is noted in the text.

I take full responsibility for any limitations. This is more than the ritual obeisance of a scholar. The idea for the book was what might be called a bright idea. The bright idea is often only a Roman candle—beautiful to behold for a short time but soon lost in darkness. Like so many inventions of the mind, the mirrored reality is much more complex.

To keep this idea from being lost in darkness, I had to read what others in many different fields had said and thought about creativity and innovation. I learned that I only had limited knowledge of the subject. Some of the authors of the chapters in this volume wanted more direction than I could offer at the time they were writing. I am sorry that I could not accommodate them but I hope the end product will compensate for some of the frustration.

Without the drafts of the chapters and the background reading I could not outline the book. Until I outlined the book, I could not formulate my thoughts about innovation and creativity. And unless I clearly formulated my thoughts, I could not subject them to criticism.

This is a rather long way of saying that writing and editing this book was not easy. It was not even always enjoyable. However, I am pleased that I did it and I am pleased with the result. In the end, an old truth emerges (perhaps one that I wished to hide from myself) that the ability to work hard and persevere is in the long run an absolute necessity if short-term bursts of ideas are to come to anything.

That aside, I do want to thank first, Mildred Mailick for reminding me that I had made a commitment to the junior faculty at Hunter College to publish the proceedings of the first conference. Without this gentle reminder, I never would have persisted. Second, my thanks to Dean Harold Lewis for urging me to accept the Chair of the doctoral program. If there had been no chair, there would have been no conferences, and no book!

Irwin Epstein provided a useful critique of an earlier draft of this volume. As always, his counsel was stimulating.

June Penkus typed the manuscript and offered quiet assurance that lost chapters would be found. For finding them and for the reassurance, thanks.

Particular thanks is owed to Bertram Beck for a stimulating critique of a second draft of the book and for serving for many years as a role model for me on how to be creative.

Last, I think anyone who reads this volume cannot help being impressed with the range and scope of ideas expressed in the chapters. For this I want to publicly express my gratitude to the authors. Without their effort and support there would be no book.

HAROLD H. WEISSMAN

Introduction

Innovation, in and of itself, is not necessarily worthwhile. In social welfare, the undifferentiated alms house, separation of services, and the deinstitutionalization of mental patients were dramatic innovations that created as many problems as they solved.

It is peculiarly American to equate change with progress. In the Middle Ages, a theologian put forward a more reasoned approach that if it was not necessary to change, it was necessary not to change. Yet this approach—conservative in the best sense of the word—really never took hold in America. Here, reform was both the creature and the creator of waves of social energy. Social workers have been both riding and helping to create these waves of reform for more than 100 years. Usually, as the waves crested, institutions and programs were created and left in their wake: for example, social settlements, social security, and Head Start.

Yet, these institutions or programs generally require stability. They need priests as well as prophets. Although this book focuses on the importance of innovation and creativity for social work, the importance of competence and craftsmanship—dependability and skill—should not be downplayed. Anyone who ever has needed help, whether it simply be directions to the next town or assistance in placing an aged parent in a nursing home, knows the value of finding a competent person. However, anyone who is faced with a "flooded out" road or a three-year waiting list for entry into a nursing home knows the value of finding a *creative* person.

Competence and creativity are viewed best as a continuum (Adams, 1976, p. 125). The goal of this book is to suggest how the individual social worker can keep from being stifled, and foster his or her movement towards the creative end of the continuum—where creativity complements competence.

The book also explains how such variables as agency structure, professional values, social climate, intellectual traditions, and cultural beliefs support, channel, or constrain individual creativity. The most well-developed trees will not bear fruit if environmental conditions are not right. Likewise, human creativity can be stifled by outside forces.

Improving one's creative capacity is not an easy task, as Edwards (1987) noted. After an exhaustive review of the literature in the field, she stated,

Creativity has been studied, analyzed, dissected, documented. Educators discuss the concept as if it were a tangible thing, a goal to be attained like the ability to divide numbers or play the violin, or golf. Cognitive scientists, fascinated by creativity, have produced volumes of bits and pieces, offering tantalizing glimpses and hints, but have not put the parts together into an understandable whole. To date we still have no generally accepted definition of creativity—no general agreement on what it is, how to teach it, or if, indeed, it can be learned or taught. (p. 2)

However, a set of heuristics, or guides, for understanding the creative process is available. Drawing on some of these guides, creative thinking is viewed here as a particular approach to identifying and solving problems. This approach is affected by a mix of personal traits and abilities. It involves both logical and nonlogical thought processes. There is no proof that "practice makes perfect" when thinking creatively. However, there is some validity to the view that working at creativity does not hurt. In fact, it may be quite valuable (Edwards, 1987, p. 31).[1]

The crucial issue is how and what should be practiced in developing creative ability. In subsequent chapters, a number of suggestions are presented. They represent an amalgam of the ideas of many authors. This book provides an original strategy for deploying these ideas, based on the view that creativity and competence represent a continuum of professional practice. The strategy points first to doing whatever it takes to be highly competent, and second, focuses on the transition area of the continuum where creativity begins to complement competence. What helps in making the transition is what will help a person be creative.

In daily work, a practitioner ordinarily selects solutions worked out by others. Occasionally some practitioners are able to invent solutions! How and why practitioners are able to invent solutions is the subject of this book. Addams' observation on social work is also true of creativity—there is both an objective and subjective necessity for both. Subjectively, it is rewarding to create. Because social work is neither a well-paid profession nor necessarily one held in high public esteem, it is absolutely imperative that social workers generate their own professional rewards.

Objectively, creativity is important because social workers deal with the highly complex problems of both people and society, currently possess

---

[1]Although the tests and exercises often are interesting and fun to do, and although the validity of some measures of creativity has been established, evidence is somewhat sparse that becoming adept at creativity exercises actually increases creative output—that is, original work or ideas. In fact, truly creative individuals—people who have been producing creative work—may or may not do well at tests or exercises in "creative" problem solving (p. 31).

a less than adequate body of professional knowledge, and operate in what often is a turbulent and changing social environment. The standard operating procedure often just will not do. Creative solutions are vital.

Finally, beyond the professionally objective and subjective needs for creativity, there is the personal. It simply is exciting, exhilarating, and satisfying to create something. It is one of life's greatest aesthetic experiences—occurring whether the task is a world-shaking or ordinary one. R. Schacter (personal communication, 1988) explained the joy of creativity as follows:

> The next day I attended a conference on the problems administrators are contending with to address the AIDS epidemic. This had nothing to do with my class assignment about school social work. . . . I listened to a social worker describe how her rehab agency went about the task of developing an AIDS educational program for its 9,000 clients and entire staff. . . . Suddenly my attention shifted from the workshop discussion to thoughts of my paper on program design. In what seemed to be no more than a moment in time, . . . my feelings of apprehension and doubt from the previous day . . . were replaced by a mental picture of how social workers practice in the public schools with children, parents, teachers, and other school personnel. This was followed by a feeling of exhilaration accompanied by the awareness that my assignment had just become clarified. I also felt relief, as if a weight had been lifted off me, but it was the feeling of exhilaration that remained with me. (p. 3)

The creative process can be described in many ways. Some theorists emphasize the use of mental skills, or the function of the brain in storing, retrieving, manipulating, and expressing ideas and feelings. Other theorists emphasize intrapsychic phenomena—the use of fantasy, archaic thought processes, and image as tools for creative thinking. Still others conclude that attitudinal and personality factors differentiate creative people from others—factors such as the openness to new experiences, the ability to persevere, and the capacity to accept or reject taboo ideas or impulses (Gelfand, 1988, pp. 21–35). Others theorize that the creative process occurs in stages: first insight, saturation, incubation, illumination, and verification. Many authors support this view. Here, the focus is on understanding the social, psychological, and cognitive determinants of the creative process. According to Rapoport, creativity is a style of thinking and acting in which logical and analogical, conscious and unconscious actions and thoughts are merged to produce novel results

(Rapoport, 1968, p. 153).[2] The subject of the text is how social workers can encourage this merger.

The product of the creative process usually is novel or unique. However, as Rogers and Schumaker note, no matter how creatively conceived it may be, an idea or concept that has social value does not become an innovation until it is adopted by an organization, group, or institution (as cited in Zaltman & Lin, 1971). Unless otherwise specified, innovation here refers to someone's introduction of something novel and unique, and its acceptance by others as something socially defined as "new." The process of innovation begins with the generation of an idea, and proceeds through its development, use, verification, and ultimate adoption by others (Thomas, 1984, p. 140). Creativity may be called for at any step in the process.

One way to conceptualize the processes of innovation and creativity is by placing innovation on a horizontal axis and creativity on a vertical axis, which can move across any or all the stages of the horizontal axis (Figure 1).

Throughout the text, references to existence of stages or phases of innovation and creativity are offered, not as verified fact, but as heuristic guides. In reality, these phases are not necessarily sharply demarcated. They may occur out of order or at considerably different times, or be omitted. At this point in the development of knowledge about innovation and creativity, however, phases are useful as anchoring points in explaining ideas. There is considerable anecdotal evidence that these phases often occur (Gruber, 1983). There even are some interesting theories that explain their recurrence. Nevertheless, a text on creativity should not encrust thinking with rigid, unproven theories.

In fact, creative ideas may occur in one burst of insight—the "Eureka" phenomenon—or may emerge piecemeal, with many partial insights, over a long period. Also, solitude is not necessary either for creativity or for innovation. The lonely solitary thinker is a poor caricature of the creative person, and an absolutely erroneous view of the innovator. The

---

[2]Rapoport (1968) suggested that imagination plays an important role in the creative process because it is the first step in generating a new idea or a fresh insight. Imagination is thought content that is divorced from its perceptual origins. It consists of mental images or ideas which have not been experienced in or derived from reality. It also involves visualizing desired goals that might be achieved through alternative possibilities, new combinations, or altogether novel pathways. It involves departure from traditional theoretical systems and from previously prescribed practice patterns.

Figure 1. Creativity and Innovation

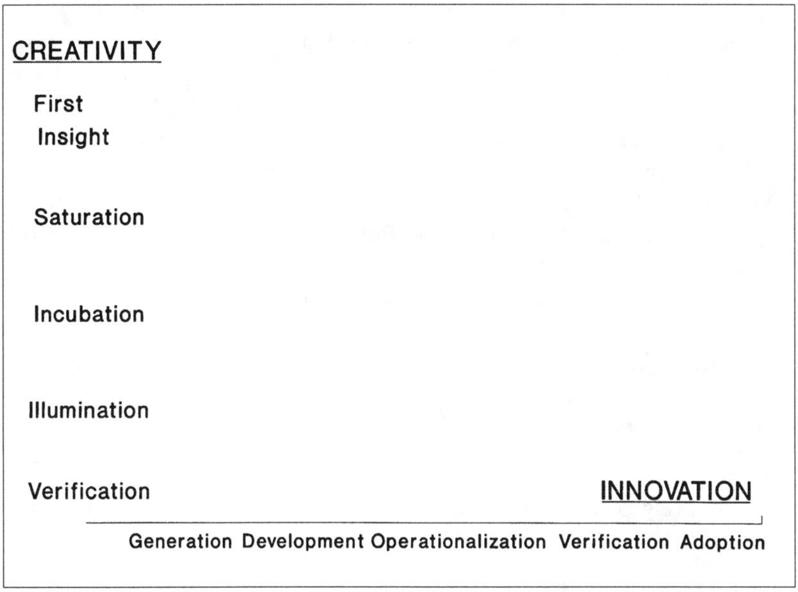

CREATIVITY

First
Insight

Saturation

Incubation

Illumination

Verification   INNOVATION

Generation Development Operationalization Verification Adoption

process of innovation is primarily a social process. Ideas usually have to be developed, prepared for use, implemented, and evaluated if there is to be innovation. As noted earlier, innovations also must be accepted by others. All of these steps involve colleagues and co-workers to a more or less considerable extent.

On the other hand, creativity appears to be mainly one individual's thought process. Yet, Gruber (1983) pointed out that "we do not need to choose between a vulgar sociology and an unqualified individualism. Exceptional creative scientists like Darwin draw on precursors and contemporaries, develop collaborations and respond to broad social forces. We need a theory of individual creative work that takes account of sociohistorical factors" (p. 4).[3] Creative social workers are affected by the social and psychological contexts in which they work.

Another issue that has confused discussions of creativity relates to its range, scope, and scale. A social worker who has novel insights about a

---

[3]Interestingly Darwin spent a great deal of time discussing his ideas, but never revealed the full scope of his theory for 15 years, fearing that it would not be accepted if it were revealed prematurely (Gruber, 1983).

client and a social worker who develops a whole new approach to therapy both are creative. Yet, the range and scale of their work is quite different. Although a creative act is one that forges something new or novel, the scale remains narrow if the insights are not generalized, verified, or adopted by others—if the insight does not become an innovation. There also is a difference in scope between a creative act that results in improving on or doing old things better, such as developing a novel outreach program, and one that results in doing things quite differently, such as changing the definition of the program. The world tends to honor or remember the big change much more than the small one. However, they both partake of creativity.

The creative product either is a discovery or an invention that was not known or did not exist before. On the other hand, an innovation usually, but not necessarily, is defined by its objective "newness" or novelty. Rogers and Schumaker (as cited in Zaltman & Linn, 1971) pointed out:

> It matters little, as far as human behavior is concerned, whether or not an idea is objectively new as measured by the lapse of time since its first use or discovery. . . . If the idea seems new and different to individuals, it is an innovation. (p. 65)

This distinction is important because it highlights the range of talents an innovator might use. Sometimes, innovation requires the innovator to be a great salesperson or a broker, at other times to possess the talents of a scientist or an engineer, and at other times to have the creative talents of an artist or inventor. And, on rare occasions, an innovator appears who has all of these talents.

In this text, the position is taken that a range of talents, including creativity, are needed if the problems of adapting, developing, implementing, and gaining acceptance for innovations are to be solved. Finding a method to distinguish creativity from other levels of capacity has been a problem. Too often the word "creativity" is used too loosely.

According to Rapoport (1968), *creativity* refers to intuitive thought or action which forges something new by making known previously unknown connections. For her, *artistry* is different than creativity. It involves the ingenious and imaginative application of what is known. (This is the transition area, where competent practice blends into creative practice.) *Craftsmanship* involves skillful execution of activities that are consciously controlled and directed, to achieve a preconceived result. It is what usually has been referred to as competence.

In this book, creativity, artistry, and craftsmanship are viewed as a continuum. The chapters that follow, therefore, flow from the premise that while the process of innovating involves germinating, designing, implementing, and institutionalizing ideas, the exact mix of required craftsmanship, artistry, and creativity is as yet unknown. Innovations are needed in social work. Innovators need creative and artistic capacities, as well as other talents associated with craftsmanship such as consistency, analytical capacity, and judgment.

The social work profession differs from a profession such as medicine, where there is a sharp split between practitioners and researchers. In social work there is a greater role for individual creativity and artistry than is allowed in medicine, as Konner (1987) pointed out:

> Doctors are not scientists, at least not in their medical roles, because, though they certainly draw on science, what they do is neither objective enough nor oriented to the production of new knowledge—nor should it be. And they are certainly not artists, since aesthetic principles and independent creativity have little or no place in practice, despite everything that has been said about the 'art' of medicine. But doctors are craftspeople of the highest order. Sometimes, like engineers, they lean very heavily on science. Sometimes, like diamond cutters, they seem to be coasting along on pure skill. And occasionally like glassblowers or goldsmiths, what they do verges on art. (p. 2)

Here, Konner suggests that doctors are neither artists nor scientists, but rather craftsmen. However, as Tims & Tims found, social workers must utilize the capacities of all three, given the unlikelihood that the social world is as orderly as the biological world (England, 1986, p. 55).

We should not allocate the task of discovery and invention to one group, that is, to scientists, and the work to another. Prior attempts and hopes that social scientists would make the intellectual discoveries for social workers proved to be disappointing and illusory.

One reason for the disappointment may be related to the fact that the history of the discovery of great ideas shows that they come to the "prepared mind." Social scientists seldom have the same preparation as social workers. Preparation for discovery and invention is another way of saying that competence in a particular field should be the first concern of professionals who want to be creative.

Frequently, for example, competence or craftsmanship in social work is defined by the no-nonsense performance of a set of job-specific capacities, which assume a level of knowledge, skill, and analytic capacity (England, 1986, p. 15). Master craftspersons, in any area, have a set of responses (ranging from how to attack a problem to how to implement a solution) in their heads—these responses are available both for use or for recombination as they pick up cues from the environment (Middleman & Rhodes, 1983, pp. 36–37).

The mastery of alternatives conveys a sense of effortlessness to an outside observer but also allows the master practitioner time to focus completely on the external cues which must be picked up in order to choose the right alternative response in particular situations. Craft here relates to the logical ability to plot a good strategy, the capacity to recognize familiar patterns and to exploit them, and to an interpersonal sense of the personality and motivation of others (Gardner, 1983, pp. 230–231). This is difficult and requires years of training and practice.

Here, a distinction is drawn between the competent who possess the above capacities, and those who are both competent and creative. The latter have a greater capacity both to recognize patterns, when fewer cues are available, and to recombine and rework them in a playful or improvisational sense, with all the risk that this entails. The less creative may be aware of alternatives, but seldom are able to see or develop the variations possible with them.

The ability to construct and recall cognitive maps—patterns of action and response—and continually rework them are important for creative work in many fields. Sessions has made the point about composers:

> He constantly has "tones in his head"—that is, he is always, somewhere near the surface of his consciousness, hearing tones, rhythms, and larger musical patterns. While many of these patterns are worth little musically . . . it is the composers' lot constantly to be monitoring and reworking [or playing with them]. (as cited in Gardner, 1983, p. 101)

Innovation, in social work as well as music, also requires a mind prepared to look at information, events, sensations, and activities from a variety of vantage points—an educated intuition. How and to what extent we can educate our intuition is the subject of this book.

Organization of the Book

Insights are intuitions expressed in words. As John-Steiner expressed it: "Metaphors, analogies, and the delineation of new patterns are the stuff of insights" (1985, p. 203).

Part One of *Serious Play: Creativity and Innovation in Social Work* discusses the importance of both insight and intuition to social work. An overview of the creative process and the role of playfulness in that creative process also is provided. Guidelines for practitioners for improving their creative skills are offered.

Social workers who can enhance their creative capacities still may have difficulty flourishing in organizations that are closed to change, in a profession that is limited by conceptual blinders, in an environment where routine and predictability are valued above all else, or in a society with sporadic and confused social concerns. There are organizational, professional, and environmental impediments to both creativity and innovation.

Thus, Parts Two and Three of the book examine these impediments— the effect of an organization's history, its ability to risk, its financial structure, its entrepreneurial roles, its culture; the profession's ability to listen to client feedback, openness to nonprofessional models of help, its model of knowledge development, and its knowledge diffusion structures. These parts also look at the considerable supports for innovation that agencies and the profession already provide. The situation is by no means completely bleak—especially when comparisons are made with other professions.

Part Four of the book examines how social movements and alternative agencies promote innovation and adaptability in the profession. It also looks at how they affect service systems, both formally and informally, and at how they affect agencies, and through this constrain or support individual creativity.

Each part of the book includes an original set of chapters and an original text or commentary. The commentary interspersed throughout the book both illustrates and expands on points made in the chapters, and also offers an original interpretation of the topic under discussion. Each part of the book also concludes with a discussion of the personal implications of the ideas, presented for those social workers who want to be innovators.

Part Five of the book synthesizes others' ideas and states the editor/ senior author's point of view about the best ways to promote innovation and creativity in social work. It suggests ways to manage a creative career. Social workers not only have to attend to their own skills and traits, but also to their work environment, their profession, and to the social environment.

References

Adams, J. (1976). *Conceptual blockbusting*. New York: W. W. Norton.

Edwards, B. (1987). *Drawing on the artist within: A guide to innovation, invention, imagination, and creativity* (Fireside ed.). New York: Simon & Schuster.

England, H. (1986). *Social work as art*. London, England: George Allen & Unwin.

Gardner, H. (1983). *Frames of mind*. New York: Basic Books.

Gelfand, B. (1988). *The creative practitioner*. New York: Haworth Press.

Gruber, H. (1983). History and creative work: From the most ordinary to the most exalted. *Journal of the History of the Behavioral Sciences, 19*, 4–14.

John-Steiner, V. (1985). *Notebooks of the mind*. Albuquerque: University of New Mexico Press.

Konner, M. (1987). *Becoming a doctor*. New York: Viking Press.

Middleman, R., & Rhodes, G. (1983). *Competent supervision*. Englewood Cliffs, NJ: Prentice–Hall.

Rapoport, L. (1968). Creativity in social work. *Smith College Studies in Social Work, 38*, 139–161.

Thomas, E. (1984). *Designing interventions for the helping professions*. Beverly Hills, CA: Sage Publications.

Weissman, G. (1987, July 26). Review of *Becoming a doctor* [book review section], *New York Times*, p. 2.

Zaltman, G., & Lin, M. (1971). On the nature of innovations. *American Behavioral Scientist, 14*, 661–673.

PART ONE

The Creative Social Worker: First Insights

The Creative Process

The uncreative mind can spot wrong answers, but it takes a creative mind to spot wrong questions.

—Antony Jay

From one perspective, creativity is something inherited—like good looks or intelligence, though somewhat rarer. If one is lucky enough to be creative, fine. If not, one should work to one's maximal capacity.

However, this point of view ignores the way individual creativity is patterned by cultural, cognitive, and social factors. It implies that one's creativity is forever fixed and ignores the effect of personal motivation or desire on creative output.

Without denying that individuals have differing innate capacities for creativity, this overview allows for the development of these capacities in its definition of creativity. It provides a framework for social workers to evaluate their own state of creative development. The joys, as well as the difficulties, of creating are explored. Here, the focus is on what a practitioner can do to further his or her own creative inspiration.[1]

No social worker can be involved seriously in the profession without, at some point, becoming frustrated by the inability to help a particular client or set of clients, being upset by continuing and worsening social problems, or being disturbed by the flawed social policies that may have to be administered. In these situations, conventional professional wisdom can become part of the problem.

Creative ideas certainly are required to deal with these frustrations. Yet, there is a good deal of at least anecdotal evidence that creativity cannot just be beckoned when needed (Fritz, 1984, pp. 44–45). Campbell (1978) theorized that individuals who develop novel ideas or innovations usually go through a creative process that includes six cycles: (1) preparation or garnering experience; (2) concentration on problem solving; (3) frustration, or lack of success; (4) incubation, relaxation, or getting away from the problem; (5) insight or solution; and (6) verification.

---

[1]This is for discussion purposes. Other chapters examine the effect of context on individual creative capability. In reality, the individual and context cannot be neatly separated. Persons aspiring to be creative must be concerned both with personal capacities and with the contexts that affect these capacities.

3

Reality seldom operates in neat phases or stages. Those who want to be creative should consider that they could be inhibited in any one of these phases. Insufficient experience, lack of concentration, inability to let problems incubate, lack of access to imagination, or lack of concern for verification—all can bring creativity to a halt (Campbell, 1978).

Rapoport (1968) found that imagination and intuition play a crucial part in the creative process.

> Imagination is thought content that is divorced from its perceptual origins. It consists of mental images or ideas which have not been experienced in or derived from reality . . . alternative possibilities, new combinations or altogether novel pathways. . . . Intuition is knowledge, perceptual rather than conceptual, based on stimuli previously received by the pre-conscious perceptual systems which are momentarily not available to conscious recall or to conceptualization. Intuition enables us to make judgments without knowing consciously how we arrived at them. (pp. 152–153)

According to Rapoport (1968), those who want to be creative must expand their imaginative and intuitive powers. However, there is considerable dispute about whether and how this can be done. Adams (1979), among others, feels that creativity *can* be taught, or at least encouraged. He noted that if Leonardo da Vinci were to read a book on creativity, he probably would be wasting his time—but most people are not da Vincis. To Adams, creativity is not Plato's "divine spark," but more a dull glow—the more fanning it receives, the brighter it will glow (p. 10).

People who aspire to be creative should consider Perkins' (1981) belief that purpose, or the desire to attain some end, "organizes the diverse means of the mind to creative ends" (p. 72). The end is not to be original, but to attain something. People whose commitment to doing something difficult tends to sag are less creative.

The Creative Process

In this text, creativity refers to thinking that uses both logical processes and analogical, visual, and perceptual processes. This distinction comes from Sperry's (1968) and others' research on the brain that showed that the right and left hemispheres use different methods of information processing for thinking (Edwards, 1987).

According to Edwards (1987), the left hemisphere, or L-mode, emphasizes logical, verbal, analytic thinking:

> It controls speech, reading, writing, and arithmetic. Naming and categorizing are among its favorite things to do. In general, its system of thought is linear: first things first, second things second. It tends to rely on general rules to reduce experience to concepts that are compatible with its style of

cognition. Its preference is for clear, sequential, logical thought, uncompli-
cated by paradox or ambiguity. The right hemisphere, or R-mode, tends to
seek relationships between parts and searches for ways parts fit together to
form wholes. Its preferences are for perceiving information, searching for
patterns or relationships that satisfy requirements for visual fit, and seeking
spatial order and coherence. It seems undaunted by ambiguity, complexity,
or paradox, perhaps because it lacks the "reducing glass" of L-mode, which
opts for general rules and resists acknowledging ambiguity and paradox. (p.
11–12)

Because of its complexity and nonverbal nature, it is difficult to describe
L-mode in words. In this overview *L-mode* and *R-mode* refer to styles of
thinking. There is still dispute about the location of functions in the brain.[2]

The two hemispheres share perceptions of reality, so that there is no
sense of two separate processes. According to Edwards (1987), "Sperry's
(1968) research on the brain suggested that creativity may occur in stages,
perhaps because the requirements of each stage cause the brain to 'shift
gears'—that is, to make cognitive shifts from one major brain mode to the
other and back again" (p. 14).

With considerable consistency, research derived from case studies of
how inventions or novel ideas were developed shows that there are stages,
or steps, in the creative process. According to Edwards (1987), creativity
often begins with a *first insight*—the first perception of a problem, or that
something is amiss. This first insight directs the search for solutions and
results from both the solving of existing problems and from finding new
problems by asking new, searching questions (p. 5).

Saturation, the second stage, follows first insight. Here, all known
information, ideas, and facts about the problem are sifted and analyzed.
Incubation occurs when one consciously stops focusing on the problem.
Edwards (1987) conjectured that it is mainly R-mode "manipulation of
visually structured verbal and visual data, performed largely outside
conscious awareness until that moment when the brain communicates the
perceptual 'aha' back to the more conscious verbal processes" (p. 225).
This is the *illumination* stage—when a flash of insight into the problem
bursts. The next stage is *verification*, when an idea is put in a form that

---

[2]The above functions, although generally attributed to the left and right hemispheres
respectively for most individuals, may vary considerably in location in the brain hemispheres of specific individuals, particularly left-handed and ambidextrous individuals.
Moreover, recent research indicates a less clear division of functions between the
hemispheres than was thought to be the case in earlier investigations (Edwards, 1987, p.
12). The editor/senior author has used the terms L-mode and R-mode to designate styles
of thinking rather than a more rigid conception of location of functions in one hemisphere
or the other.

makes it accessible to others. In this stage, the idea is checked for usefulness and error.

The saturation and verification stages seem to fit best with logical, analytical thinking. The first insight, incubation, and illumination steps fit the conceptions of imagination and insight. However, a basic problem with discussing creativity in terms of stages is the elusiveness of describing, for example, how to incubate or illuminate. Is the L-mode of thinking and describing really adequate to describing a process that also utilizes R-mode thinking?

How does one know when one is "saturated"? Is incubation a set of procedures that has a controlled beginning and end? Are some stages skipped or do they always occur sequentially? If the insight is only partial, must the process begin again? There are no proven answers to these questions (Edwards, 1987, p. 5).

Creative people often report going through stages of creativity. The idea that the brain shifts mode in moving from some stages to other stages makes these reports plausible. What these people may be reporting are alterations in types of thinking. People are usually aware of when they are concentrating and thinking in a linear, logical fashion, and when they are not.

Whether or not there are stages of creativity or noticeable shifts in thinking, those interested in being creative should concern themselves with their ability to use the brain's R-mode. In most peoples' experience, school emphasized L-mode or logical, verbal, linear thinking. The L-mode is dominant in Western culture. However, Hunt (1982) made the point that there is no convincing evidence that "courses in problem solving [or creativity] can increase one's ability to make the imaginative leaps that are often crucial in problem solving" (p. 31). On the other hand, there is evidence that intuition and imagination (R-mode) play a crucial part in the development of creative ideas and products. Edwards (1987) suggested a way out of the dilemma:

> Mainly, I think, that looking at things upside down forces one to "see differently." Things are seen apart from their usual connections. A line that is just a line, interesting in itself when viewed upside down, seems to disappear into a familiar form when viewed in the usual orientation.
>
> I believe that this phenomenon of things sinking into a familiar context is one of the true blocks to creativity. Upside down, one sees things—parts and wholes—with a separate clarity that becomes lost in normal orientation. In drawing as in creative thinking—again, paradoxically—it is sometimes extremely valuable not to know what you are seeing, or what you are looking for. Preconceptions, whether they are visual or verbal, can blind one to innovative discoveries. (p. 26)

Research shows that it is the "prepared mind" that has the first insight. Yet, paradoxically, it is the prepared mind that has the most preconceptions. One way to gain access to the R-mode is to trick the repository of preconceptions in the L-mode. "In order to gain access to the subdominant visual perceptual [R-] brain mode, it is necessary to present the brain with a task the dominant verbal analytic [L-] mode will turn down" (Hunt, as cited in Edwards, 1987, p. 137) such as doodling or solitude. Another is to accept the limitations of words. "Words most often distill, simplify and abstract complexity. . . . The relationship of words to images is similar to that of titles of drawings to the actual drawings" (p. 53). Thus, our preconceptions and ideas are always in danger of being shown to be only partial ones—not the whole story.

Another way to gain access to the R-mode is to be seriously playful—to temporarily relax rules and to cross previously forbidden boundaries. Here, the essence of creative practice is the ability to develop, then monitor and rework a large repertoire of *cognitive maps* or models, that are accessible to recall from the memory. In the following chapter, Hartman and Laird give examples of how this development and reworking takes place and how playfulness helps overcome preconceptions.

Harold H. Weissman
Editor/Senior Author

References

Adams, J. (1979). *Conceptual blockbusting.* New York: W. W. Norton.

Campbell, D. (1978). *The psychology of creativity* [Audiotape]. Available from the Center for Creative Leadership, Greensboro, NC.

Edwards, B. (1987). *Drawing on the artist within: A guide to innovation, invention, imagination, and creativity* (Fireside ed.). New York: Simon & Schuster.

Fritz, R. (1984). *The path of least resistance.* Salem, MA: DMA Inc.

Hunt, M. (1982). *The universe within.* New York: Simon & Schuster.

Perkins, D. (1981). *The mind's best work.* Cambridge, MA: Harvard University Press.

Rapoport, L. (1968). Creativity in social work. *Smith College Studies in Social Work, 38*, 139–161.

Sperry, R. (1968). Hemisphere disconnection and unity in consciousness awareness. *American Psychologist, 23*, 723–733.

Crossing Boundaries and Exploring Metaphors

Joan Laird and Ann Hartman

After the final counseling appointment with a married couple, one of the authors received a gift in the mail—a dictionary. The enclosed note read, "Turn to page 555." There, carefully pasted among the other definitions, was the following:

> Hartman. Heart, akin to having heart. Good listener. Patient. Wise. Sympathetic. Helpful.

Here, we thought, was something creative, something imaginative and innovative. This couple had created something different by combining two familiar things—a dictionary definition and a meaningful experience. The gift was touching and amusing, but also surprising because it had broken an unspoken rule that dictionaries are sacred and inviolable. What audacity to carefully type and insert one's own words in those neat and permanent columns—to alter a dictionary! Like many creative acts, it was not difficult to *do*, it was difficult to *think* of. It was difficult to have the idea!

As teachers and social work practitioners, we are constantly searching for ways to tap into and expand our own creative potentials as well as those of our students and clients. Here, creativity is examined in a rather personal way, using our own journeys in social work and particularly in the family therapy field, highlighting those stops along the way that have seemed "special," thought-expanding and, perhaps, productive of more creativity in our own work. Because we believe that analogue is one of the great sources of creativity, perhaps the personalizing of the story can be justified by its analogic potential for the reader.

In this chapter, we begin with a brief exploration of creativity. This definitional effort is followed by an overview of prevailing theories of creativity. The notions of boundary crossing and rule breaking are central to our own thinking about creativity as are the concepts of metaphor and analogy, so it is these issues that are central in our discussion. We describe some of our own experiences with crossing boundaries and with the search for more useful and less restrictive metaphors and analogues in understanding and helping people. We conclude with a brief discussion of social work's current relationship with creativity, past and future.

Defining Creativity

What does creativity mean? In the same dictionary as the gift dictionary, (*Webster's*, 1985) we find two definitions: (1) "to produce through imaginative skill" and (2) "to make or bring into existence something new." Thus, on one hand, creativity involves action—implying a skillful actor with "imagination" who can "produce" something. Creativity also implies a product that has not existed previously in quite the same form; something that may be seen, heard, or otherwise experienced in a new way. This "something new" can be as momentous and globally important as the hydrogen bomb, or as delicate and personal as a child's first handmade gift to mother or father. Creativity can refer to a concrete product, such as a great building, a mechanical invention, or a poem; or it can refer to an idea or an action—to thinking about or doing something in a new or imaginative way.

Barron and Harrington (1985) wrote that

> Creative products are distinguished by their originality, their aptness, their validity, their usefulness, and very often by a subtle additional property which we may call aesthetic fit. . . . The ingredients of the creative process are related functionally to the creative forms produced: seeing things in a new way, making connections, taking risks, being alerted to chance and to the opportunities present[ed] by contradictions and complexities, recognizing familiar patterns in the unfamiliar so that new patterns may be formed by transforming old ones, being alert to the contingencies which may arise from such transformations. (p. 168)

Imagination, actor, action, product, pattern, connection, the familiar, novelty, transformation: these seem to be some of the major ingredients of creativity. Creativity, then, implies an expansion of human experience, a way of liberating oneself from one's own conditioning, rigidities, and usual choices (Arieti, 1976). Creative work is not solely an internal act. The action stirs a new vision of truth, establishing a new bond between the creator and the environment and generating a range of potential responses: aesthetic pleasure, laughter, a feeling of transcendence, new understanding, and the ability to predict experience in new ways (Arieti, 1976, p. 5).

Theories of Creativity

The puzzle of creativity has intrigued scholars from ancient to modern times. Unlocking the secrets of the creative process is an effort that respects no disciplinary boundaries. Artists, scientists, philosophers, and practitioners of many persuasions have sought to discover the sources of creativity, to draw on them for their own work, or to harness their inspirations in teaching or helping others. The philosopher Bergson (1911), for example, was interested in the role of will in creative production. Both he and Jung (1976) explored individual intuition as a source of creativity. Others have been interested in the relationship between intelligence and imagination. Since the 1940s, there have been many empirical studies concerning the relationship between personality and creativity, and on creativity in education. According to Barron and Harrington (1985), however, these efforts have produced inconclusive results because of unreliability in choice of measures, and because of inconsistent and extremely complex definitional criteria.

Some scholars have stressed the role of conscious and unconscious psychological processes in creativity. For example, creativity was seen by Kris (1952) as a result of regression in the service of the ego, a process in which primary process is central. For Jung, the creative process represented a reemergence of primordial experiences from the collective unconscious; for Greenacre (1957), the potentially creative person possesses both greater than normal sensitivity and a greater ability to dissociate the ego from real objects, thus developing a love affair with the world. Other scholars have attempted to analyze the creative process as a series of stages, a pursuit perhaps more appropriately applied to the creative process in science than in art. However, creativity often may be more a matter of seemingly sudden illumination, of spontaneous or discontinuous process.

If some have stressed essence and structure, other thinkers believe that creativity emerges from ambiguity, contradiction, and complexity, that it is stimulated at the boundaries of margins of life. Koestler (1964), for example, argued that bisociation underpins the creative process. He viewed the creative act as a mental occurrence in which two habitually incompatible contexts are simultaneously associated. For Koestler, the creative act "is always a leap into the dark, a dive into the deep," although "the diver is more likely to come up with a handful of mud than a coral" (cited in Papp, 1984, p. 25).

Novelty, contradiction, complexity, humor, absurdity, and risk-taking—these too are part of the creative process. In describing the skilled, creative lecturer, Goffman (1983) spoke of "breaking frames," of the planned and controlled "aside," the introduction of the unexpected, the "marginal" notes that make an ordinary speech a special one. Similarly, it is often the deviant, the revolutionary, the thinker at the boundaries, who gives birth to the most original ideas. Thus, creativity is a matter of allowing oneself to be challenged by new ideas, to cross disciplinary and other kinds of boundaries, and to break the frame. Still other scholars argue that pattern, connection, and relationship lie at the heart of creativity. In this perspective, creativity is neither static nor inherited, neither attribute of person or environment, nor something created out of nothing. Except perhaps for the God of Genesis, most great creators have not created something ex nihilo. In this sense there *is* nothing new under the sun.

Rather, creativity is a process of putting things together in a new way. This is as true for our clients and their dictionary as it is for the great scientists and artists of past and present. For example, in both mathematics and linguistics, the focus is on the relationships among symbols. Mathematics historian Bell (cited in Holenstein, 1976) argued that "it is not the things that matter but the relations between them" (p. 23). Einstein named his central contribution to physics the theory of *relativity*. Indeed, experimental scientists search for the relationship between a variable and one or more others, seeking to create new knowledge. The famous linguist Jakobson defined his task as the exploration of relations among different tenses and linguistic entities, and the cubist painter Braque's (cited in Holenstein, 1976) credo was "I do not believe in things, I believe only in their relationship" (p. 23). For Koestler (1964), great drama emerged from a process of uncovering, selecting, reshuffling, combining, and synthesizing.

Another issue concerns the product of creativity. If creativity is the process of bringing something new into existence, must this "something new" make a significant, aesthetic, or valuable addition to society, or might it simply enrich one person's mundane everyday world? Significant, valuable, beautiful, aesthetically pleasing in whose opinion? Is creativity

11

something that exists in the eye of the beholder? How are such judgments made? When is an idea or production "creative"? When is it "new"? Is it the answer, the product, the thing of beauty that best expresses creativity? Or, might the greater creativity, the richer meanings and meaningfulness, reside in the question, in, as the existentialists tell us, the search itself? Can creativity be predicted or taught? What nurtures creativity? Can we at least construct teaching and practice environments that hold greater promise for its emergence?

In attempting to explore these questions, we found ourselves turning to our own experiences, to an examination of the events, the turning points, the paradigm shifts, the ideas, and the contexts that we found freeing, exciting, challenging, that seemed to open up new possibilities for our own thinking, writing, teaching, and practice.

As narrative and story have become major interests for both of us, we have found ourselves drawn to these communicative forms. The story we find ourselves telling is set in the contexts of the rich and vital field of family therapy and of the social work profession. We have, of course, individually taken different routes and explored different byways. However, we share a common interest in integrating into social work practice knowledge, insights, and world views that have developed and continue to emerge from the family therapy field. At one stage, our efforts in this direction culminated in the publication of *Family-Centered Social Work Practice* (Hartman & Laird, 1983). But like most such works, that book represents a dip into a rapidly moving stream of thought at one point. The stream has traveled on, new tributaries swelling and shifting its course. The creative energy in the family field has not waned; instead, it continues to excite and challenge those who would follow its movements. Here, we describe some of the events, ideas, and themes that, in our respective stories, have enriched our thinking and practice.

Crossing Boundaries and Breaking Rules

Boundaries provide order, coherence, protection, and continuity. Crossing boundaries, allowing oneself to become a stranger in a strange land, challenges assumptions and provides access to alternate world views and new options. Moving back and forth across the boundary between social work and family therapy both challenges some of our social work theory and practice assumptions and also brings some of the special and valued aspects of our social work identity and heritage to the family perspective. For example, although family therapists changed the unit of attention from the inner life of the individual to the individual in the context of the family and to the family itself, many have been slower to place the family in its larger sociocultural context. Family therapists who are also social workers, such as Aponte (1976), Hoffman and Long (1969), and McGoldrick, Pearce, and Giordano (1982), have emphasized the importance of this perspective.

Boundary crossing also has occurred among the mental health professions as they joined forces in the family field. In more traditional mental health disciplines, a team model is the norm. Different roles and functions generally are arranged hierarchically according to discipline and thus also often by gender. In the family field boundaries between professional disciplines have dissolved, creating a shared family therapy identity. This boundary crossing has resulted in some identity confusion, as well as some losses for the social work profession (Hartman & Laird, 1987). However, it also has cleared the way for more egalitarian collaboration and creativity.

Such was our experience at Ann Arbor Center for the Family, a program we helped to create and shape. For many years, the center provided us with a context of collaborative sharing in a system unconstrained by rigidly prescribed roles or rules based on discipline, experience, age, or gender. Other kinds of boundaries were crossed as we made our own work available for observation, through sharing cases, watching video-tapes, sitting behind the one-way mirror, or participating in lively discussion groups. Weekly staff meetings provided a professional culture that encouraged the noncompetitive presentation and discussion of ideas, cases, research, and writing. This stimulating environment nurtured the creative capacities of everyone involved.

Family therapists also have reached across boundaries into the academic disciplines and arts for sources of knowledge and creativity in ways that are reminiscent of the creative period in the early years of the professionalization of social work. Bateson (1971, 1979), one of the spiritual and intellectual parents of the family therapy field, set the example. He, like many innovative thinkers, was a master at blurring the genres, at erasing the distinctions between the physical and biological sciences and the social sciences and between art and science, at finding art in science, science in art, and social theory in all human creation and activity (Geertz, 1980). Bateson (1979) searched endlessly across these boundaries for illuminating connections. He asked,

What pattern connects the crab to the lobster and the orchid to the primrose and all four of them to me? And me to you? And all of the six of us to the amoeba in one direction and to the back-ward schizophrenic in another? (p. 8)

Thus were the Balinese, the Iatmul, the schizophrenic, the porpoise, the mind, nature, his daughter, his self sources of inspiration for Bateson's own learning about learning. His questions suggest that the material, the "stuff" of creative process, is all around us; our task is to put it together in new ways—perhaps to *see* familiar things differently, to transcend the cognitive snares that entrap us in familiar patterns of thought and action.

If creativity often involves a challenge to worldview, a new integration, a breaking of frame, many family leaders are known for their genius in challenging entrenched family "stories," and of holding out the possibility of an alternative "reality." Minuchin's (1974) theory and technique of reframing, the use of positive connotation by Selvini-Palazzoli, Cecchin, Prata, and Boscolo (1978), and the use of strategic interventions such as paradoxes and reversals (Watzlawick, Weakland, & Fisch, 1974) are frame-breaking interventions that call to question entrenched and un-workable solutions, challenging stale ideas and habitual solutions. Whitaker (1975, 1979) turns family paradigms upside down, creating a virtual theater of the absurd in which little is sacred and families can learn to laugh at (and give up) some of their most rigid and uncreative ideas.

In 1985, we had several profound boundary-crossing experiences when we attended a small conference honoring Bateson, held at the College of Saint Benedict in Saint Cloud, Minnesota. Here we exchanged ideas with biologists, poets, family therapists, theologians, astronomers, linguists, three or four social workers, and one sign painter. Not only did the presentations stretch our minds and challenge us to seek and find analogies, to think, and to think about how we think, but the aesthetic context provided by the gracious and enormously talented Benedictine sisters who organized and hosted the event transformed the experience. Beautifully performed Gregorian chants, ample and artistically displayed food, art, film, drama, and the special and welcoming atmosphere that encouraged sharing among all participants created an unusually rich and memorable context for learning.

Two months later, in the social work world, a conference celebrating the centennial of the birth of Bertha Capen Reynolds provided yet another rich experience of boundary crossing. In a merger of art, history, and the profession, the conference began with a docudrama composed from the letters and writings of Bertha Reynolds, a powerful and moving experience that achieved a special immediacy, merging past and present knowledge in a way rarely communicated in scholarly presentation. Throughout the weekend, creative energy was mobilized and insights developed out of another kind of boundary crossing—that between the generations. Men and women in their seventies and eighties, who had worked at the side of Bertha Reynolds several decades ago, social workers of the left, met in small discussion groups with young clinical social workers of the 1980s, teaching, learning, and renewing her legacy.

The boundary crossing that has had perhaps the most significant impact on our work has been the journey into anthropology. Like the earlier leap from psychodynamic to ecological, systemic, and structural views of person-in-situation, this journey has not been merely a search for new knowledge from yet another quarter. It has meant a change in worldview, a new language, a new set of metaphors and modes of understanding and action, and a new understanding of the person, the family, and the surround. Some of the specific ways these ideas have been influencing our work will be shared later.

Yet a third small gathering has had immeasurable impact on the family field and on those who attended, a gathering organized by three women family therapists whose roots are in social work. In September 1984, 50 women family therapists who were in leadership positions, teaching, or writing in the field met together at a small inn in Connecticut for 3 days. For women to gather in such a way broke the organizational rules of the tribe, stimulating a good deal of grumbling from and uneasiness among those who controlled access to the field's ideology and symbols. We were accused of trying to break up the family of family therapists. It was a boundary crossing group, because we came from different disciplines and different "schools" of family therapy, yet it also drew, at least temporarily, a new boundary, a boundary between the sexes. Many of us felt that this boundary needed to be clarified, this extended period of time marked off, if women were to be able to clearly share their concerns and views about this issue of gender in the family therapy field.

The meeting was repeated 2 years later. Together these gatherings were highly generative, both in expressing and further catalyzing the feminist critique of the field and in encouraging the rich contributions to be made by women to family-centered theory and practice and to the political structures that shape future directions. We will return to some of these themes and to an elaboration of this swiftly moving current as it is shaping our own thinking and our work.

Finally, another rule-breaking, boundary-crossing theme in family work has entailed the opening up and redefinition of the boundaries between therapist and family, between helper and client. Family therapists Furman and Ahola (1988) have called this the new "glasnost" in psychotherapy. Glasnost opens boundaries, surfaces secrets, and enhances communication and creative sharing among professionals. More recently this notion of sharing and openness has taken on new meaning for the therapist–client relationship.

An early and dramatic example of glasnost in family therapy occurred at a 1967 conference of family therapists and researchers when Murray Bowen (1972) presented his research on, and interventions with, his own family of origin. In this presentation, Bowen modeled the use of self as a source of learning, demonstrated openness and sharing, and tested the traditional boundary between therapist and client. Following Bowen's lead, open sharing of work and personal history among professionals became a rich source of creativity.

Returning to our own journey, at Ann Arbor Center for the Family the staff adopted and expanded upon the Bowen model, meeting regularly in a family of origin group. Here we explored our own family themes, the prescriptions and proscriptions, the intergenerational transmission processes that shaped our work and personal lives. A similar experience was instituted as part of the center's postgraduate training program. These processes, separate from, but parallel to, those explored in therapy and in the lives of our clients deserve an extended analysis. For our purposes here, there is space to say only that the boundaries between informal and formal collegial structures were perceived in new and, what we all believed to be, facilitating ways; mutual understanding was promoted and problem-solving mechanisms strengthened. Opening the boundary to our own family experiences made lifetimes of experience and understanding available for the generation and testing of ideas, much in the same way that many researchers, particularly anthropologists, have sought to merge experience-near and experience-far (Geertz, 1976). In our view, both practice and research frequently are constricted by rigid boundaries between "investigator" and subject, isolating, distancing, and distorting the relationship. At the same time that this experience rendered our learning more immediate and more powerful, the work served to stimulate our respect and humility in terms of the power of families, enhancing our empathy for client families, enriching our learning about how to help, and freeing us to work on new ways of using "self" in the helping relationship.

16

Recently, the spirit of glasnost has challenged the boundary of secrecy between professional and client in other ways. Therapists are sharing their thinking more openly with clients. This is expressed dramatically in the recent use of the "reflecting team" (Andersen, 1987). In a stunning reversal, the lights have been turned on behind the mirror and the sound system goes both ways: The family can watch and listen to the observing team's discussion and interpretation of the family's situation and are invited to dialogue. L. Hoffman (personal communication, July 1988), for example, largely has abandoned the use of paradoxical, surprise, or secretive/strategic interventions. She now presents ideas to the family as possibilities for change, which they may or may not choose to try.

Changing the Metaphors

It is with words that we create our worlds. Words endow events with meaning, creating what we then term "reality." In this sense, then, theories may be thought of as languages created to describe what we think we perceive. We, as professionals, use these languages as explanatory metaphors and sometimes we reify them, turning them into powerful systems of belief that color subsequent interpretations. Such has been the power of psychoanalytic language—for who ever has touched, seen, heard, or smelled a superego? Family therapy language has similar power—has one ever seen a structure? A family triangle? These concepts serve as symbols and templates for making sense of the world, for naming and ordering phenomena. Increasingly, therapists have become aware of the creative power of language and its ability to generate analogy and metaphor, stimulating openness, boundary crossing, and creativity.

Throughout his career, Bateson was intrigued with the power of analogy and of analogic thinking. He believed that all phenomena should be understood from multiple perspectives, or what he termed "double description" (1979, pp. 142–144). Bateson was inspired by the work of philosopher Charles S. Pierce (1908), who argued that the two stances of scientific thinking—(1) inductive and (2) deductive reasoning—were insufficient for full understanding of any phenomenon. Pierce coined the term *abduction*, or reasoning through metaphor. In his last speech, Bateson discussed metaphor and thought processes, challenging the Aristotelian syllogism that has served as a template for thought in Western society:

All men die.
Socrates is a man.
Socrates will die.

17

Bateson argued for a different syllogism, first suggested by Dutch psychiatrist von Domarus to illustrate schizophrenic thought:

Grass dies.
Men die.
Men are grass. (cited in Opitz, 1984)

This syllogism can represent poetry or disordered thought, depending on the perspective. It suggests the power of metaphor and of analogy, implying that connections are made not only through subjects but through predicates, through sharing the same experiences rather than the same morphology. Through metaphor and analogy we can discover patterns that connect phenomena in different contexts.

Common family therapy metaphors have borrowed concepts and "languages" from, among other sources, physics, biology, the corporate world, and even from the military. Families are characterized by "homeostasis," they are "fusing and differentiating organisms," machine-like "cybernetic systems," organizations characterized by "hierarchy." The therapist, weak in comparison, needs "strategies," "maneuvers"—in fact, a full complement of "weapons" to "win" in the game of change. These powerful, generative metaphors are more familiar and comfortable to male patterns of knowing and to male experiences in public life. After all, the family is composed of people in relationships with its own culture and its own meanings. Perhaps women's ways of knowing, women's experiences in domestic life—perhaps their central metaphors—might have other things to offer.

One of us, immersed in doctoral work in anthropology, began to explore the possibilities of cultural categories and metaphors as heuristic devices in understanding family life. A hypothetical question freed us to follow new paths as we asked ourselves, "What if the family is viewed through an anthropologist's eyes as a sociocultural system—as a small society?" Of course, a family is something both like and quite different from a small society. However, adopting the sociocultural metaphor shifts the direction away from the more commonly accepted systemic and structural metaphors. It leads us to the concepts and categories symbolic anthropologists lean on and to ethnographic methodology itself. It leads us away from the normative notions of structure and process now being challenged by constructivist thinkers and toward the notion of "culture" and the concepts and modes of action that help us understand culture. It also opens up new ways of thinking about thinking and knowing. Anthropologists attempt to understand wholeness, pattern, complexity, personal and social ideology, and a society's system of meanings and beliefs. Like the psychoanalyst or the family therapist, they try to include everything that might deepen the interpretation rather than to isolate particular correlations. What categories, what modes of human action useful in studying small societies might be useful in understanding the family?

Use of Family Ritual in Therapy

The first concept that captured our interest and imagination was that of ritual, a mode of human action that, until recently, largely had been ignored in both family therapy and in social work (Laird, 1984). Rituals stand at the core of human experience but, like religion, mythology, folklore, and other sources of meaning, had been obscured in social workers' rush to embrace more "scientific" ways of understanding the human condition. Scholars study ritual to gain access to the deepest levels of shared meanings, of values, and of organization in a society. As symbolic enactments, rituals analogically and metaphorically communicate a group's shared constructions of reality and they legitimize particular social prescriptions, moral stances, or world views. Rituals also can be powerful instruments for change, because they can alter and shape meanings and behaviors.

If rituals stand at the core of culture, and if families develop their own cultures and probably are also the most central force in transmitting larger sociocultural values and perspectives, it can be hypothesized that the understanding and use of ritual form and process are central to the therapist–client relationship.

This path of investigation in time led us to the exploration of rituals in family life as a part of assessment, to an awareness that some families are underritualized, lacking in a family choreography that would lend pattern, coherence, and analogic communication of meaning and values to family life (Laird, 1984). Some families seem too rigidly ritualized, preempting possibilities for flexibility and growth. Other families bypass important transition rituals, which leaves painful issues unresolved. The nontraditional family needs to create new rituals, or to adapt traditional rituals, to consolidate and communicate a sense of itself as a family unit. Learning about ritual can help social workers and family therapists better understand client family values, meanings, and world views, in the process becoming more aware of when their family, ethnic, and other cultural biases are intruding. The important work of Wolin and Bennett

(1984) and Imber-Black (1988) has greatly enhanced understanding of ritual themes and the possibilities of ritual in work with families.

This growing understanding was translated into practice as we began working with families and individual clients around constructing rituals when they were missing, helping families replace oppressive rituals, or devising ritual enactments that might help family members communicate their meanings to self and others more clearly. Ritualized assignments, for some time used by family therapists such as Erickson (cited in Haley, 1973), Haley (1977), and Selvini-Palazzoli et al. (1974, 1977), were expanded and took on new meaning.

Thinking about the family as a small society led us down another path. Small societies also tend to have rich oral traditions, fashioning their experiences with stories, legends, and myths that are told and retold, communicating the group's history, its values, and its culture. In family therapy theory, the importance of family stories largely has been ignored. Family myths have been viewed as defensive and homeostasis-maintaining (for example, Byng-Hall, 1973, 1979; Ferreira, 1963; Stierlin, 1973). However, this view is far too narrow. These oral traditions, through which people symbolize and explain themselves, their thinking, and their actions, are among the richest possible sources of meaning. They are part of the creative core of culture.

In our next exploration, we sought to learn about storying in families and to discover if family narratives, stories, and myths would help us tap into the deeper and often obscure layers of meaning in families. Again, using ourselves and our colleagues as part of a laboratory for learning, we first looked to our own families, gathering and trying to make sense of the family stories that had been told and retold. We then involved our colleagues at Ann Arbor Center in reminiscing about and sharing their own family stories. These experiences taught us many things. First, it became clear that most families had relatively few stories that were told repetitively. How was it that families, with scores of members and hundreds of memorable events as raw material for drama, selected and fashioned only a few central stories as part of the family mythology? These stories, which often seemed to be linked, to form patterns over time, seemed to be expressive of the family's individual worldview, its core themes. The stories, although often brief and frequently cautionary, were clearly packed with meaning and metaphor. They dealt with important events and issues in family life: birth, death, the founding of the family, important migrations, family heroes and heroines, issues of gender, and fate.

Storytelling became an important part of our work with individuals and families and of our research, as we began to listen for and encourage such modes of narrative, rather than treating them as digressions. In fact, therapy itself can be thought of as the building of a "best text" (Draeger, 1983), as worker and client select from, and amend, the rich variety of detail possible in understanding relevant events of the past and construct- ing a "story" for the future. Bettelheim (1977) maintained that such creations of narrative order may be essential in giving one's life a sense of meaning and direction. The disciplines of narrative and literary theory, folklore, anthropology, linguistics, and others offer potential metaphors for new ways of tapping, understanding, cointerpreting, and reconstruct- ing the narratives that become part of our work.

The Feminist Critique

The final stream we wish to explore in our search for sources of creativity takes us to feminist scholarship and to the feminist critique in the mental health professions. Slipping the lens of gender into one's eyeglasses changes the colors, shapes, and configurations of many of one's assumptions or "truths." It challenges one's language, one's perceptions of reality, provoking an often painful reexamination of our most prized explanatory modes. Social work and family therapy have lagged well behind other disciplines in incorporating feminist ideas. The systems and ecological notions, the organismic, mechanistic, cybernetic, and corporate metaphors were thought to avoid gender bias. Instead these metaphors drew inappropriate boundaries around the family, leading us down an ahistorical path (Luepnitz, 1988) and blinding us to the issues of oppression of women and differential access to power and resources. In fact, MacKinnon and Miller (1987) and Taggart (1988) warned that even the new and so-called radical constructivist epistemol- ogy of the 1980s largely ignores the politics of the social construction of gender. Clearly, men and women have unequal power in defining their lives and in convincing others of their constructions.

The studies of history and of culture largely have been studies of men. Women's voices either have been unheard or discounted. For the most part, their stories have been untold throughout the world and their very modes of narrating have gone unrecognized (Laird, 1989). Women's ritual lives in most societies have been less public, dramatic, and colorful than those of men. Women's ritual lives have been contingent on how others— husbands, parents, and children—progress through the life cycle. In many societies, women lack meaningful celebration and transition rituals. Existing rituals can be demeaning, defining women as sexual objects and/ or as property (Laird, 1988; Laird & Hartman, 1987). As social workers and family therapists become more sensitized to the meanings of gender, they learn how to listen for the stories that women tell and to search for and respect the ways in which they tell their stories. Most important, women need to more clearly take charge of their own mythmaking; they need to interpret their own stories. They must make choices about the ways they wish to construct their own rituals and to story their own futures.

The feminist critique and the lens of gender hold enormous, still largely untapped potential for a creative leap in the mental health professions. If women's ways of knowing and their voices are indeed different from those of men, social workers have much to learn as women continue to emerge from the domestic world and fully enter public life. Women are now calling attention to and questioning male gender influences in current therapy models and in prevailing research paradigms (Davis, 1985; Keller, 1985). As women cross boundaries into leadership positions, the possibility for the generation of new metaphors, of new ways of knowing, is immeasurable.

Art in Science and Science in Art

In theory building and in practice, some family therapists have turned primarily to the biological and social sciences for their explanatory analogies and central metaphors. Others have used the metaphors of the arts and humanities. For example, Papp (1984) believed that the language of science is too abstract and the metaphors too mechanistic to describe human systems. She argued that we cannot measure beliefs, weigh myths, or apply equations to human perceptions. She wrote,

> What artists have always known is that in order to deal with human dilemmas and ambiguities, one must bypass the rigid corridors of reason, science, and logical analysis and concern oneself with imagery, dreams, symbols, and metaphors. Artists don't explain their work, but reveal deepest human truths through universal codes, codes that turn those locks that remain resistant to conceptual thought. (p. 22)

In her own highly creative work, Papp has turned to sculpture, dance, Greek drama, and the enacted dream as sources for therapeutic change. Others, such as Erickson (cited in Haley, 1973) and Friedman (1984, 1985), have drawn upon the genres of poetry and metaphor, and of legend and fable, to present possibilities for change. Still other therapists are turning to literature, linguistics, and the metaphors of story and conversation (Laird & Hartman, 1984), as well as to the research techniques of conversational and narrative analysis for models (Mishler, 1986; Riessman, 1989).

According to Germain (1970), "Both modern science and modern art seek to eliminate the dichotomy of object and space, of person and situation" (p. 29). Our restricted view of knowledge closes us off from other genres that may offer much richer metaphors, analogies, and sources of understanding the human story. Such limitations build walls that keep out dangerous new ideas and conserve the status quo. As Deutsch (1958) said,

> If one is too strongly attached to one's preconceived model, one will of necessity miss all radical discoveries. It is amazing to what degree one may fail to register mentally an observation which does not fit the initial image. (p. 102)

Kuhn (1965) made a similar point:

> Novelty emerges only with difficulty, manifested by resistance, against a background provided by expectation. Initially only the anticipated and usual are experienced even under circumstances where anomaly is later to be observed. . . . (p. 64)

Goals for a Creative Future

There is, of course, no conclusion to the creative journey. Perhaps we can end with some wishes and some hopes—wishes that our profession could take more risks, could open its boundaries, could worry less about counting and more about understanding—hopes that we can open ourselves to all available sources of learning and creativity, even those that seem irrelevant. Social work is a profession that should strive to be scientific and pragmatic, but also aesthetic and humanistic. Social workers can alter the structures and the processes that constrain our creativity and limit our development.

Twenty years ago, Rapoport (1968) argued that the primary motivation for the exodus to private practice from social work institutions and public agencies largely was the desire to practice one's art. The same argument may pertain today. If social workers cannot practice creatively and flexibly in established settings, they, too, will go into business for themselves.

References

Andersen, T. (1987). The reflecting team: Dialogue and meta-dialogue in clinical work. *Family Process, 26*, 415–428.

Aponte, H. (1976). The family–school interview: An ecological approach. *Family Process, 15*, 303–311.

Arieti, S. (1976). *Creativity: The magic synthesis.* New York: Basic Books.

Barron, F., & Harrington, D. (1985). Creativity. In A. Kuper & J. Kuper (Eds.), *The social science encyclopedia* (pp. 167–169). London: Routledge & Kegan Paul.

Bateson, G. (1971). *Steps to an ecology of mind.* New York: Ballantine Books.

Bateson, G. (1979). *Mind and nature: A necessary unity.* New York: E. P. Dutton.

Bergson, H. (1911). *Creative evolution.* New York: Henry Holt. Translated by A. Mitchell.

Bettelheim, B. (1977). *The uses of enchantment.* New York: Vintage Books.

Bowen, M. (1972). Anonymous: Toward the differentiation of a self in one's own family. In J. Framo (Ed.), *Family interaction: A dialogue between family researchers and family therapists* (pp. 111–174). New York: Springer.

Byng-Hall, J. (1973). Family myths used as defence in conjoint family therapy. *British Journal of Medical Psychology, 46*, 239–250.

Byng-Hall, J. (1979). Re-editing family mythology during family therapy. *Journal of Family Therapy, 1*, 103–116.

Davis, L. (1985). Females and male voices in social work. *Social Work, 30*, 106–113.

Deutsch, M. (1958). Evidence and inference in nuclear research. In D. Lerner (Ed.), *Evidence and inference.* Glencoe: Free Press.

Draeger, J. (1983). The problem of truth in psychotherapy: A phenomenological approach to treatment. *Social Science Medicine, 17*, 371–378.

Ferreira, A. (1963). Family myth and homeostasis. *Archives of General Psychiatry, 9*, 456–463.

Friedman, E. (1984). The play's the thing. *Family Therapy Networker, 8*, 23–29.

Friedman, E. (1985). Friedman's fables. *Family Therapy Networker, 9*, 30–35.

Furman, B., & Ahola, T. (1988). *Glasnost in psychiatry, psychotherapy, and related fields.* Unpublished manuscript.

Geertz, C. (1976). From the native's point of view: On the nature of anthropological understanding. In K. Basso & H. Selby (Eds.), *Meaning in anthropology* (pp. 221–237). Albuquerque, NM: University of New Mexico Press.

Geertz, C. (1980). Blurred genres: The refiguration of social thought. *American Scholar, 49*, 165–179.

Germain, C. (1970). Casework and science: A historical encounter. In R. Roberts & R. Nee (Eds.), *Theories of social casework* (pp. 3–32). Chicago: University of Chicago Press.

Goffman, E. (1983). *Forms of talk.* Philadelphia: University of Pennsylvania Press.

Greenacre, P. (1957). The childhood of the artist. *Psychoanalytic Study of the Child, 12*, 47–72.

Haley, J. (1973). *Uncommon therapy*. New York: W. W. Norton.

Haley, J. (1977). *Problem-solving therapy*. San Francisco: Jossey–Bass.

Hartman, A., & Laird, J. (1983). *Family-centered social work practice*. New York: Free Press.

Hartman, A., & Laird, J. (1987). Family practice. In A. Minahan et al. (Eds.), *Encyclopedia of social work* (18th Ed.; Vol. 1; pp. 575–589). Silver Spring, MD: National Association of Social Workers.

Hoffman, L., & Long, L. (1969). A systems dilemma. *Family Process, 8*, 211–234.

Holenstein, E. (1976). *Roman Jakobson's approach to language*. Bloomington: Indiana University Press.

Imber-Black, E. (1988). Idiosyncratic life cycle transitions and therapeutic rituals. In B. Carter & M. McGoldrick (Eds.), *The changing family life cycle: A framework for family therapy* (pp. 149–163). New York: Gardner Press.

Jung, C. (1976). On the relation of analytic psychology to poetic art. In A. Rothenberg & C. Hausman (Eds.), *The creativity question* (pp. 120–126). Durham, NC: Duke University Press.

Keller, E. (1985). *Reflections on gender and science*. New Haven: Yale University Press.

Koestler, A. (1964). *The act of creation*. New York: Macmillan.

Kris, E. (1952). On preconscious mental processes. In E. Kris (Ed.), *Psychoanalytic explorations in art* (pp. 303, 310–318). New York: International Universities Press.

Kuhn, T. (1965). *The structure of scientific revolutions*. Chicago: University of Chicago Press.

Laird, J. (1984). Shamans, sorcerers, and social workers. *Social Work, 29*, 123–129.

Laird, J. (1988). Women and ritual in family therapy. In E. Imber-Black, J. Roberts, & R. Whiting (Eds.), *Rituals in families and in family therapy* (pp. 331–362). New York: W. W. Norton.

Laird, J. (1989). Women and stories: Restoring women's self-constructions. In M. McGoldrick, C. Anderson, & F. Walsh (Eds.), *Women in families* (pp. 427–450). New York: W. W. Norton.

Laird, J., & Hartman, A. (1984, April). *Meanings, beliefs, and spirituality: The role of myths and stories in family life*. Paper presented at the American Orthopsychiatric Association Conference, Toronto, Canada.

Laird, J., & Hartman, A. (1987). Women, rituals, and family therapy. *Journal of Psychotherapy and the Family, 3*, 157–173.

Luepnitz, D. (1988). *The family interpreted: Feminist theory in clinical practice*. New York: Basic Books.

MacKinnon, L., & Miller, D. (1987). The new epistemology and the Milan approach: Feminist and sociopolitical considerations. *Journal of Marital and Family Therapy, 13*, 139–155.

McGoldrick, M., Pearce, J., & Giordano, J. (Eds.). (1982). *Ethnicity and family therapy*. New York: Guilford Press.

Minuchin, S. (1974). *Families and family therapy*. Cambridge, MA: Harvard University Press.

Mishler, E. (1986). *Research interviewing: Context and narrative.* Cambridge, MA: Harvard University Press.

Opitz, M. (1984). Thoughts on a theory of metaphor. *Proceedings of a symposium on the ideas of Gregory Bateson.* Saint Joseph, MO: The College of Saint Benedict.

Papp, P. (1984). The creative leap. *Family Therapy Networker, 8,* 20–29.

Pierce, C. (1908). A neglected argument for the reality of God. In P. Wiener (Ed.), *Charles Saunders Pierce: Selected writings* (pp. 358–379). Garden City, NY: Doubleday.

Rapoport, L. (1968). Creativity in social work. *Smith College Studies in Social Work, 38,* 139–161.

Riessman, C. (1989). From victim to survivor: A woman's narrative reconstruction of marital sexual abuse. *Smith College Studies in Social Work, 59,* 232–251.

Selvini-Palazzoli, M., Boscolo, L., Cecchin, G., & Prata, G. (1974). The treatment of children through brief therapy of their parents. *Family Process, 13,* 429–442.

Selvini-Palazzoli, M., Boscolo, L., Cecchin, G., & Prata, G. (1977). Family rituals: A powerful tool in family therapy. *Family Process, 16,* 445–453.

Selvini-Palazzoli, M., Cecchin, G., Prata, G., & Boscolo, L. (1978). *Paradox and counterparadox.* New York: Jason Aronson.

Stierlin, H. (1973). Group fantasies and family myths: Some theoretical and practical aspects. *Family Process, 12,* 111–125.

Taggart, M. (1988). Epistemological equality as the fulfillment of family therapy. In M. McGoldrick, C. Anderson, & F. Walsh (Eds.), *Women in families* (pp. 97–116). New York: W. W. Norton.

Watzlawick, P., Weakland, J., & Fisch, R. (1974). *Change: Principles of problem formation and problem resolution.* New York: W. W. Norton.

Webster's Ninth New Collegiate Dictionary. (1985). Springfield, MA: Merriam-Webster, Inc.

Whitaker, C. (1975). Psychotherapy of the absurd: With special emphasis on the psychotherapy of aggression. *Family Process, 14,* 1–16.

Whitaker, C. (1979). The importance of the family therapist being impotent. *The Family, 4,* 120–126.

Wolin, S., & Bennett, L. (1984). Family rituals. *Family Process, 23,* 401–420.

Origins of Creativity

Creativity begins with doubt and questions. In social work, creativity starts when practitioners doubt the value of their work or question the methods they are using. Without these doubts and questions, there is no need for insight. However, an insight sometimes comes before a question or doubt. For example, a social worker may have a new insight about a client. The insight then stimulates a set of questions or doubts about therapeutic method. Ironically, the role that social work research could play in stimulating these questions and first insights usually has not been a focus of discussion. Instead, much of the current debate has centered around the relative merits of quantitative or qualitative methods, summative or formative, hard or soft, science or art. Yet if research is to promote innovation, initially proof is not so much needed as timely and accurate information. Epstein (1986) has reasoned that social work is neither science nor art, but rather a set of practical activities designed to help people in distress. Therefore, the criteria social workers use to assess the value of research should involve questions of practicality, purpose, and cost. To do otherwise is to limit the potential of research to stimulate new directions and insights.

In a dynamic profession such as social work, research never should be the exclusive province of paid researchers. In their chapter, Epstein and Grasso suggest how practitioners can carry out practice research, and use practice research to generate innovative ideas for themselves and their colleagues. Epstein and Grasso also discuss the latent function of research for creativity.

By introducing new information, research legitimizes social workers asking questions which otherwise might be considered unprofessional, disloyal, or unimportant. By stimulating enthusiasm and concern, research also generates new ideas that often are not directly related to the topics being researched.

Epstein and Grasso's chapter also suggests that first insight is more likely to come to the mind that is fed information—for such information is vital to creative practitioners for use in reworking and remolding their cognitive maps.

Harold H. Weissman
Editor/Senior Author

Reference

Epstein, I. (1986, May). *The positivists' lament: Qualitative faddism vs. quantitative pragmatism.* Paper presented at a conference—Clinical Creativity: An Antidote to Agency Doldrums—of the Hunter College School of Social Work, New York.

Using Agency-Based Available Information to Further Practice Innovations

Irwin Epstein and Anthony J. Grasso

Many social work clinicians, supervisors, and administrators have excellent ideas for practice innovations. Frequently, because of time pressures, competitiveness, procrastination, or other preoccupations, these ideas are never specified, tested, and shared. These failures to describe, test, and disseminate personally constructed innovations are losses to the social work field. More problematic, from the client's standpoint, is the tendency for some "intuitionists" to hold onto their clinical perceptions and diagnostic judgments irrespective of past, present, and future client behavior. Today's intuitive leap can become tomorrow's intellectual straitjacket. The words "first insight" used in the literature on creativity should be taken literally. The insight needs to be examined.

No matter how deeply felt, intuitions can be wrong. Unless social workers have ways of independently collecting data about their perceptions and subjecting them to logical and empirical testing and scrutiny they cannot tell much about the value of their intuitiveness. The same is true of the design of interventions and services based solely on ideology that are untested by empirical investigation and systematic evaluation. Unfortunately, social workers are least likely to subject our most deeply held practice assumptions to rigorous specification, scrutiny, and testing.

With the advent of the computer, the potential applications of available agency data are just beginning to be recognized. This quantitative information can serve as a source of new knowledge about clients, staff, program, and policy. To illustrate, the examples presented are based on a highly sophisticated computerized information system that the authors developed at Boysville of Michigan, a child and family service agency. However, a system of this complexity is not necessary to provide useful data. Any agency that routinely collects information about its clients, staff, or programs can put this information to innovative use.

For definitional purposes here, *research* is considered to be the *relatively* systematic collection, analysis, and interpretation of information routinely available to direct service practitioners, supervisors, and administrators. Potential data sources include case records, statistical reports, community surveys, census data, client diagnostic data, and so forth. Obviously, this definition of research is not restricted to classical experimental designs. Also, although the sources listed are predominantly quantitative, qualitative methods are not excluded from the definition. Any and all forms of inquiry that rely on practical experience, logic, and external validation should be endorsed.

Boysville Management Information System (BOMIS)

Boysville of Michigan is the state's largest private agency, serving 550 troubled adolescents and their families. Treatment centers are located at its main campus in Clinton, a smaller campus in Saginaw, and nine group homes. The original Boysville treatment program was based on a modified version of "positive peer culture" in which the natural influences of the adolescent peer group were enlisted to change client behavior and attitude. Over the past few years, Boysville also has introduced an intensive family therapy program on the main campus for all youths in placement, specialized family foster care for youths unable to return to their natural families, and a metro-area emergency placement program. Although a growing number of the Boysville clients are neglect-abused, most are adjudicated delinquents with serious behavioral, social, and educational problems.

The information system (BOMIS) designed and employed at Boysville is a fully integrated, computerized management information, program evaluation, practice decision-making, and applied research effort. It also is intended to promote basic research on adolescent development and family function. Its primary purposes are to maximize the effectiveness of Boysville's efforts to help troubled children and their families and to describe these efforts accurately to funding and accountability agencies (Tripodi, Fellin, & Epstein, 1978). In this chapter, the contribution of BOMIS to innovation and testing within the agency is emphasized.

BOMIS information is gathered at four stages of client involvement with the agency—(1) input, (2) throughput, (3) output, and (4) outcome. At the input stage, client information such as previous placement in other programs, seriousness of offense, and family composition, as well as more standard demographic information such as race, sex, and so on, is gathered. The diagnostic information also is added. With these background and diagnostic data, agency staff are able to systematically assess clients who come to Boysville and plan a treatment strategy.

At the throughput stage, BOMIS stores and analyzes information on worker interventions, client critical incidents, and staff rating of client behavior and of behavioral change during their involvement in the program. This information is used primarily for modifying and improving treatment interventions but also for some program management decisions at the supervisory level.

At the output stage, BOMIS collects information on the conditions of client termination. This information includes data regarding successful completion of the program, placement destination, and completion of the family work program, as well as individual and family coping scores at time of termination. This information is used to determine whether individual clients and their families have achieved treatment goals. Through aggregation, it also makes possible individual worker, unit, and program level evaluation.

At the outcome stage, information is gathered at 3, 12, and 18 months after client termination. This data set includes information on current client placement status—that is, whether the client is placed in the family, jail, or other settings; whether the client is in school and/or is working; whether the client has had other contacts with the police—and family and client coping measures. This information allows Boysville to make inferences about the impact the program has had on clients after termination.

In addition to the data on client progress, BOMIS also gathers information concerning staff activity and effectiveness on an individual and unit basis. Using this information, supervisors can provide more effective individual and group supervision and identify staff training needs. At the middle management level, staff receive regular reports concerning program performance and contract compliance. Finally, BOMIS provides executive staff with data that are used for assessing broad agency policies, influencing public policy external to the agency, and procuring additional funding.

BOMIS as a Source of Practice Innovations

In the relatively short time that BOMIS has been used it has provided an empirical base for both clinical and program evaluation. Grasso and Epstein (in press) have described elsewhere the significance of a length-of-stay study for agency discharge policy and state funding policy reformulation. In addition, BOMIS has generated both policy and practice innovations. The following are data-based innovations that have direct implications for the structuring of practice and implications also for staff development and training.

Reconfiguration of Home Visitation

One example of how BOMIS has contributed to family treatment involves the restructuring of home visitation patterns. A family treatment worker is assigned to work with every Boysville child's family while the child is in care and for 6 months after placement. The agency's contract with the state Department of Social Services requires that family contacts are to average, at a minimum, one per month for the duration of service delivery to the family.

Analysis of family contact and client outcome data generated by BOMIS revealed two independent patterns that, when combined, had innovative practical significance. First, it was found that family workers tended to structure their family contacts at roughly equal intervals throughout the course of client placement and family treatment. Second, clients were most likely to become recidivists during their first 3 months after their return home. Because there were no additional resources available for increasing family outreach activity, a decision was made to intensify family contacts during the first 3 months of placement to maximize family engagement; reduce family contacts during the middle period (usually about 6 months); intensify family contacts during the last 3 months of placement; and intensify family contacts during the first 3 months after placement.

Although this reconfiguration of service is not ideal, it considers resource constraints, satisfies the requirements of funding and accountability sources, and possibly might increase the effectiveness of the family treatment program. It also will be possible to empirically assess its effectiveness and efficiency by comparing recidivism rates before and after reconfiguration.

Client's Acting Out and Staff Responses

All residential child care settings must deal with critical incidents in which clients "act out" their frustrations and anger. Sometimes youths go "AWOL" (absent without leave). At other times, they may require isolation to protect themselves and others. At Boysville, as in other progressive settings, the use of "lock-up" is a last resort. In this context, running away is seen as a program failure. Information about such "critical incidents" routinely is incorporated into BOMIS.

Recently, analysis of the use of lock-up at Boysville revealed that in the campus-based program black clients showed significantly higher rates of lock-up than white clients. This finding initially was alarming to staff who were concerned that it might reflect a pattern of institutional racism at the campus. Further analysis, however, revealed that white youths were most likely to go AWOL. Considering the rural location of the campus and that most black youths in placement were from inner-city Detroit, it made no sense to run. Their "acting out" behavior, as a result, was more likely to land them in isolation. For white youths who were closer to home, going AWOL meant, among other things, avoidance of lock-up.

Although the racial differences were now explained, it was determined that both kinds of critical incidents were indicators of the program's failure to more effectively handle client "acting out." As a result, a training program in conflict management was introduced for line staff. Upon completion of the program, analysis of precritical and postcritical incident patterns will determine whether the desired reduction has been achieved and whether specific units on campus or individual workers are associated with higher rates of such incidents.

Uncovering Patterns of Sexual Abuse

A final and more complex example of the use of BOMIS and a survey of qualitative case records for generating clinical innovation involves the sensitive issue of sexual abuse. Generally speaking, information about prior sexual abuse tends to be lacking at intake. Understandably, youths do not volunteer this kind of information in their initial contacts with intake workers, their parents do not reveal it, and referral sources do not provide it. However, clinical staff report that during placement clients often reveal, directly or inadvertently, evidence of having been sexually abused or that they have sexually abused others.

This perception was supported by Trepper and Barrett (1986) who described family coping profiles of incestuous families. In their article, they also employed the FACES II instrument routinely administered by BOMIS. A comparison of the family profiles of Boysville client families indicated a remarkable similarity between the profiles of many of the Boysville families and the patterns of incestuous families described by Trepper and Barrett. A systematic survey of qualitative case record data conducted by treatment staff validated this perception. That survey, which reviewed intake information as well as information revealed through client careers in the agency, indicated that nearly 60 percent of the males and 93 percent of the females in placement had been involved in sexual abuse before placement at the agency.

Based on this disturbing finding, Boysville Department of Clinical Staff Development has developed an extensive training program for all Boysville staff to more effectively deal with this problem. Evaluation of that program will focus on the success with which family coping patterns change over the course of treatment, with particular attention to those family profiles that are associated with sexual abuse.

Simple Studies Can Produce Surprising Discoveries

BOMIS is an example of a state-of-the-art computerized information system. However, a research-oriented clinician or clinical administrator sometimes can learn a great deal about the effectiveness of practice and the need for innovation by simply counting and calculating percentages of relevant data. For example, in a post-master's degree program evaluation course (Dane & Epstein, 1985), numerous examples of simple studies that involved hand counting but produced true "discoveries" emerged. Although these studies might not appear in scientific journals, the inelegance of their subject matter should not detract from their programmatic significance.

One study involved a breakfast program for senior citizens. The program director noticed that food was discarded despite her best effort to introduce variety into the meals. Encouraged to count the types of food and the quantity thrown away, she inferred that program participants preferred the same menu daily rather than variety. A return to daily bagels from trendier muffins saved money and reduced waste.

Another agency was losing potential clients because of lengthy intake processing and turnaround time. The agency employed full- and part-time workers who all were involved to some degree in intake activities.

A student working at the agency was encouraged to compute the average time in processing applicants by full- and part-time workers. She discovered that part-time workers were significantly more efficient in processing intake applications. Regardless of the reasons for this pattern, once part-time workers were reassigned primarily to intake, the problem of client loss was significantly reduced. Both sets of workers were pleased with this solution.

Finally, a director of a family treatment training program for psychiatric residents indicated that her program had been in operation for 3 years and that she had trained three cohorts of psychiatric residents but had never been evaluated. She reluctantly reviewed case records compiled during 3 years to determine what percentage of resident interviews with patients were conducted with a patient's family member present. Although she resisted this "simplistic" and crude indicator, she was astonished to discover that more than 80 percent of the treatment interviews were conducted with only the patient. She agreed that a more extensive program review was in order.

Data May Challenge Cherished Beliefs

Although quantitative research provides a means for describing, collecting, analyzing, and interpreting data about monitoring and testing practice innovations, it does not always provide pleasing results. For example, in a study of the adoption of practice innovations in community organization, Rothman, Teresa, Kay, and Morningstar (1983) found that appeals to social workers' bureaucratic commitments were more potent than those appeals pitched to professional or client concerns. For proponents of professionalization, these findings are not heartening. However, it is precisely this capacity for self-refutation that recommends quantitative research so strongly. The opportunity to systematically test and challenge cherished beliefs is what makes quantitative research and hypothesis testing so valuable.

In this regard, quantitative researchers sometimes refer to Type 1 and Type 2 errors. These valuable concepts warn against the assumption that an intervention has an effect when it does not, or that it has no effect when it does. In clinical social work research, this typology of inference provides a logical and statistical means by which researchers can reject those interventions that are meaningless or possibly harmful and accept those that seem to help. Alternatively, the quantitative researcher must guard against the tendency to equate statistical and social significance, or to assume that anything that cannot be counted does not exist. Thus, in advocating the use of available quantitative information for generating and testing practice innovations, the authors propose an approach that recognizes the strengths as well as the potential abuses of this approach.

Putting Information to Creative Use

It should be clear that a system of continuous collection, analysis, and interpretation of relevant data not only suggests innovations but also can be used to assess the impact of innovations once they have been implemented. Agency-based quantitative research for generating first insights and testing practice innovations is important and useful. Although the most elegant examples are drawn from a highly sophisticated computerized information system, some more methodologically mundane but no less programmatically significant examples are provided. All of these examples are meant to demonstrate that the disregard for agency-based, quantitative information does not serve the goals of clinical creativity or building knowledge in social work.

To take full advantage of these data, the profession will have to reassess its commitment to a single model of research. Students will have to be trained to have a broader perspective on how research can affect practice. Not the least important change will be an understanding of the importance of knowing as precisely as possible what is actually happening to all concerned parties when services are rendered. Information is a stimulus to creativity.

References

Dane, E., & Epstein, I. (1985). A dark horse in continuing education programming at the post-master's level: Monitoring and evaluation skills for social workers in middle management. *Journal of Continuing Social Work Education, 3*(2), 3–8.

Grasso, T., & Epstein, I. (in press). Management by measurement: Organizational dilemmas and opportunities. *Journal of Administration in Social Work.*

Rothman, J., Teresa, J. G., Kay, T. L., & Morningstar, G. C. (1983). *Marketing human service innovations.* Beverly Hills, CA: Sage Publications.

Trepper, T. F., & Barrett, M. J. (1986). Vulnerability to incest: A framework for assessment. In T. F. Trepper & M. J. Barrett (Eds.) *Treating incest: A multiple systems perspective* (pp. 13–25). New York: Haworth Press.

Tripodi, T., Fellin, P., & Epstein, I. (1978). *Differential social program evaluation.* Itasca, IL: F. E. Peacock.

First Insight

His public strategies reflect the project of his art, the joyful disruption of the conventional, the refusal of complacency. . . .
—Richard Ellman, on Oscar Wilde

What provides that first insight that something is not quite right with the usual way of thinking about a problem—that insight that provides a guide for the search for a creative solution? Experience is one source. For example, by working with deaf people, Alexander Graham Bell was able to see relationships that led to the invention of the telephone. Thomas (1984) suggested that new social work ideas and techniques come from four sources: (1) applied and basic research, (2) transfer from other fields, (3) legal application, and (4) personal and professional experiences (p. 130). New concepts may be stimulated by practitioners' exposure to advances in scientific technology, such as computers and pharmacology. Ideas also may be drawn from other fields, such as public administration or psychology, or even from self-help groups. Still other innovations are stimulated by changes in laws or governmental regulations. Professional and personal experiences also are fruitful for generating ideas.

The fresh insight is most likely to come when one is exposed to a variety of related, but different, experiences and conceptions of the world. A jolt to our usual ways of thought and expression often is needed. For example, a student began his senior thesis with the phrase "after a great deal of thought and extensive research I have concluded that. . . ." It was returned with a red line drawn through "after a great deal of thought and extensive research." Above the red line his professor had written, "I'll be the judge of that."

Von Oech (1988) suggested that the key to the relationships between one's experience and creativity is the ability to see analogies. At times, a different way of thinking—the "whack on the side of the head," as Von Oech (1988) said—is needed to dislodge assumptions and thought patterns that constrict the ability to see new analogies and be innovative. Necessity often provides this whack.

To ensure that new ideas occur when innovation is needed, it is important for social workers not to restrict their thinking, as Imre suggests in the following chapter. The creative search for both solutions and problems needing solutions is shaped by what people think the world is like, and in what ways they think they can explain or predict what people will do in it.

37

Is the world complete and governed by universal laws that only can be discovered through scientific study? Or is the world a place where order always is in danger of giving way to disorder, where knowledge is not discovered, it is made, based on how people make sense of the world, and how that sense-making changes the world. According to Middleman and Rhodes (1985), "Change is to be expected in this worldview. Uncertainty, instability, and fluctuation are natural as new levels of order are apprehended. This is the world where limitations may be possibilities if one can see the evolutionary trends (p. 50).

As Imre notes, social work has been dominated by the views that knowledge can be based only on careful observation and experimentation, that there is social cause and effect, and that when there are multiple causes, statistical analyses can determine the amount of variance different factors produce. However, there are other, quite different views of the world, that posit that a certain amount of flexibility or "play" exists among its parts. As Hackman (1985) stated,

> For example, where contingency theory assumes that if we knew the right moderating variables, we would be able to predict and control behavior in virtually any situation, multiple possibility theory holds that such an aspiration is ill conceived.
>
> Instead, the theory maintains, there are many possible outcomes that can emerge in any situation, and the particular outcome that is actualized is not completely determined by the causal factors that precede it. Thus, multiple possibility theory envisions a world with some "play" in the system, and it encourages attention to human choice as a factor that transforms multiple possibilities into single courses of action.
>
> Multiple possibility theory nicely complements the system theorists' notion of equifinality. Where equifinality alerts us to the fact that the same outcome can occur in response to many causes, multiple possibility theory posits that the same cause can generate a variety of outcomes. Taken together, the two notions call into question standard stimulus–response models in which situational causes are tightly linked to behavioral effects—whether directly ("Introduce this management practice and performance will improve") or contingently (". . . performance will improve, but only for certain kinds of people under certain circumstances"). (pp. 141–142)

If creativity involves breaking out of existing cognitive limits, multiple possibility theory offers a way of transcending the limitations of stimulus–response thinking (Weick, 1979). The creative person no longer is looking for an answer, but is open to the possibility that there are many answers.[1]

Imre suggests certain nets that can limit the ability to develop first insights. The primary net, she proposes, is the definition of "knowledge." Is it something "out there" in the world to be discovered, uncontaminated by feelings or interests? Or is knowledge embedded in the knower—are the meanings that are attached to an event as important as the event?

The meanings people give events often provide the key to insight. For example, envision a dispute between a social worker and a child care worker over treatment of an adolescent who has been disrupting life in a group home. The social worker reasons on the basis of developmental theory about adolescents who are "acting out." Yet, would this social worker make the same arguments if he or she had had experience as a child care worker? Perhaps, but at least the social worker would have a completely different understanding of the meaning of the child care worker's point of view. From that understanding, different ideas might emerge.

Harold H. Weissman
Editor/Senior Author

References

Hackman, J. R. (1985). Doing research that makes a difference. In E. Lawler, A. Mohrman, S. Mohrman, G. Ledford, & T. Cummings (Eds.), *Doing research that is useful for theory and practice* (pp. 222–248). San Francisco: Jossey–Bass.

Middleman, R., & Rhodes, G. (1985). *Competent supervision.* Englewood Cliffs, NJ: Prentice–Hall.

Thomas, E. (1984). *Designing interventions for the helping professions.* Beverly Hills, CA: Sage Publications.

Von Oech, R. (1988). *Whack on the side of the head: How to unlock your mind for innovation.* New York: Warner Books.

Weick, K. (1979). Cognitive processes in organizations. In B. Staw (Ed.), *Research in organizational behavior* (pp. 41–74). Greenwich, CT: JAI.

[1]Weick (1979) pointed out that there are some models of action, such as organized anarchies, garbage cans, and loose coupling, where rational sequences seldom are thought to unfold in a rational order. Steps either are omitted or occur at odd points (p. 64). For example, on the basis of data about the effectiveness of treatment, physicians often make a diagnosis after the fact, but a priori diagnosis seems to have little to do with treatment effectiveness (p. 64).

The Effect of Words, Knowing, and Meaning on Practice

Roberta Wells Imre

Students who study social work practice inevitably encounter the subjective versus objective dilemma. The problem is particularly acute in social work because a connection commonly is made between the word "objective" and a conventional and limited definition of science. The result is a tendency to associate objectivity with rationality and science and to view intuition as subjectivity with its implied emotionality as contaminants to be avoided. This oversimplified view of science fails to note that whatever is known about the world is known by a self inevitably involved in the knowing—a perspective that raises serious doubts about the existence of a clear-cut separation between objective and subjective aspects of knowing.

Social workers are just beginning to realize the limitations of this simplified view of science which generally had been accepted without question until recently (Heineman, 1981; Imre, 1982; Weick, 1987). This conventional view is based on the philosophy of *logical positivism*, which holds that all that counts as knowledge can only be known through direct observation. Subjectivity is to be guarded against by the use of various, often highly sophisticated, mathematical techniques. Ideas and information so derived are considered to represent the objective world from which the influence of the human participant has been rigorously excluded.

In fact, science is much more complicated than positivism would suggest. New scientific paradigms have grown out of developments in relativity and quantum mechanics. Techniques based on Newtonian principles fit the positivist paradigm and continue to be useful. Yet the limitations of this perspective generally are taken for granted in the physical sciences where theoretical research goes on apace utilizing different paradigms and perspectives as well as the Newtonian.

As new frontiers in science advance, it becomes clearer that what can be learned through scientific methods involves the personal participation of the scientist using all of the resources of the self. These resources include intuitive feelings and a recognition that nature does not stand still for human observation. The process of observation itself may influence what is there to be seen. In addition, it is human beings who are doing the observing. The sense they impose on what they see comes from the resources of the human mind. They construct what is believed to be reality, often using metaphors to represent what nature itself appears to be like. It is logical then to expect that the personal involvement of the social worker will be an inevitable part of professional practice and of the methods used to understand it.

Tacit Knowledge and the Nature of Human Relationships

One of the primary resources of the mind is what Michael Polanyi (1966) called the "tacit dimension," which refers to all that has been learned by a person through prior experience of various kinds and now is used in efforts to perform a task or to make sense of what currently is focused on. Polanyi emphasized that knowing involves more than can be put into language. He meant that it is impossible to be aware of all the tacit resources or all the knowledge being used at any given time to understand a complex situation.

The way the crucial concept of relationship, for example, has been considered in social work often makes it difficult to realize the presence of tacit consent. Although it actually is being used, it is not recognized as being there (Imre, 1985). Even research building on the pioneering effort of Truax and Carkhuff (1967), work based on Carl Roger's work, tends to treat the concept of relationship as if the necessary qualities could be isolated without reference to this tacit content.

In the psychoanalytic literature, the influence of early relationships is considered to be important, even critical, yet the use of an objectifying term such as "love object" predominates. This language is a stumbling block to recognizing the truly interpersonal nature of love relationships and implies the existence of a kind of objectivity that prevents a deeper

41

understanding of what it means to be connected to another person in a loving way. Objects have an "out there" quality to them. Objects can impinge on, and in turn themselves be acted on by others, but they do not respond as other persons do with the complex mix of thought and feelings, and attributions of meaning, which characterizes relationships between persons.

The difficulties social work has with this kind of content are shared by a number of other professions. Several years ago, a symposium on love was sponsored by two organizations, the Columbia University Center for Psychoanalytic Training and Research and the Association for Psychoanalytic Medicine (Gaylin & Person, 1988). In her paper for this meeting, Gilligan (1988) noted that in psychology the use of a technical language objectifies love and obscures the true nature of love, in which the participants are subjects, not objects. She turned to literature to find a deeper understanding of the love that is found in relationships between subjects, not objects.

The difficulty in understanding this difference does seem to reside in the choice and use of words that reflect the emphases of a society greatly concerned with technology and its associated sciences. The result of such a selective process, however, is to leave out references to the personal, which is deemed to be too subjective to be a proper subject for academic study. Yet, how else can one understand relationships between people, and what people need from each other, without addressing what it means to be a person who lives in relationship?

What seems to be missing in a language where another person becomes a "love object," or in recent social work jargon where the client is referred to as "the client system," is a perception of relationships as involving real and continuing emotional connections between and among people. These connections are fed by deep roots that become entangled with each other in ways that make a true separation at the very least difficult and in some respects impossible. When attention is paid to this aspect of human life, it becomes apparent that the self cannot be understood in isolation, but only in relationship—in relationship to a variety of others beginning with earliest experiences with parenting figures and including all those others who have been, or currently are, a part of any individual's social milieu. These relationships account for many aspects of the self, including the meanings, conscious and unconscious, that become attached to everyday experiences as well as to those of life's more dramatic moments.

Gilligan's (1982) provocative suggestion that women tend to think differently about moral matters because they have had different developmental experiences suggests important ways in which experience in relationships contributes to how a person thinks. Some researchers believe that the dichotomies of objective and subjective, reason and emotion, so characteristic of thought in Western culture, have contributed to a tendency to demean and undervalue the contributions of women to understanding the nature of knowing in human life (Belenky, Clinchy, Goldberger, & Tarule, 1986). It is only relatively recently that the voices of women have been heard in enough numbers to require that attention be paid to what they are saying.

The difficulties women have had both in expressing themselves and in being heard illustrate how easy it is to believe that knowledge is objective and out there, while in fact basing this picture of reality on all of the presuppositions and assumptions one has acquired in the process of growing through relationships, as all humans do. It is then easy to believe that the resulting picture represents a world from which the self and the personal have been eliminated. However, as the physicist Bohm (1981) has said: "Our whole approach to life is evidently full of presupposition, which deeply affect not only our actions, but also our thoughts, feelings, urges, desires, motivations, the contents of the will, and, indeed, our general way of experiencing almost everything" (p. 381).

Using Intuition in Practice

Human beings grow up in interaction with others and in these interactions the self is continuously created. This self, as H. R. Niebuhr (1963) has said, "is fundamentally social, in this sense that it is a being which not only knows itself in relation to other selves but exists as self only in that relationship" (p. 71). Because all selves have this quality of embeddedness in a social milieu of relationships, past and present, the social worker brings a reservoir of tacit resources to the situation of trying to understand another person or persons who develop through the same general processes, albeit in a variety of different situations and cultural environments.

Intuition involves a tapping of these tacit resources in a process whereby the focus on the other calls forth often inchoate reactions in the self. These reactions often are responses to some similarity in the other person—a similarity that the imagination utilizes in trying to make sense out of what is going on in this person's life and what is needed in the present relationship. Such intuitive feelings often come from personal experiences and their origins rarely are clear at the time. It would be a great mistake to say, however, that they either are not there at all or that they are meaningless.

What is required is a checking of these responses in terms of the client's reality. An intuitive response can be mistaken, but it also can be an accurate, even indispensable guide. When a social worker finds such feelings stirring in the self, whether or not they can be immediately accounted for by the specific content of what has been said, it is important to note the intuitive response. It is potentially a clue and should be recognized as such.

England (1986) sees an important place for theory in this process. The mind of the social worker weaves together the intuitive responses and various theories in an effort to give meaning and coherence to what is being experienced. "The worker uses theoretical knowledge not to apply formulae, but to construct coherence from immediate complexity" (p. 202). Intuitive feelings are a vital part of this complexity.

Practice as "Knowing-in-Action"

In his discussion about the importance of reflection in the various kinds of practices, Schön (1983, 1987) made an interesting suggestion. He started from the position that not enough is understood about how professionals actually work. Schön proposed looking more closely at the place of what he called "reflecting-in-practice" (1983, pp. 59–69) or "knowing-in-action" (1983, pp. 49–69). He suggested that the artistry of a profession is lost in the "technical rationality" of the research university (1987, pp. 12–13).

Although he focused primarily on other professions, including architecture and engineering, as well as medicine, one of the potential contributions of Schön's thought to social work is the recognition that a good, creative practice involves a discipline that needs to be understood. He suggested that this practice can best be learned by studying what practitioners actually do. This is a crucial point for discussion. Recognizing in social work that the separation of the objective from the subjective is a questionable division at best does not mean that practitioners are free to do whatever feels right to them. What it does mean is that there is a need to be clearer about the kinds of discipline involved in good, creative practice and the standards by which it can be evaluated by others as well as by the participants.

Given the complexity of life, and human propensities for error and self deception, there are many ways studies of these aspects of practice can be derailed. If real understanding of practice is to be furthered, however, there needs to be a recognition of the complexity of the inevitable involvement of the self in this practice. The person of the social worker, with all its capacities for experiencing and knowing learned through relationships, provides resources for understanding the stories of other selves lived in relationship. To help others, it is necessary to listen for the imaginative meanings they attribute to their relationships, as well as to the interpretations of events that people weave into the narratives of their lives.

Katherine Morton (1984) suggested that one of the values of literature is to expand these imaginative resources and meanings:

> So you say that reading a novel is a way to kill time when the real world needs attending to. I tell you that the only world I know is the world as I know it, and I am still learning how to comprehend that. These books are showing me ways of being I could never have managed alone. I am not killing time, I'm trying to make a life. (p. 2)

Practitioners are always being recalled to the concrete, the present, and the clearly "real." The roles of imagination and intuition as part of the artistry of practice seldom are noted amid the constant necessity to respond to unremitting human need.

Social workers, like other human service workers, need breathing room to reflect on their work without having to do something, and do it now. Because of this characteristic immersion in concrete situations—so many clients to see, to refer, to arrange placement for, to help somehow in the allotted time before the next client must be seen—the importance of the intuitive and artistic resources of the self are obscured easily, and hence to some degree endangered. More attention needs to be given to how the integration of thinking, feeling, and imagining in the self of the social worker makes possible a disciplined practice more fully responsive to the complex needs of the other human beings who are seeking help.

References

Belenky, M. F., Clinchy, B. M., Goldberger, N. R., & Tarule, J. M. (1986). *Women's ways of knowing*. New York: Basic Books.

Bohm, D. (1981). Insight, knowledge, science, and human values. *Teachers College Record, 82*(3), 380–402.

England, H. (1986) *Social work as art*. London: Allen & Unwin.

Gaylin, W., & Person, E. (1988). *Passionate attachments: Thinking about love*. New York: Free Press.

Gilligan, C. (1982). *In a different voice*. Cambridge, MA: Harvard University Press.

Gilligan, C. (1988). The riddle of femininity and the psychology of love. In W. Gaylin & E. Person (Eds.), *Passionate attachments: Thinking about love* (pp. 101–114). New York: Free Press.

Heineman, M. B. (1981). The obsolete scientific imperative in social work research. *Social Service Review, 55*, 371–397.

Imre, R. W. (1982). *Knowing and caring: Philosophical issues in social work*. Lanham, MD: University Press of America.

Imre, R. W. (1985). Tacit knowledge in social work research and practice. *Smith College Studies in Social Work, 55*(2), 137–149.

Morton, K. (1984, December 23). The story telling animal [Book review]. *The New York Times*, pp. 1–2.

Niebuhr, H. R. (1963). *The responsible self*. New York: Harper & Row.

Polanyi, M. (1966). *The tacit dimension*. New York: Doubleday.

Schön, D. A. (1983). *The reflective practitioner*. New York: Basic Books.

Schön, D. A. (1987). *Educating the reflective practitioner*. San Francisco: Jossey–Bass.

Truax, C., & Carkhuff, R. R. (1967). *Toward effective counseling and psychotherapy: Training and practice*. Chicago: Aldine.

Weick, A. (1987). Reconceptualizing the philosophical perspective of social work. *Social Service Review, 61*, 218–230.

Use of Metaphor

The chapter by Imre calls attention to the gravitational pull of accepted ways of looking at the unknown. Competent practitioners use cognitive maps in the area of their expertise. These practitioners also use meta models of thinking—such as rules about logic, consistency, and analysis—which can bar or aid their capacity to rework and recombine practice patterns. Flexible application of these rules is one of the keys to making the transition to creative practice. There is a difference between the new ideas that come from insight and the kind of knowledge that comes from merely rearranging what already is known. As Sloan (1983) pointed out, "Technical and discursive reason, logic, and classification all may be useful in ordering our thought, and sometimes even in rearranging them in new patterns and relationships. But they work with the given, and do not bring any new elements into play" (p. 129). To gain a fresh perspective—a new grasp—insight is required.

The dictionary (Neufeldt, 1988) defines metaphor as "a figure of speech containing an implied comparison, in which a word or phrase ordinarily and primarily used of one thing is applied to another . . . [such as] the 'curtain of night' " (p. 852). Metaphor makes it possible to accommodate apparent differences, to maintain both the literal sense of words and the new sense to which the metaphor refers. By introducing new meanings and understandings, metaphor overcomes some of the limitations of logic, in which the same word must mean the same thing in one sentence as it does in another (Sloan, 1983). Metaphor maintains the separate meanings of words, and at the same time, generates a new meaning.

Steinman (as cited in Frazier, 1988) described metaphor as ". . . a way of saying what you don't mean in order to say what you don't say" (p. 2). Metaphor exponentially increases the communicative power of vocabulary, according to Steinman. It is the window of the imagination, from which one sees new meanings in events and situations.

To grasp the new meaning, what Gardner (1983) called "spatial intelligence" often is required. To Gardner, *spatial intelligence* is different from logical mathematical intelligence. It is the ability to capture in words a "kind of resemblance that may have occurred . . . initially in spatial form. Indeed, underlying many scientific theories are "images of wide scope: Darwin's vision of the 'tree of life,' Freud's notion of the unconscious as submerged like an iceberg, Dalton's view of the atom as a tiny solar system" (p. 177). However, intuitions or imaginings can be deceptive. Often, desire substitutes for analysis, and what is intuited is wrong.

Gould (1987) gave an example of how the wish for harmony distorts reality:

> I find it both depressing and amusing that so many of our intellectual efforts, though masquerading as attempts to understand nature, are really anodynes for justifying our hopes and calming our fears. (p. 227)

> Accordingly, the systems view of health can be applied to different systems levels, with the corresponding levels of health mutually interconnected. In particular we can discern three interdependent levels of health—individual, social, and ecological. What is unhealthy for the individual is generally also unhealthy for the society and for the embedding ecosystem. (Capra, as cited in Gould, 1987, p. 227)

> Would it were so. The world would be an easier place if this hope of interacting harmony followed inevitably from a concept of levels. But it doesn't. If levels have substantial independence, then advantages to individuals at one level may or may not yield benefits to individuals at adjacent levels. Blessings to persons need not benefit collectivities—unless we are trying to graft our hopes for harmony upon an ultimately uncooperative world. (Gould, 1987, p. 227)

> At best, we get hints from people who have worked out a holistic system only halfway (von Bertalanffy), or in an oracular fashion (Gregory Bateson), or in the pop mode (Arthur Koestler). (p. 221)

Intuition can be expanded by crossing boundaries and finding fruitful analogies. However, once they are created these new analogies and metaphors must be questioned.

Schön's (1987) study of five professions described another way to expand intuition—by observing how professionals use the information they have when they are faced with ambiguous situations. Schön argued that professionals do not simply operate as problem solvers, deducing their actions and solutions to problems in a logical, objective, value-free way. Rather, he saw them as often involved in a creative or artistic process in which they had to deal with uncertainty, instability, and value conflict.

Professionals have to manage large amounts of information selectively, spin out long lines of invention and inference, examine several ways of looking at a situation at once, and, thus, reflect on unique, uncertain situations. Schön (1987) called this kind of patterned yet informal improvisation having a reflective conversation, or letting the situation "talk back." (pp. 26–27).

Much of professional thinking involves implicit conversations with phantom others. Who are these phantoms, under what conditions are they invoked, and what are their basic beliefs? Professionals who want to be creative cannot avoid considering who it is that they talk with when they think, and how these people think.

The Davidson chapter that follows gives examples of these conversations with others and where such conversations can lead. The chapter also shows how a person's talks with himself or herself about personal experiences can lead to improvisations and new insights.

Harold H. Weissman
Editor/Senior Author

References

Frazier, J. (1988, March). *Metaphor, imagination and clinical practice.* Paper presented at the Symposium of the Study Group for Philosophical Issues in Social Work conducted at the meeting of the Council on Social Work Education.

Gardner, H. (1983). *Frames of mind.* New York: Basic Books.

Gould, S. J. (1987). *An urchin in the storm.* New York: W. W. Norton.

Neufeldt, V. (Ed.-in-chief.). (1988). *Webster's new world dictionary* (3rd college ed.). New York: Simon & Schuster.

Schön, D. (1987). *Educating the reflective practitioner.* San Francisco: Jossey–Bass.

Sloan, D. (1983). *Insight–imagination: The emancipation of thought in the modern world.* Westport, CT: Greenwood Press.

Gaining Insight through Conversations with Clients, Peers, and Ourselves

Kay W. Davidson

In familiar situations, social workers can call on procedures derived from a body of professional theory and knowledge. However, in new and unforeseen circumstances, doubt that traditional practice is appropriate can be the stimulus for development of new ideas. When traditional practice is not effective, and when, in Schön's (1987) terms, the case is not "in the book," social workers, like other professionals, must find new ways to solve problems using improvisation and innovation (p. 5). Doubt about traditional practices can be a spur either to innovation or to burnout. Steps social workers can take to ensure a spur to innovation are described in this chapter.

The process of moving from doubt to new forms of practice requires that social workers undertake what Schön calls "reflection-in-action" (p. 27) by holding conversations about their doubts with clients, peers, and themselves, thereby stimulating innovation. For example, this process is especially important in the area of social work services to families, where multiple and rapid changes in family forms and life-styles have led to reexamination and redefinition of the concept of family (Hartman & Laird, 1983).

From Certainty to Doubt

Despite its strong family services roots, the social work profession developed with an emphasis on individually oriented, psychotherapeutic services. Even with the systemic approach of family therapy, the model of family practice that did evolve was designed for and accommodated the needs of middle-class, two-parent families. For the most part, service delivery systems remained physically based in agencies with schedules and patterns of service that led to problems of access, availability, and engagement for many families and cultural groups.

Traditional services for families presupposed the ideal type of two-parent family with emotional supports, and sought to move families toward stability around that model. There was little doubt that other family forms were "less than normal" and the "broken home" was a cause for pity. Questions of choice of life-style, or the consideration that there might be more viable, potentially healthier forms of family life than that of a stressful and unhappy marriage, were given minimal attention.

Traditional family services also emphasized the need for clients to think through, reflect on, and move toward improved behavioral and relationship patterns primarily through individual, long-term counseling. Although extra resources frequently were provided to meet gaps and deficits, the practice model focused on self-sufficiency. It was based on the assumption that the ideal family type applied to, and was aspired to, by all families.

As the process of reformulation of social work practice has evolved (Goldstein, 1986), uncertainty about long-standing assumptions has been expressed.

Today, 50 percent of first and second marriages are ending in divorce, many families are disrupted, and their membership and life-styles have changed. Many families are coping with problems such as divorce, poverty and unemployment, early parenthood, inadequate housing or homelessness, social isolation and lack of supportive networks, poor education, and ill health, and sometimes with most or all of these factors simultaneously. Often, no role division is possible in such highly stressed families, especially those with single parents. This lack of role division places a heavy responsibility on the mother, and, at times, on the children (Wallerstein & Kelly, 1979). As Rhodes (1977) has suggested, "The single adult of a one-parent family is particularly dependent on refueling sources outside the family which the society is not providing, thereby making the single-parent family vulnerable to disorganization" (p. 305). Yet, practice innovation has not met single parents' needs.

Doubt about Practice Environments

As some social workers became aware that many families found traditional services inaccessible, unwelcoming, and difficult to use

51

because of agency location, hours of service, eligibility requirements, and formality of intake procedures, their doubts were the stimulus for innovative practices that reached out to potential clients and eased eligibility requirements. The social workers' goals were minimum disruption of the already beleaguered life-style of clients, and maximum flexibility, to encourage clients to participate and benefit from services.

These innovative social workers set aside their assumptions, and, through their conversations with clients, recognized the importance of the clients' self-knowledge. The recognition that even the most overwhelmed and highly stressed clients could participate both in defining their problems and in seeking solutions led to greater readiness to actively seek out the client's contribution.

When clients drop out of programs, break appointments, or do not follow through on referrals, they often are dissatisfied with the fit between the service and their needs. For example, remodeling waiting areas, providing appropriate reading materials, caring for the visual impact of the setting, respecting privacy, and assuring safe play areas for children are all innovations that reduce client discomfort and diminish the sense of not belonging in formal and often forbidding environments.

As Smith and Thrasher (1986) have noted, social workers have begun to view their agencies as "facilitating environments" (p. 2). They describe the establishment of a mental health clinic in an attractive brownstone in a poor neighborhood. The agency emphasizes physical comfort for clients and extends a positive message as a well-cared-for, but not intimidating, environment. This facilitating environment extends to the social work practice of the agency, which offers flexibility and the willingness to explore any potentially therapeutic effort. The clinic seeks not to fit clients to its approach but "to make itself suitable for clients" (p. 2). For example, in a mental health clinic in an impoverished urban neighborhood, clients from overwhelmed families who had appeared to be nonverbal and interested only in minimal concrete services took part in a program that relied on creative use of clinic hours (Smith & Thrasher, 1986). Through conversations with clients about what they perceived their needs to be, the staff recognized that highly stressed clients had problems that might not be resolved by a weekly hour with a worker, but that could be approached through a flexible day treatment program. Thus, the length of a client and social worker session might exceed an hour or be as brief as 20 minutes. Clients were encouraged to make short, unscheduled visits to the agency called *do-drop-ins* (p. 5). Clients were informed that

> their own worker would not necessarily be available for each drop-in visit, but that they were free to interact with available clinical and support staff. The most frequent reasons clients dropped in were for information or for emotional refueling. One client described it as "getting my battery charged." (p. 9)

These efforts require agency openness and flexibility while clients test the usefulness of the service. Smith and Thrasher (1986) noted that staff rarely found the use of do-drop-in services to be excessive or disruptive of their general work routines.

Such practice innovations are developed by listening, improvising on clients' leads, and accepting their goals. Making use of these implicit and explicit conversations requires that social workers move beyond their reluctance to settle for the client's understanding of the problem, even though it may seem like role reversal if the social worker identifies the client's expertise and self-knowledge as taking precedence over the professional's contribution.

Taking the risk of suggesting or testing an innovation requires a social worker to have confidence that his or her efforts will be supported by others in the agency (Brager & Holloway, 1978). Peer support plays a vital role in the social worker's readiness to face doubts about accepted practices, to reflect on conversations with clients, and to explore possibilities for change.

Sharing the Doubt

Continuing reports that many highly stressed families needed help, yet failed to keep appointments, failed to verbalize problems seen as within the agency's domain, did not share cultural backgrounds and values with agency staff, and led some social workers to improvise in family programs. Because many clients' situations failed to improve with individually focused care, family group treatment was proposed as a method of choice by Levine (1964) and Minuchin (1967).

Availability to clients on their own terms was emphasized, and the home visit was rediscovered as a "new" technique for reaching out to highly stressed families (Levine, 1964; Bryant, 1980). Reflection and dissatisfaction with the limited results of traditional services led social workers to examine their assumptions with colleagues, to allow the entry of doubt, to check with colleagues about the relevance of services, and to open the door to innovation.

The innovative intervention termed the "Chattanooga choo choo" by its creators was used in a ghetto neighborhood to help families who had to place their child outside the home (Smith & Thrasher, 1986). Local members of the extended family, a traditional source of support in the black community, rarely were able to offer substitute care because they already were overburdened.

The social workers' readiness to explore alternatives and their attention to the complex family networks described by many clients led to the discovery that southern or Caribbean branches of clients' families often had the emotional and financial resources to care for a child. Thus, institutional placement could be avoided. When it was learned that these children had previous relationships with family members, they were sent to live with those families. This arrangement provided security and bonds of affection for the child. It also followed clients' wishes and enabled parents to retain a greater sense of integrity and self-worth than if the child had been placed in an institution.

The program was developed after conversations among colleagues in which social workers shared common childhood memories and considered their potential relevance for practice. Thus, when there appears to be a poor fit between the service delivery program and the needs of clients, the change process must be initiated by someone who is willing to raise questions such as

• Why are we doing things this way?
• What would happen if we did something different?
• What other ways of helping do we know?

Asking these questions and taking the steps to find answers to them create risks for a social worker. Questioning the program in which one is employed may endanger chances for promotion or place the job in jeopardy. The element of risk may to some extent account for the tendency of practitioners to undertake small, incremental innovations that do not threaten to destroy entire programs if they fail to thrive (Brager & Holloway, 1978; Patti, 1980). It is only by taking risks, however, that social workers can talk with peers to discover whether their doubts and questions are shared. Taking risks is easier in an agency that encourages open communication; supports collegial relations through structures such as supervision, in-service training, and support groups; and rewards the development of new ideas.

Doubt and Innovation

Considering client feedback on the appropriateness of services provided is a crucial aspect of professional accountability. The increasing readiness of social workers to take their clients' opinions and views of practice seriously as a means of actually scrutinizing their practice is evident in recent practice literature and research (Mayer & Timms, 1970; Maluccio, 1979; Weissman, 1987). Innovations are likely to occur when social workers have the courage to pause and reflect on what they are doing.

The following example illustrates the value of openness and self-scrutiny. Here, social workers once viewed the "putative" father as the cause of the social difficulties experienced by the mother and baby. They now take the initiative in educating the medical team to the importance of the participation of the father and his family members to the infant's ongoing health and family life.

In a prenatal clinic serving many poor, black, unmarried teenage parents, the desire of teenage fathers to be present at prenatal examinations was initially perceived by staff as unhelpful, intrusive, and inappropriate. Only when social workers began to allow themselves to hold doubts about their assumptions were they able to stop and listen more closely to their clients' reactions to the clinic program and its policies. They learned that the fathers' concern to be involved in the examinations included considerable anxiety, in large measure due to lack of knowledge about pregnancy and childbirth.

When their message of concern and anxiety about the young pregnant women was understood, the fathers' presence was seen as an opportunity for vital education, as a strong support to the mothers and as a valuable resource for ensuring the maintenance of good prenatal care. Once they had reflected on their own values and the actions based on them, they could orient other staff to the value of the father's participation, both for active care of the mother and as an opportunity for future planning for the baby's care. This innovation has become the basis for developing new service programs with male workers employed to reach out to and engage teenage fathers who had not been actively involved in prenatal care of their children. (Littlejohn, 1986)

Social workers should take time to reflect on and scrutinize their underlying values. The reflective process requires the social worker to experience doubt, which may bring confusion and uncertainty. Yet, it is this uncertainty that helps the social worker integrate the ideas and questions developed from conversations with clients and peers, to arrive at a new understanding of practice needs.

Taking Risks to Create Innovations

The wish to avoid uncertainty is strong and must be balanced by readiness to venture into uncharted territory. A social worker needs self-confidence and a readiness to risk rethinking accepted practice. Social workers must have a sense of competence and autonomy to begin to allow themselves to raise doubts, to challenge assumptions, and to admit uncertainty. Too much doubt can prevent social workers from trusting their ability to help and can affect their service to families. However, some degree of questioning is an essential ingredient in the development of innovation. A critic does not have to be a cynic.

Beginning social workers try to overcome a lack of confidence in their competence and may be reluctant to question established practice methods. However, scientific method is as essential for social work practice as it is for research. Social workers must learn that doubt not only is permissible but desirable for professional accountability and continued learning.

This concept is critical for the practitioner to retain readiness to learn, to permit doubt and questioning, to seek out new information, and to remain sensitive to changing needs. Reflective conversations with ourselves, peers, and clients are the means by which social workers can rethink their practice and move toward improvisation and innovation.

References

Brager, G., & Holloway, S. (1978). *Changing human service organizations.* New York: Free Press.

Bryant, C. (1980, December). Introducing students to treatment of inner city families. *Social Casework, 61*(10), 629–636.

Goldstein, H. (1986, September/October). Toward integration of theory and practice: A humanistic approach. *Social Work, 31*(5), 352–357.

Hartman, A., & Laird, J. (1983). *Family-centered social work practice.* New York: Free Press.

Levine, R. A. (1964). Treatment in the home. *Social Work, 9*(1), 19–27.

Littlejohn, M. (1986, May). *Family services.* Paper presented at a conference on Clinical Creativity: An Antidote to Agency Doldrums, Hunter College, School of Social Work, New York.

Maluccio, A. N. (1979). *Learning from clients.* New York: Free Press.

Mayer, J. E., & Timms, N. (1970). *The client speaks.* New York: Atherton Press.

Minuchin, S., Montalvo, B., Guerney, B. G., Jr., Rosman, B. L., & Schumer, F. (Eds.) (1967). *Families of the slums.* New York: Basic Books.

Patti, R. J. (1980). Internal advocacy and human service practitioners: An exploratory study. In H. Resnick & R. J. Patti (Eds.), *Change from within: Humanizing social welfare organizations* (pp. 287–301). Philadelphia: Temple University Press.

Rhodes, S. (1977, May). A developmental approach to the life-cycle of the family. *Social Casework, 58*(5), 301–311.

Schön, D. A. (1987). *Educating the reflective practitioner: Toward a new design for teaching and learning in the professions.* San Francisco: Jossey-Bass.

Smith, L., & Thrasher, S. (1986). *Working with overwhelmed families.* Unpublished manuscript.

Wallerstein, J. S., & Kelly, J. B. (1979, November). Children and divorce: A review. *Social Work, 24*(6), 468–475.

Weissman, H. H. (1987). Planning for client feedback: Content and context. In R. J. Patti, J. Poertner, & C. A. Rapp (Eds.) *Managing for service effectiveness in social welfare organizations* (pp. 205–220). New York: Haworth Press.

Play and Creativity

The social workers described in the chapter by Davidson got their first insight into their clients' problems by using the analogy of "fit"—by asking whether the service fit the clients' lives. Once they looked at the fit they had a powerful guide for their search for new solutions.

Laird and Hartman suggested that innovative thinkers try to understand the illumination to be found in analogy, the creativity of metaphor, the power of words to make new worlds, and the meaning in story and myth. One important way to gain a first insight is to make explicit the implied metaphors, stories, or analogies that underlie one's thinking about a problem. Thought processes usually are patterned. Many patterns are beliefs, such as that there is only one right answer, that ideas must be logical, that accepted rules or canons of procedure cannot be violated, and that one cannot be impractical (Von Oech, 1988).

The way such beliefs affect thought processes can be quite limiting. Gardner (1978) illustrated one such limited mind-set:

> A banana was suspended from the center of the ceiling, at a height that the chimp could not reach by jumping. The room was bare of all objects except several packing crates placed around the room at random. The test was to see whether a lady chimp would think of first stacking the crates in the center of the room, and then of climbing on top of the crates to get the banana.
>
> The chimp sat quietly in a corner, watching the psychologist arrange the crates. She waited patiently until the professor crossed the middle of the room. When he was directly below the fruit, the chimp suddenly jumped on his shoulder, then leaped into the air and grabbed the banana. (p. vi)

The professor's problem was "how to construct a test." The chimpanzee had to solve the problem of "how to get lunch." A problem that seems difficult may have a simple, unexpected solution, if the problem is seen from a different perspective.

Albrecht (1980) offered some useful suggestions that can be used to examine the ways one thinks which can limit the ability to shift perspectives and improvise solutions. Albrecht suggested: "Study your patterns for arguing, for compromising . . . [for] listening to another person explain an idea you believe you already understand . . . [for] making a decision when you don't have as many facts as you would like . . . [for] hearing an opinion with which you strongly disagree" (pp. 35–36).

For example, because most people hold countless fruitless discussions with others, a little time spent reflecting on how one discusses or argues offers large rewards in gaining access to new insights. Maslow noted some time ago that "when the only tool you have is a hammer, you tend to treat everything as if it were a nail" (Albrecht, 1980, p. 36)

Creativity and Relaxation

There are different types of thought processes. The focus of thought can be classified as either divergent or convergent. *Divergent thinking* is expansive. A problem is seen from various points of view—looking both at the big picture and at many pictures. *Convergent thinking* narrows down the problem to a smaller, more manageable size and perspective (Albrecht, 1980, p. 91). Both types of thinking are necessary for problem solving. Yet, in concentrating, in wanting to be logical, most people tend to shift quickly into convergent thinking.

Metaphors exemplify divergent thinking. They enable people to relax the usual structures of clarity and logic and look at things in a new way. In a sense, the concept of metaphor embodies two traits that are closely related to creative capacity: (1) playfulness and (2) relaxation.

When Archimedes uttered his famous "Eureka," he was relaxing in the bath. He did not get into the bathtub to do a hydraulic experiment, but the answer to such a problem came to him during his bath. The ability to "let go" of a problem is often an important part of the creative process.

Von Oech (1988) categorized the answers that he received to the question "During what kinds of activities and situations do you get your ideas?" One category of answer related to necessity: "When I'm faced with a problem, when things break down and I have to fix them, when the deadline is near." The other category of answer implied exactly the opposite of necessity: "When I'm just playing around, when doing an unrelated activity, when I'm toying with the problem, when I'm not taking myself too seriously" (pp. 96–97). Von Oech concluded that necessity may be the mother of invention, but play is the father. In a mental playground, defenses are down, mental locks are loosened, and there is little concern with rules, practicality, or being wrong (p. 97). Insights can bubble up.

Creativity through Playfulness

Ordinarily, a variety of factors impede a person's ability to make intuitive leaps. Seeing what one expects to see, defining a problem too narrowly, imposing false limits, lacking the ability to see a problem from various viewpoints, and failing to use all sensory inputs keep people from accurately perceiving problems and solutions (Adams, 1979).

Though there are some guides for overcoming these perceptual limitations, the concept of playfulness offers an easier, and potentially more fruitful, approach to increasing one's intuition and insight.

"No playing around" is the implicit credo of most professions. Doctors, lawyers, and social workers are expected to be serious. Yet, seeing only childishness in "playing around" is a limited view of playfulness.

March and Olsen (1979) suggested that play can be an instrument of intelligence. They noted that strict insistence on purpose, consistency, and rationality paradoxically limits one's ability to solve problems. Intellectual playfulness makes it possible to escape the traps of our assumptions, and the logic built in these assumptions, without relinquishing a commitment to the necessity of intelligence (p. 77). March and Olsen found that

> Playfulness is the deliberate, temporary relaxation of rules in order to explore the possibilities of alternative rules. When we are playful we challenge the necessity of consistency. . . . Playfulness allows experimentation. At the same time, it acknowledges reason. It accepts an obligation that at some point either the playful behavior will be stopped or it will be integrated into the structure of intelligence in some way that makes sense. (p. 77)

A playful stance can help people out of the desire to see purposes as always preexisting rather than, at times, emerging; the compulsion to be consistent; and the desire to see the world as a rational series of tightly coupled causes and effects. Such intellectual cages must be opened if intuition is to have a freer reign. Playfulness aids the ability to defer judgment, shift perspectives, and challenge assumptions and in doing so frees imagination and intuition (Heus & Pincus, 1986).

March and Olsen (1979) advised treating memory as an enemy.

> The rules of consistency and rationality require a technology of memory. For most purposes, good memories make good choices. But the ability to forget, or overlook, is also useful. If I do not know what I did yesterday or what other people in the organization are doing today, I can act within the system of reason and still do things that are foolish. (p. 79)

March and Olsen also suggested a novel way of making experience the best teacher:

> Experience can be changed retrospectively. By changing our interpretive concepts now, we modify what we learned earlier. Thus, we expose the possibility of experimenting with alternative histories. The usual structures against "self-deception" in experience need occasionally to be tempered with an awareness of the extent to which all experience is an interpretation subject to conscious revision. (p. 79)

Certainly, playfulness is difficult in a profession dealing with some of the world's most serious situations. Yet, too much emphasis on consistency, logic, and order can limit severely creative potential.

One other reason to be intellectually playful is that "one of play's products is fun—one of the most powerful motivators around" (Von Oech, 1988, p. 98). It is likely that people who have fun at work will come up with more ideas because they are more likely to persist at their tasks. This is important if the old adage is correct—that creativity is 10 percent inspiration and 90 percent perspiration.

Blocks to Creativity

How do our perceptions form into creative ideas, conceptions, or solutions? Freud (as cited in Adams, 1979) focused on the role of repression in creativity. If the id and superego are too selective, not many creative ideas will surface. If they are not selective, a person would be inundated with ideas that would seem to be useless.

Kubie (as cited in Adams, 1979) located creativity in the preconscious, rather than the unconscious. Neurosis is thought to distort the creative process. Humanistic psychologists see creativity as a response to a broader range of human needs—not just a way of solving conflicts between id and superego. People want to grow and develop to the fullest, to realize their potential.

Whatever is accepted as the source of creative ideas, most people will suffer from occasional blocks, which interfere with the ability to explore and manipulate ideas, prevent their communication to others, and limit the ability to conceptualize.

Gelfand (1988) suggested that there are three basic types of blocks: (1) psychological, (2) characterological, and (3) socioeconomic. Psychological blocks include the fear of failure, unwillingness to risk, and the need to conform to existing norms. Characterological blocks, or gaps in inner development, include the lack of self-discipline, the focus on external rather than internal rewards, and the inability to center on problems rather than on the self. Socioeconomic blocks include an oppressive social milieu, cultural preferences and taboos, professional rivalries, and so forth.

Adams (1979) found that there also are intellectual blocks. Social workers usually use a problem-solving language that is mainly verbal and logical. At times, a visual approach or an empathic approach may be far more appropriate, because creativity is related to the ability to connect or combine various elements into new forms. Adams also noted that most students are highly verbal and are relatively less competent visually. Students are not used to relying on taste, smell, or feel for problem solving. Yet various sensory inputs—most notably vision—are important to people who are extremely innovative. Words alone often are insufficient to capture the complexity of situations.

In problem solving, analysis, judgment, and synthesis are three distinct types of thinking. According to Adams (1979), "Logic is the tool that is used to dig holes deeper and bigger to make them altogether better holes. And if the hole's in the wrong place, no amount of improvement is going to put it into the right place" (p. 34).

Logical analysis is used to find the correct answer. Judgment generally is used when a problem has several answers and one must be chosen. Synthesis is used in situations where there are an infinite number of answers.

> If one analyzes or judges too early in the problem-solving process, one will reject many ideas. This is what students learn and it is detrimental to them and the profession. First of all, newly formed ideas are fragile and imperfect— they need time to mature and acquire the detail to make them believable. Secondly, ideas often lead to other ideas. (Adams, 1979, p. 46)

A highly competent social worker is not simply logical. He or she should possess the ability to construct and recall patterns of action and re-sponse—cognitive maps—and continually rework or remold them. At a high level of competence in particular fields of social work practice, practitioners have sophisticated schemas in mind.

Mozart reputedly could compose a whole symphony while walking down the street. Although such aspirations are beyond the reach of almost everyone, the approach is constructive. The ability to recall large numbers of patterns and responses in a field of practice, to compare these with each new kind of situation, then rework and remold them on the job—impro-vise—is an important step toward making the transition to creativity.

Gardner (1982) described sophisticated schemas:

> These schemas are sufficiently general and abstract to apply to a (variety of situations). . . . Some slots of the schemas are relatively inflexible. . . . Other slots are quite flexible . . . and may be entirely different from one embodiment of the schema to another . . . Moreover, the realization of each future instance is helped immeasurably by the prior existence of the schema—the mold with its recesses of various shapes and sizes into which particular ingredients are poured. (p. 362)

What distinguishes the creative practitioner from simply the competent is the ability to come up with novel deviations and changes which add a distinctive touch to the schemas, or ultimately result in a new schema—doing something better, or doing something quite different.

Yet, rather than leading to creativity, mastering the cognitive schemas in a particular field could also lead to the "trained incapacity" to entertain any new or original thoughts noted in many experts.

Yet, without cognitive maps, there would be no context against which to judge anomalies, no basis for realizing that anything is wrong with the usual approach (Perkins, 1981). In addition to assisting the highly competent in avoiding trained incapacities, a seriously playful approach is worth considering for other reasons.

Serious Play: Breaking Societal Boundaries

Playfulness, with an emphasis on the temporary relaxation of rules, the need for consistency, the need for rewards, and enjoyment, can help to overcome certain blocks, such as the fear of risking, the need to conform, and the need for external rewards. On the other hand, it may be difficult for some people to be playful, even if such an attitude is sanctioned by authority. There are a number of pressures against developing a playful attitude in our society. For example, Adams (1979) suggested that "Intelligence is often associated with the amount of knowledge we possess. Accumulating knowledge can keep one in the boundary of what is known yet to question and 'see problems' in a different light is one of the more important qualities of a creative person" (p. 104).

According to Campbell (1978), research studies show besides being personally more playful, creative people see themselves as working harder than others, have a high energy level, are intellectually curious, tend to have a wide range of skills, tend to be strong willed, and have a sense of destiny. Although the research shows considerable variations among individuals, many of the traits noted support playfulness in a culture that does not value this trait in adults.

Perhaps because creative people tend to be hard working, they receive a certain license from others to be more playful. In a culture that rejects playfulness, the willfulness of creative people may be necessary to sustain a questioning attitude. If one cannot be strong willed, one may not be able to be playful.

Harold H. Weissman
Editor/Senior Author

References

Adams, J. (1979). *Conceptual blockbusting.* New York: W. W. Norton.
Albrecht, K. (1980). *Brain power.* Englewood Cliffs, NJ: Prentice–Hall.
Campbell, D. (1978). The psychology of creativity. [Audiotape.] Available from the Center for Creative Leadership, Greensboro, NC.
Gardner, H. (1982). *Art, mind, and brain.* New York: Basic Books.
Gardner, M. (1978). *Aha! Insight.* San Francisco: W. H. Freeman & Co.

Gelfand, B. (1988). *The creative practitioner.* New York: Haworth Press.
Heus, M., & Pincus, A. (1986). *The creative generalist: A guide to social work practice.* Barneveld, WI: Micamar.
March, J., & Olsen, J. (1979). *Ambiguity and choice in organizations.* Bergen, Norway: Universitetsforlaget.
Perkins, D. N. (1981). *The mind's best work.* Cambridge, MA: Harvard University Press.
Von Oech, R. (1988). *A whack on the side of the head: How to unlock your mind for innovation.* New York: Warner Books.

Summation of Part One

Where does the first insight into a problem come from? Ordinarily, if the usual thought patterns do not work, then a different approach is called for, one where rules are broken or boundaries crossed.

To begin to think differently, social workers should think about their thinking about a problem. What assumptions are being made? What metaphors, analogies, or stories are buried in conversations about the problem? Must clinical problems have a "cure"? Must administrative solutions be efficient? If cure is a goal, creative ways to achieve remission may be missed. If efficiency is a must, the value of redundancy in certain situations could be lost.

A philosophy teacher once offered an analogy to a class at the beginning of the term. Like Moses, he said he would lead them through the wilderness but not into the promised land. In the same vein, Part One of this book has offered a few guides through the transitional wilderness between competent and creative practice.

Social workers taking this journey should first consider to what extent they can visualize different cognitive maps of their area of expertise at various levels and times—similar to what a grandmaster at chess does.[1] It is important for practitioners to

• recognize the concepts, metaphors, analogies, and stories which direct and precondition their cognitive maps

• question whether the range of their personal and professional experiences that can be related to the problem limits their maps

• consider the cognitive maps of other fields and professions concerned with the problem

• consider what additional information they need to verify their maps

• consider to what extent and about what they can entertain doubts about a problem

In addition, practitioners should play with the above mental models or schemas, by

---

[1] For a useful discussion of how to do this visualization, see Hampden-Turner, C. (1981). *Maps of the mind*. New York: Macmillan.

- temporarily relaxing their logical and professional rules, which can constrain thinking
- being aware of how their knowledge paradigm puts limits on their cognitive ability
- constructing "glitches" in their usual way of approaching problems
- improvising actions to test new cognitive maps or develop additions to old maps[2,3]

The above suggestions should promote fluency of ideas or first insights. Yet the suggestions do not convey a full sense of serious play. If playfulness and enjoyment play a part in creativity, another set of issues must be addressed.

Scheffler (as cited in Perkins, 1981) pointed out that although some emotions can stifle inquiry, others inspire it, such as those related to a spirit of adventure, a sense of intellectual derring-do, and the joy of discovery. He also suggested "cognitive emotions," such as the joy of verification and simple everyday surprises when something contradicts our expectations, do something more—". . . Besides enriching, rewarding and policing our efforts at inquiry, [they] inform us about the course of these efforts, providing insights we can use rationally to guide inquiry" (p. 119).

Most creative people like to solve problems, despite the frustration of dealing with difficult ones. The effort is intrinsically rewarding to these people and probably helps them persevere in the face of frustration. Thus the more people know about making confronting problems enjoyable, the more creative people are likely to be. The "how tos" of cognitive enjoyment may be required before the above suggestions for reworking our cognitive maps can be put to use.

Part One has focused on individuals, without taking into account the context in which they function. In the following parts, the way agencies and the organized profession affect individuals' cognitive capacities, as well as their capacity to enjoy utilizing these capacities, will be explored.

Harold H. Weissman
Editor/Senior Author

---

[2]This is not an exhaustive list. Intrapsychic and motivational issues and techniques such as imaging and perseverance are dealt with in other chapters.

[3]Artful inquiry, or "artistry," is seen in part as the selective management of large amounts of information, the practitioner's ability to spin out long lines of invention and inference, and the capacity to hold several ways of looking at a situation at once, thus conducting a pattern of reflection-in-action in a unique and uncertain situation. This *reflection-in-action*, a kind of patterned yet informal improvisation, Schön calls having a reflective conversation with the situation (as cited in Pettigrew, 1985).

References

Perkins, D. N. (1981). *The mind's best work.* Cambridge, MA: Harvard University Press.

Pettigrew, A. (1985). Contextualist research: A natural way to link theory and practice. In E. Lawler, A. Mohrman, S. Mohrman, G. Ledford, & T. Cummings (Eds.), *Doing research that is useful for theory and practice* (pp. 222–248). San Francisco: Jossey–Bass.

PART TWO

Professional Supports for Creativity: The Saturation Phase

Knowledge and Creativity

Chance favors the prepared mind.

—Louis Pasteur

In any profession, practitioners often are accused of being blinded by their favorite conceptions, unreceptive to any criticism or fact that challenges their conceptions. The old jibe expresses this well—the operation was a success but the patient died.

One of the functions of professionalism is to accumulate and add to the store of knowledge in particular fields. Studies of creative people show that they almost always possess a great deal of knowledge about the problems with which they were concerned. Kneller (as cited by Edwards, 1987) made the point that "it seems then, to be one of the paradoxes of creativity that in order to think originally, we must familiarize ourselves with the ideas of others" (p. 126).

Saturation is a phase in the creative process where one is immersed in and grasps all that is known about a topic. Yet, in this phase as in others, it is difficult to know when one is ready to move on. When does one really know everything about a topic?

Unfortunately, there is no pat answer to this question. One practical approach to the saturation phase is to systematically study a topic. In the chapter that follows, Rothman and Ayala suggest social research and development as a paradigm. For them, saturation not only is searching the literature, but also generalizing from it, trying ideas on a trial and error basis, revising, and then repeating the cycle.

Social research and development can enable the practitioner to begin the process of constructing cognitive maps of patterns of action and response around a particular problem. A *cognitive map* (Tolman, as cited in Middleman, 1983) is an internal representation of routes to goals, how one intends to get from here to there. Although Tolman's concept joins purposefulness, meanings, and expectations, the exact relationship between persons' judgments and behavior remains unclear—does a person judge the act, or act and then judge?

Yet there is practical utility in making intentions or plans explicit even though there may be gaps or lacunae in them. People can deviate from or improvise on their cognitive maps in a systematic way. New maps also can be constructed.

Middleman and Rhodes (1985) suggested that cognitive maps are affected by our individual cognitive style—convergent versus divergent, analytic versus holistic, impersonal versus social, risk-taking versus cautious, rigid versus flexible; cultural influences—such as a preference for inductive and pragmatic reasoning; professional conventions—worldviews, career incentives, bureaucratic and collegial norms; and so forth.

The more one knows about one's usual way of constructing these maps, the more likely one is to recognize the possibility of alternative interpretations. In addition, not the least value of constructing cognitive maps is knowing where the blank spaces or the disputed areas are on the maps. Here is the area for improvisation, for the use of intuition when trial and error approaches do not close the gap or fill in the blanks.

In any particular field or problem there are different levels of maps. The term *process* refers to an overarching map—one with beginnings, middles, and ends. There are smaller maps that suggest in each part of a process how individuals will react to certain situations, for example, how groups organize themselves or how programs or service systems interrelate.

Visualize these maps as containing arteries, veins, blood vessels, and capillaries, as well as anticipations and expectations of how these parts interrelate and react under certain circumstances. For example, a teacher planning a class must have an overall sense of what a two-hour class is like in terms of sequence, time, place; have ideas about how students learn, understand something about the complexity of the particular material and how it might best be taught; know how individual differences among students can be managed to promote learning; be aware of what assignments or exercises might assist students in retaining or applying the material; and know how one class will affect the next class, and so forth.

Our cognitive maps represent our "know-how" in an area. The maps show its parts and levels and how they react and relate. Know-how is the trademark of competence—the more sophisticated the mapping in a particular field, the more likely one can make the transition to creativity in that area, provided the trained incapacity that can go along with know-how can be transcended.

Harold H. Weissman
Editor/Senior Author

References

Edwards, B. (1987). *Drawing on the artist within: A guide to innovation, invention, imagination, and creativity* (Fireside ed). New York: Simon & Schuster.

Middleman, R. (1983). Role of perception and cognition in change. In A. Rosenblatt, & D. Waldfogel (Eds), *Handbook of clinical social work* (pp. 229–251). San Francisco: Jossey–Bass.

Middleman, R., & Rhodes, G. (1985). *Competent supervision.* Englewood Cliffs, NJ: Prentice–Hall.

Social Research and Development: First and N^{th} Insights

Jack Rothman and Frank Ayala, Jr.

The social work profession has lagged in using knowledge from research for practice innovation. The social worker's intuition, experience, and values, and the client's self-direction often have substituted for the systematic application of empirical knowledge. The authors have taken part in the design of a social work innovation that was based on explicit empirical research. Working with the Los Angeles County Department of Children's Services (DCS), the authors participated in a 1985 study of status offender issues that investigated the problems of runaway and homeless teenagers. The objective was to design an innovative program to meet the needs of these youths, using a social research and development strategy.

The research and development model used was formulated by Rothman (1980). This approach to program development links social research and practice need. It is based on beliefs that effective, innovative practice is informed practice and that existing empirical studies in the social sciences are a major, underutilized source of information for innovation. The objective of this approach is described aptly by Reid (1987):

> A new strategy for the construction, testing, and modification of social work programs and models has emerged in recent years. [It] has as its objective the creation of empirically based service approaches. . . . The primary goal is not the [conventional] generation of knowledge . . . but rather the building of intervention technology. (p. 480)

The project focused on the problem of teenage runaways. The information-gathering phase of the research began with a comprehensive,

73

computerized search of existing social science research on this population. Results of 79 previous studies on homeless and runaway teenagers were combined. From this synthesis, a number of generalizations were made. Not surprisingly, given the nature of social science research, results usually were given in descriptive form. To be useful to social workers, however, these results had to be converted into "action guidelines" or "application concepts."

A more specific look at this conversion and design operation is provided by the following example. Based on the research review, the authors formulated a generalization that the responsibility for runaways became widely diffused or nonexistent in the community, particularly after legislation was enacted that put this population outside the jurisdiction of the juvenile justice system. Among the adverse consequences noted were poor coordination and assessment of the varied problems of these youths, and faulty follow-up by responsible agencies.

From this descriptive observation, an inferential leap was taken toward application through the formulation of prescriptive statements. From the social research, the following related practice guidelines were developed:

> Mechanisms should be established to promote cooperation and coordination among service providers in order to optimize their effect in delivering proper services or configurations of services to youth.
>
> The point of entry into the service system must exhibit sound professional characteristics in order for clients to receive fair and effective service. (Rothman & David, 1985, p. 8)

However, before DCS presented the project findings to the county board of supervisors for approval and the funding required for implementation, the actual action guidelines were restated in the final report. Presented as a recommendation, the above example read as follows:

> Establish a rational, integrated, systematic approach to providing services for runaway and homeless youth. . . . This should involve several regional central intake, screening, diagnostic, and dispositional centers . . . administered by the DCS in collaboration with appropriate private agencies. . . . All agencies would be informed of these service centers. (Rothman & David, 1985, p. 4)

Action guidelines like this example are more useful to the practitioner than the aforementioned practice guidelines, although they still tend to be stated in rather abstract terms. In the next stages of the research and development process, however, more concrete implementation occurs. In effect, the guidelines are now hypotheses, which have been derived systematically from the combined findings of the earlier studies. These hypotheses now can be tested and operationalized.

In the example presented here, program development was directed by a specially created central intake planning committee. With membership from DCS, various community agencies, and the University of California–Los Angeles research staff, this committee developed the principles that guided program design and operation.

In 1986, the Runaway Adolescent Pilot Project (RAPP) opened in the Hollywood, California, area. The project is housed in an old-fashioned residence and operates 7 days a week, 10 hours a day. It has a director and a professional staff of 11. This neighborhood intake facility offers a centralized location where the target population can go for help. Empirical knowledge from the combined research has been put into practice and transformed into a concrete and testable program innovation. RAPP now represents a trial effort to determine whether the action guidelines will work under specific, real conditions.

When the RAPP project opens, the stage will be set for the evaluation and refinement of this new program. At this point, the research and development function involves formative and outcome evaluation assessments, which determine whether the program is being carried out as intended, and what results are being obtained. With this "real world" testing of the program design concepts in concrete form, the development phase of the research and development process has begun.

At this stage in the development of RAPP, the implementation of other action guidelines is being considered. For example, research showed that volunteers were highly effective "in vocational counseling and placement, academic tutoring, personal and social counseling, establishing intimate relationships with youth, using behavioral contracting, and engaging in youth advocacy" (Rothman & David, 1985, p. 8). Consequently, the prescriptive formulation called for the active use of volunteers. The actual recommendation in the report to the county reads: "Volunteers, especially college students, should be employed more extensively in work with runaway and homeless youth" (p. 5). Currently, a plan is being developed to use volunteers to enhance RAPP efforts.

Now that this working model of an innovative central intake facility has been created, however, further development research remains. Expanded field testing and evaluation in a variety of sites is needed. Once this main field testing and evaluation phase is completed, useful practice and policy outcomes are expected. A positively evaluated intake center for runaways then becomes a program that can be prepared for use by social workers who are faced with a similar social problem in other localities. At this knowledge utilization and transformation stage of the research model, the emphasis is on dissemination efforts that transmit ready-to-use information on the program to practitioners. Some examples of linkage media are videotapes of the program in operation, handbooks and manuals detailing the strategies of the program and its response to the teen runaway problem, and a variety of explanatory charts and documents.

References

Reid, W. (1987). Research in education. In A. Minahan et al. (Eds.), *Encyclopedia of Social Work: Vol. 2* (18th ed.) (pp. 474–487). Silver Spring, MD: National Association of Social Workers.

Rothman, J. (1980). *Social R & D: Research and development in the human services.* Englewood Cliffs, NJ: Prentice–Hall.

Rothman, J., & Rothman, D. T. (1985). *Status offenders in Los Angeles County: Focus on runaway and homeless youth.* Los Angeles: UCLA School of Social Welfare and Department of Children's Services, Los Angeles County.

Examining Information

Rothman and Ayala make no claim that social research and development is the only means of developing innovations or achieving saturation in the creative process. Without denigrating its potential value, however, Patti (1981) suggested that there are three shortcomings to this particular approach: (1) the lack of a substantial body of social science research on many problems; (2) given the state of knowledge, the need to give more attention to the use and synthesis of existing practice, rather than social research experience, and (3) a lack of clarity on how to generalize practice guidelines.[1]

Similarly, in many situations there may be no first insight to guide saturation. As noted, stages do not necessarily flow in order. The best that can be done is a systematic search of what is known, which depends on one's ability to define the search objectives, identify relevant knowledge areas and data sources, and establish boundaries and screening criteria that can help determine when one is saturated.

Saturation probably is related to people's ability to map their practice wisdom and compare this with the maps that can be drawn from research. If gaps or discrepancies are found during this process, problems may be reframed or new problems may be discovered. Often, this is a key to creativity.

Whatever approach is taken, saturation with all of the existing ideas related to a particular topic mainly is a function of the logical, analytical L-mode way of thinking. Yet, simply gathering and pondering information and ideas will not ensure a creative solution. A new way of looking at the information is needed. This need introduces elements of the R-mode of thinking.

The problem, then, is how to develop this new way of looking at, or recombining, information. The first insight provides something of a guide, such as when a new metaphor or analogy is used. Edwards (1987)

---

[1]Bertram Beck (personal communication, May 2, 1989) also suggested that social research and development is remote from the political and financial wellsprings of program development.

suggested that the issue is one of perception, of presenting information to the mind in a new way by "arranging and manipulating it by means of visual strategies" (p. 132).

To be able to see differently, one first must be aware of the way an organized profession provides its members with a range of accepted ideas, techniques, and models for use in interpreting the world. The following chapter on working with abused children illustrates how different views of the world are reflected in different programs and service techniques. Yet, what is most important about the chapter is its focus on a strategy for searching for solutions. Here, strategy is defined as a guide for action as opposed to tactics, the proximate steps or action dictated by the strategy or approach to the problem. Is it a search for a cause, a cure, or a reduction in symptoms?

This search strategy acts as a filter for the mass of information and ideas about social issues or problems. Without such a strategy, one can become mired in the mass of detail. Saturation without strategy can lead to despair.

Edwards (1987) suggested a number of innovative strategies for looking at material differently during the saturation stage. In the following chapter, Anderson offers excellent illustrations of the first two of the steps outlined by Edwards:

1. Perceive the edges of a problem. Where does one thing end and another begin? Where are the boundaries of the problem—the edges that separate the problem from what surrounds it?

2. Perceive the negative spaces of a problem. What is in the space (or spaces) around or behind the objects (or objectives) of the problem? Because the edges of the spaces (background) are shared with the objects (foreground), can the spaces help define the objects? (p. 127)

It is absolutely crucial that cognitive maps are evaluated in the above manner to avoid *group think*. According to Weick (1979), people caught in group think are

dominated by a single schema and this domination becomes self-reinforcing. Having become true believers of a specific schema, group members direct their attention toward an environment and sample it in such a way that the true belief becomes self-validating and the group becomes even more fervent in its attachment to the schema. (p. 52)

Harold H. Weissman
Editor/Senior Author

References

Edwards, B. (1987). *Drawing on the artist within: A guide to innovation, invention, imagination, and creativity* (Fireside ed.) New York: Simon & Schuster.

Patti, R. (1981). The prospects for social R & D: An essay review. *Social Work Research and Abstracts, 17*(2), 38–42.

Weick, K. (1979). Cognitive processes in organizations. In B. Staw (Ed.), *Research in organizational behavior* (pp. 41–74). Greenwich, CT: JAI Press.

Child Abuse and Neglect: Wicked Problems and Professional Paradigms

Gary R. Anderson with Harold H. Weissman

Cases of child abuse and neglect provide a difficult challenge to creativity and innovation. In these cases, action must be taken quickly, with little time to think and act creatively. There are great demands on services, and limited resources to provide those services. If an innovative plan or program is unsuccessful, the consequences may be catastrophic. Risk is high, and failure can result in serious injury or a child's death. In addition, most child protective services are provided by workers employed in large bureaucratic organizations, whose structure and mandate to "get the job done" may resist a change in service delivery.

However, despite these obstacles, social workers have developed and used a range of innovative approaches and programs in dealing with child abuse and neglect. However, there can be *too many* innovations. A single, appropriate professional stance or approach to deal with these problems is needed.

Innovative Responses to Child Abuse

The magnitude of the problem of child abuse has almost overwhelmed social agencies. However, it also has stimulated a search for effective interventions, and the willingness to develop and implement fresh approaches to service. These innovations can be classified according to how they accomplish primary tasks in child protection: the investigation of child abuse and child neglect, the treatment of child abuse and child neglect, and the societal and organizational response to child abuse and child neglect.

Who, if anyone, should be served and how he or she should be treated depend on the social worker's understanding of abuse and neglect. For example, Freud searched for intrapsychic explanations for his adult female patients' childhood sexual encounters with their fathers, because he could not accept that these accounts were descriptions of reality.

At times, particularly earlier in the twentieth century, abused children have been described in terms that blamed them for their maltreatment by their parents. In the past 25 years, the blame for child abuse has often fallen upon mothers. The failure to recognize abuse by explaining it as imaginary, or the identification of one family member as the culprit who should be punished, has resulted in the failure to provide children with needed treatment.

Even when treatment has been given, the concepts behind the treatment have serious implications for services. If child abuse is defined as a psychiatric illness and if evidence of psychopathology exists, long-term therapy and medication for the abusing parent and separation from the child may be prescribed. If child abuse is seen as learned behavior, the abusing parent will be subject to controls through punishment and reinforcement. Again, the child may be kept from the parent until re-education is complete.

However, newer views on child abuse and neglect are taking hold in the field. These include the following:

• A child's temperament and behavior affect the parent's behavior and response to the child. The interaction of parental and child temperament and behavior are described as their "fit," and the degree of comfort or conflict this produces influences the assessment of risk in a family. This recognition of the child's interactive role in a family does not excuse adult maltreatment, nor does it blame the child for a parent's harmful act (Chess & Thomas, 1985).

• The mother's important role in a child's development and experience is undeniable. However, blaming the mother for abuse reduces the worker's understanding of the family and encourages a punitive, rather than therapeutic, attitude and treatment plan.

• Clinical work with troubled families requires a family-centered approach, rather than isolated understanding and treatment of one family member.

• Although there is disagreement with regard to a precise and universal definition of child abuse and neglect, there is agreement that there are multiple dynamics at work in child maltreatment, including

social, economic, and cultural conditions, as well as psychiatric considerations. Therefore, clinical work with troubled families requires attention
to a variety of causes and conditions affecting family functioning (Meier,
1985).

These views have popularized the use of family treatment approaches
and an ecosystems theoretical perspective (Cardonna, 1985), and fostered
a rich range of resources created to address the multiple needs of troubled
families. For example, other resources for parents include

• Parent aides—volunteers who assist referred families with practical
child management advice, errands and appointments, and supportive
friendship (Kempe & Helfer, 1972)

• Homemakers and home health aides—volunteers or paid workers
who assist parents with household chores such as cleaning, cooking, and
general organization, some of whom may be trained to assist with health
related concerns and care (Kempe & Helfer, 1972)

• Parent counseling groups—groups of abusive or potentially abusive
parents designed to discuss parenting patterns and gain understanding of
their own behavior and how to stop abusing their children (Gentry, 1985)

• Self-help groups for adults—including Parents Anonymous, Mothers
Anonymous, and Parents United—in which participants learn to cope
with their feelings and function better in their everyday lives (Meier, 1985)

• Offenders groups—therapist-directed groups of sexual or physically
assaultive parents that address the causes of abuse and the offenders'
lives, feelings, actions and problems

As this partial list indicates, the profession indeed has been innovative,
willing to change perspectives, and adapt to a new and emerging understanding of the problem. Yet, although there is an impressive array of
innovations noted, the knowledge or theory of how and when to use them
is underdeveloped. The field of child welfare remains in disarray for a
variety of reasons—legal, financial, bureaucratic, and political. One reason for the lack of effectiveness is that the field of child neglect and abuse
has a Sisyphean quality—no matter how many innovations are introduced, there seems to be little, if any, progress. Running has been
necessary simply not to lose ground.

One of the central issues may revolve around the fact that neglect and
abuse is what Rittel and Webber (1977) call a wicked problem. A wicked
problem has five distinguishing features: (1) there can be no quick test
of a proposed solution; (2) there are unlimited ways to deal with the
problem; (3) the problem can be seen as a symptom of another problem;

(4) there is no rule for determining the correct explanation of a problem; and (5) the solutions are not true or false, but good or bad, depending on one's values. Because of all of the above, a wicked problem cannot be formulated until its solution has been formulated. "The process of formulating the problem and of conceiving of a solution (or re-solution) are identical, since every specification of the problem is a specification of the direction in which a treatment is considered" (Rittel & Webber, 1977, p. 137).

As Rittel and Webber (1977) noted, social workers cannot depend on traditional scientific method to solve wicked problems. These researchers indicated that

> the difficulties attached to rationality are tenacious, and we have so far been unable to get untangled from their web. This is partly because the classical paradigm of science and engineering—the paradigm that has underlain modern professionalism—is not applicable to the problems of open societal systems.
>
> One reason the publics have been attacking the social professions, we believe, is that the cognitive and occupational styles of the professions— mimicking the cognitive style of science and the occupational style of engineering—have just not worked on a wide array of social problems. The lay customers are complaining because planners and other professionals have not succeeded in solving the problems they claimed they could solve.
>
> We shall want to suggest that the social professions were misled somewhere along the line into assuming they could be applied scientists— that they could solve problems in the ways scientists can solve their sorts of problems. The error has been a serious one.
>
> The kinds of problems that planners deal with—societal problems—are inherently different from the problems that scientists and perhaps some classes of engineers deal with. Planning problems are inherently wicked.
>
> As distinguished from problems in the natural sciences, which are definable and separable, and may have solutions that are definable, the problems of governmental planning—and especially those of social or policy planning—are ill-defined; and they rely upon elusive political judgment for resolution. [Not "solution." Social problems are never solved. At best they are only re-solved—over and over again.] (p. 135)

Clearly, the social work profession has espoused the concept of rational, cause and effect social engineering, but the paradigm actually used has been more attuned to resolving, instead of solving, the problems of child neglect and abuse. From this confusion, a number of complications emerge. These complications make dealing with an already wicked problem even more wicked.

First, accountability mechanisms tied to funding are set up to be appropriate only for simple problems. When applied to a wicked problem, these inappropriate standards produce frustration, burnout, and cynicism. Second, the failure to acknowledge that the challenge is posed by wicked problems or taking money on the basis that one can *solve* the problem, leads to adverse media coverage, which then leads to service organization paralysis. This view also creates the false impression that social problems are like social diseases—that a social worker or "doctor" can be hired to "cure" them. The public does not have to be concerned personally or involved in dealing with the problem. Finally, the search for the all-encompassing solution limits the time, money, and effort needed to develop ideas whose value may not be immediately apparent.

If one expects to find an answer, one asks a certain kind of question about an innovation, focusing on an outcome. If one expects to find a partial explanation and perhaps data to use to more sharply focus one's questions, then one is likely to look at innovations in a quite different manner. The focus shifts to process, as well as outcome.

Buried in social work practice are levels of preconceptions, or "stories," which precondition what practitioners do and think about the problems they encounter. For example, when a social worker faces a child abuse or neglect problem, his or her view of the problem will include stories about "good boys," "bad girls," and "mean stepmothers," and what happens to them.

Abuse and neglect is the subject of a variety of stories in our culture. In a sense, it is easy to shift perspectives and create different types of programs, based on alternative stories. In other fields of practice, the stories often are not so culturally accessible or varied. Yet "hearing" a different story often is the key to a fresh insight.

References

Cardonna, R. (May, 1985). *Child abuse and family system theory.* Paper presented at the Hunter College School of Social Work Doctoral Conference, New York.

Chess, A., & Thomas, S. (1985). *Origin and evolution of behavior disorders.* New York: Brunner/Mazel.

Gentry, T. (May, 1985). *Parent education groups and child abuse.* Paper presented at the Hunter College School of Social Work Doctoral Conference, New York.

Kempe, C. H., & Helfer, R. E. (1972). *Helping the battered child and his family.* Philadelphia: J. B. Lippincott.

Meier, J. (1985). *Assault against children: Why it happens, how to stop it.* San Diego: College Press.

Rittel, H., & Webber, M. (1977). Dilemmas in a general theory of planning. In G. Gilbert & H. Specht (Eds.), *Planning for social welfare* (pp. 133–145). Englewood Cliffs, NJ: Prentice–Hall.

Professional Playfulness

Many of the differing perspectives on child abuse Anderson noted probably developed from someone's ability to perceive the edges or negative spaces of a problem—in this case, the mother, the family, and the system. Shifting the perspective, from blaming the parents for child abuse to seeing family interaction as a source of the problem, is a way of seeing something formerly in the space around the problem—the family interaction—as part of the problem.

In a profession such as social work where precise knowledge is not always available, there is a push to improvise, because real life problems cannot wait. Inevitably, the necessity to improvise leads to many different practices among professionals. Practice knowledge and new perspectives are invented or improvised, rather than discovered. Saturation involves improvisation.

Edwards (1987) suggested that one key to success in the saturation stage is to try not to name, or frame, the problem too quickly. She found that "our aim is to 'fly by' the net of words in order to see, and premature naming of the problem may draw in the net of words too closely, perhaps excluding something that is in fact part of the problem. If you say something to yourself in words, try to limit the words to 'What I know about this situation is . . .' or 'What's bothering me is . . .' or 'At this point, the way I see it is. . . .'" (p. 103).

The object of saturation is to try to form images, apart from verbal language, that reflect spatial, relational, and visual arrangements—a non-verbal visual language. This is not an easy task for professional social workers, who depend heavily on verbalizations.

Part of the problem is that social workers usually see clients away from their usual environments, in places like the welfare office, the school, courts, community meetings, and so forth. In these situations, social workers talk and reason. Because clients may not be seen in their natural environments, practitioners' views of their lives can be limited.

March and Olsen (1979) commented that "many of the most influential, best educated [people] . . . have experienced a powerful overlearning with respect to rationality. They are exceptionally poor at a playful attitude toward their own beliefs, toward the logic of consistency, or toward the way they see things as being connected in the world" (p. 78).

The Importance of Unlearning

A profession should be structured to encourage its members in a certain amount of "unlearning" and seeing things differently if saturation is to result in a creative "illumination." To accomplish this task, Heus and Pincus (1986) recommended the encouragement of professional relationships, which involve the capacity of persons, forces, and ideas to optimize and enhance each other. Learning and unlearning then would reinforce each other.

This learning and unlearning are difficult tasks, but ones for which playfulness is admirably suited. As a supplement to the usual panoply of papers, professionals need intellectual "potlatches"—chances to discuss both their successes and failures with others in the field. What could be more salutory than to have a regular conference series devoted to topics such as "My Biggest Policy Error and Why I Made It," "The Worst Class I Ever Taught," or a mandatory talk by every retiring dean, "My Biggest Administrative Errors"? We need intellectual potlatches. Here, the community benefits from the errors of the mighty and the mighty are sustained by their willingness to admit these errors.

Another conference session could be entitled "Myths and Realities," devoted to analyzing the difference between what people say they do and what they actually do. Argyris (1983) referred to this as the difference between "espoused theories" and "theories in use" (p. 390). Papers delivered would deal with what accounts for the differences, when and how they were recognized, the effect of discrepancies on relationships to colleagues and clients, and the like.

To illustrate the creative benefits of nonverbal language, professionals could attempt to express problems without words—such as by trying to draw them or dance them (Anderson, 1981). This approach uses a different set of thought processes—the spatial and relational. Edwards (1987) believed that drawing is an excellent exercise for revealing interconnections that might be missed in verbal, logical, analytic ways of thinking.

Playfulness makes it possible to do and think in new ways. Professional playfulness is a means of getting social workers moving in new professional directions. However, much more than structured playfulness is required to encourage full use of creativity and innovation in dealing with the problems social workers face.

Changed Perceptions and New Views

In the next chapter, Mailick deals with another of the techniques of creatively saturating one's mind with all available information about a problem. To enable one to do this, Edwards (1987) suggested the following:

Perceive the relationships and proportions of a problem. Relative to your point of view, what is the state of the problem in relation to the constants of the situation—the things that don't change (or can't be changed)? What are the relationships of the parts to each other and to the whole? (p. 127)

Mailick suggests one means to ensure that one's theory does not blind one to other views of reality, to other possible relationships among the parts of a problem. Her antidote is exposure to, and intimate understanding of, at least one other competing view. She also reminds social workers that theories always should be considered provisional.

Rapoport (1968) issued the following warning, which offers a good summation of Mailick's concerns to social work educators many decades ago:

We also undervalue intuitive thinking. Academic education, while forced to acknowledge its existence, does not pay explicit attention to the development of intuitive thinking, the training of hunches, the courageous leap to tentative conclusions, all those nonrigorous methods of achieving solutions which Jerome Bruner calls heuristic procedures.

A related problem to the danger of overconceptualization is the trend toward overintegration of knowledge. There is a danger in our field of overintegration—of linking knowledge and concepts particularly from different theoretical frames of reference or from different levels of abstraction. We tend to force a premature integration which puts a kind of closure to theory. This prevents the learner from doing his own intellectual work, from identifying theoretical inconsistencies and flaws, and from discovering fresh connections which might lead to better insights and integration. (p. 160)

Harold H. Weissman
Editor/Senior Author

References

Anderson, J. (1981, August 23). Danceview. *New York Times* (sec. 2), p. 12.

Argyris, C. (1983). Usable knowledge for double loop problems. In T. Kilmann, K. Thomas, D. Slevin, R. Nath, & S. Jerrell (Eds.), *Producing useful knowledge for organizations* (pp. 377–394). New York: Praeger.

Edwards, B. (1987). *Drawing on the artist within: A guide to innovation, invention, imagination, and creativity* (Fireside ed.). New York: Simon & Schuster.

Heus, M., & Pincus, A. (1986). *The creative generalist: A guide to social work practice*. Barneveld, WI: Micamar.

March, J., & Olsen, J. (1979). *Ambiguity and choice in organizations*. Bergen, Norway: Universitetsforlaget.

Rapoport, L. (1968). Creativity in social work. *Smith College Studies in Social Work, 38*, 139–161.

Social Work Practice with Adolescents: Theoretical Saturation

Mildred D. Mailick

Visions of reality can be expanded or constricted by the use of theory in social work practice. Theories can encourage greater clarity or confusion, depth or superficiality, integration or fragmentation, flexibility or rigidity, simplicity or complexity. Theories can be beneficial and rewarding or, alternatively, place obstacles in the way of creativity and innovation in clinical practice and program design.

The dictionary (Neufeldt, 1988) defines theory as "a mental viewing," a "formulation of apparent relationships . . . of certain observed phenomena," "a systematic statement of principles," and finally, as an ". . . idea or plan as to how something might be done" (p. 1387). Popularly, according to the dictionary, it means "a conjecture or guess." All of these definitions can be applied to the use of theory in social work with adolescents.

In social work practice, the most widely acknowledged function of theory is to understand, explain, or conceptualize behavior, relationships, or developmental phenomena. In this sense, it is "mental viewing," and used as a guide to thinking about clients or some aspect of their environment (Rychlak, 1981, p. 54). Theories define the scope of observations, and implicitly set up a hierarchy of values that define the importance or relevance of data. Theory also can provide a structure, or frame of reference, creating a systematic way to order and integrate observations. Social workers are trained to use the conceptual models provided by theories in organizing their understanding of the complexities of clients' lives, and in planning interventions designed to help clients

89

(Lewis, 1982, p. 61). In addition to providing a frame of reference, theories also have the potential to generate new ideas. When relationships among events or characteristics are observed regularly, they naturally lead to new hypotheses, which then can be tested and integrated into the existing knowledge base.

A broad range of biological, psychological, sociological, and environmental theories are available to practitioners as a source of information for use in social work practice. These "orienting" theories, derived from other disciplines, offer knowledge on which social workers can draw to help to explain or understand client behavior within the context of the environment.

Practice theories are of a different order. They explain and justify strategies of practice. They synthesize knowledge derived from the disciplines and generalized from practice experience, and organize them into a framework for action. Lewis (1972) suggested, however, that "no systematic theoretical model attempting to explain all social work practice has thus far been proposed, though many ad hoc models of a limited nature have been entertained" (p. 81). Social work is not alone in not having arrived at an overall, or grand, theory. This is the situation in most social sciences.

Social workers are influenced strongly by both orienting and practice theories in working with adolescents. The personal and social problems of adolescents are so complex that they require recourse to intrapsychic, interpersonal, sociocultural, and environmental knowledge bases. When one theory is given too much attention and consideration is given only to those facets of adolescents' behavior that support it, other important aspects of the adolescent and his or her social environment will be ignored. Although a narrowed theoretical lens may offer clarity of detail, this may occur at the expense of a comprehensive view. Similarly, adherence to a limited treatment technology or theory of practice may constrict flexibility, and may thus reduce possible effectiveness.

The complexity of the problems of adolescents is reflected in current statistical trends. Death rates from accidents, suicides, and other forms of violence have increased steadily since the 1960s (Rickloff & Klemanski, 1979). Drug and alcohol addictions are associated with physical illness, school dropouts, and trouble with the law (Needle, Glynn, & Needle, 1983). Early sexual activity leading to unintended pregnancies has created long-term social, health, educational, and economic consequences that are difficult to reverse (Chilman, 1983). Current social conditions have contributed to the growing number of homeless adolescents, and to unemployment rates far higher than for any other group within society. The severity of these problems, the turbulence of the external environment, and the lack of community resources are cause for serious concern. It is clear that the current service delivery patterns and treatment technologies have not proved markedly effective or successful.

Agencies and practitioners serving adolescent populations currently are going through a period of vigorous reappraisal. A bewildering number of innovative practice approaches have been developed. Many appear, are used, and then vanish without being sufficiently noted or tested. Some are haphazard or unsystematic, and involve subjectively valued theories or techniques. Others are more systematically developed and durable and can be taught, replicated, and evaluated (Norcross, 1986).

In the face of the need for creativity and effectiveness, individual practitioners and agency program planners have developed differing responses. Some of these practitioners and planners deny the need for a reexamination of theories of adolescence, rejecting those potential clients whose behavior cannot be explained or redefined by their existing formulations. Others develop new programs and treatment techniques, integrating them into the existing framework of their preferred theoretical orientation. Still others draw on new theoretical frameworks and create novel treatment technologies and program initiatives. Some abandon theory completely.

Perhaps of greatest concern are practitioners and agency program planners who recognize that the traditional theory they use does not fit their own empirical observations of clients. In the press of getting services to these clients, practitioners and planners may ignore or informally explain away the discrepancies that they notice, and avoid the discomfort of cognitive dissonance (Ginsberg, 1975). Although they may change or adapt their programs or treatment technologies, they perhaps do not report their findings in the professional literature. Their innovative practice or services cannot be replicated, and the opportunity to generate new theories or practice ideas and to test their potential uses and limitations is lost.

Intellectually, at least, this may occur because, for some people, understanding adolescence can be like trying to comprehend and use concepts of quantum physics. Just as theories of classical physics remain useful in understanding many phenomena of the physical world, other explanations are necessary to account for the complexities of the subatomic quantum world (Gribbin, 1984). The chaotic quality of adolescent clients and the turbulence of their environments are like the quantum reality, where the theories that are familiar in the everyday world do not seem to apply. Psychosexual and psychosocial developmental theory and cognitive and object relations theory explain aspects of adolescence, which, like classical theories of physics, fit under some circumstances and cannot be ignored. However, social work with multistressed and troubled adolescents enters a special domain, a reality in which classical theories are not sufficiently applicable.

There are an overwhelming number of journal articles and books devoted to the subject of adolescence. However, many are not developed in ways that are useful or relevant when applied to a large segment of adolescent clients that social workers see in their agency practice. The developmental stages and tasks, the interests and conflicts, and the preoccupations and behavior of this group of adolescents do not seem to agree with the theory. Lamb (1978) expressed the attitude of many social workers with the observation that "there are shelves of books on adolescence, but in this torrent of words and theories little is relevant to what therapists see in the troubled adolescents that come, or are even dragged to them for help. Worse yet, therapists can find almost no practical advice on how they can resolve the problems of the disturbed youth whom they wish to help" (p. 1).

An examination of major social work journals published in the past 5 years reveals that most of the articles in which the authors speculate about theories of adolescence are published by academics, and most of the articles in which the authors describe innovations in the delivery of services to adolescents are written or co-authored by practitioners. It is clear that this dichotomy is not based on a lack of competence in either group. Rather, the interests, experiences, and expertise of each are shaped by priorities imposed by the clientele and by the rewards given by the systems in which those social workers are employed.

The problem engendered by this division is that theories tend to become isolated from practice. Academics continue to teach about adolescents in ways that no longer effectively support practice. They formulate research within a theoretical framework that produces knowledge that is not broadly helpful to practitioners. Social work practitioners and program planners adapt and innovate, creating programs and treatment approaches that "make sense" to them, but are deprived of the sanction and guidance of a theory-based practice.

Theories of Adolescence

The world of the adolescent has three major domains. The first is the inner domain of drives, wishes, impulses, and conflicts. The second is the domain of the self, and the third is the domain of the external or social reality. Periodically, adolescents seem to inhabit one of these domains to the exclusion of the other two. Sometimes, they seem particularly preoccupied or driven by their inner impulses. At others, they may be sensitive only to the stimuli of the external reality, and then, they unpredictably become submerged in contemplation of their selves, their ideals, values, and beliefs (Coppolillo, 1980). These rapid shifts from one domain to another are most characteristic of younger adolescents and those emotionally or socially troubled youths who have limited capacity to regulate, manage, and integrate the three parts of their world.

Each of these three domains has a group of theories that help to make sense of the unique problems of the adolescent. Some theories have been used extensively by social workers. Other theories, for lack of a frame of reference, knowledge, institutional support or of a method of applying them in practice, are ignored.

Inner Domain

Social workers have made extensive use of psychodynamic theories of the inner domain to explain adolescent behavior. It is difficult to conceive of work with adolescents that does not consider some understanding of psychodynamic theories. However, psychodynamic theories do not sufficiently consider the vast array of sociocultural, economic, and political realities that compose the external environment of adolescents. Concepts of class, race, gender, role expectations, ethnicity, cultural patterns and values, family dynamics, peer groups, societal pressures and prejudices, and access to resources in the environment often are given too little attention.

For example, how instructive are classical psychodynamic theories alone as a basis for effective program development and clinical practice with pregnant adolescents, or those at high risk of becoming pregnant? Can the theoretical explanation rest only on such considerations as early deficits in nurturing, the acting out of Oedipal conflicts, a need to seek a separate identity, or an unconscious wish to fill an inner emptiness? Or do social workers need to consider the adolescent's attitudes toward a locus of control, a cultural belief in fate, a sense of hopelessness about achievement, a feeling of being rejected by society, and so on (Group for the Advancement of Psychiatry, 1986)? These latter considerations are illuminated by the application of theories drawn from sociology, anthropology, and other social science disciplines.

Do Eriksonian stage theory and ego psychological formulations, with their emphasis on the dynamics of separation/individuation, autonomy, and an independent identity, fully fit the adolescent's experiences or realities? Considerable doubt is raised by some researchers over whether the search for identity, for example, is most central to the experience of the *majority* of adolescents (Marcia, 1980). Is the adolescence that Erikson so eloquently described an artifact of his focus on moderately affluent, intellectually competent, North American or Western European male adolescents whose value system encourages individualism and whose environment offers freedom to choose among a variety of opportunities (Chilman, 1983)?

On the other hand, cross-cultural research on female development among Mexican American, Puerto Rican, and black adolescents supports the idea that independence and autonomy may not be issues of primary importance. Among these young women, researchers found an absence of emphasis on separation from parental figures. An interesting study of Hispanic, low-income adolescent mothers from English- and Spanish-speaking homes in California revealed that an overwhelming majority of the young women in both groups reported that their mothers were their major source of influence and support. Those questioned seemed to have experienced relatively little stress from issues of the wish for independence and separation from parents (deAnda, 1985).

Another earlier study in New York by Young, Berkman, and Rehr (1975) supports this same idea. In a sample of 48 low-income, black and Puerto Rican pregnant adolescents, more than 80 percent (*n* = 38) of the respondents considered their relationship with their mother as the most significant, and it was mothers who had the most influence on daughters in making decisions about whether to continue a pregnancy or to have an abortion.

Is the central theoretical issue in serving adolescent girls the problem of the foreclosure of personal identity? Or should social workers and agencies be using a theory that informs them about the adolescent's need to define her identity through a caring and intimate relationship? A poignant comment by one young woman is quoted in Luker's (1975) book. When asked by the interviewer if she thought a maternal urge was a factor in her becoming pregnant, the young woman replied,

I think so, yeah. I don't know exactly, but taking a wild stab, I think it would be that getting pregnant means having someone who will take my love and care, 'cause lots of times I think no one else wants it. (p. 68)

Does traditional theory alone offer social workers enough understanding of the adolescent's perspective of the risks and benefits of being sexually active? Do social workers acknowledge those theories that suggest that to the adolescent, sexual activity, pregnancy, and childbearing may offer proof of feminine identity and self-worth, as well as the hope for increased attention and a caring relationship, either with her lover, her parents, or her child (Luker, 1975)? Are these young women more consciously concerned with the attitudes of their partners and their perception of the realities of their opportunities in the adult world than with cognitive considerations of the undisputed negative consequences of early parenthood, such as interrupted education and reduced potential for remunerative work?

Domain of the Self

Regarding the domain of the self, what theories seem useful in understanding adolescent clients? The self traditionally is defined as the sum of the self and object representations and their related affective states (Masterson, 1985). Elkind (1975) summarizes cross-cultural research that suggests that the self-concept evolves in somewhat dissimilar ways in different cultures. Constitutional factors, early childhood developmental experiences, and socialization create the core of the psychological self. However, by the time of adolescence, situational and environmental norms become important (Elkind, 1975).

Adolescents are affected in different ways by their family, social, cultural, and physical environments. Their concepts of self are strongly influenced by the formal and informal norms of subgroups that surround them. Congruence between their attitudes, behavior, or values and those of their immediate social groups help to support their capacity to maintain self-esteem. The importance to adolescents of the feeling of being in harmony with their peers is generally accepted. Conspicuous departures from the norms of any of these groups disrupts the adolescent's unsteady sense of self. Disparity between adolescents and their reference group norms may be the result of such status differences as religion, social class, race, sexual orientation, or ethnicity; or they may be the result of differences of values in relation to performance variables such as school achievement, competence in sports, social skills, sexual activity, drug use, or illegal behavior. Issues of self-esteem, so central to the development of the adolescent, depend on the relative impact that each of the multiple contexts has on their assessment of self (Rosenberg, 1975). When groups conflict in their standards and expectations, adolescents are subject to further assaults on their identity, their sense of competence, and the stability of their personally held value systems. There is a rich, well-articulated set of theories about the effects of reference groups on individuals that are used by social psychologists, but that social work clinicians have not integrated effectively into practice yet.

Domain of the Environment

The impact of the environment is ambiguous and difficult to define. Traditional theory contends that aspects of the environment are introjected and become part of the mental representations lodged in the personality. How the adolescent internalizes representations of the environment and responds to its stimuli and challenges largely have been unexplored. Social workers long have recognized the importance of the family in the early development and in the later socialization of the child. Yet at the research and practice level, the focus on the need of the adolescent for separation and independence has reduced the understanding of the continued importance of the family and the use of family systems theory in treatment or in the organization of services.

Theories of the larger external environment, which have an important part to play in understanding adolescent clients, often have been ignored even more. Some of these sociologically based theories are well-conceptualized and can accurately describe a number of important variables in the outside world that social workers need to consider, such as stress and support, receptiveness of the environment to the needs of the individual, the opportunities offered by access to resources, and the potential of the environment for change. However, practitioners find it difficult to use knowledge of these variables in their clinical work with clients. Application of research on the different responses of adolescents to negative environmental situations and on the importance of intervening variables, such as the culture, family, social support systems, and small group dynamics, clearly is needed.

Practice Dilemmas

Drucker (1973) suggested that the introduction of innovative theories and practices depends on the readiness of practitioners to change their perceptions of people, their problems, and the external environment. It requires sufficient professional willingness and programmatic flexibility to reconsider existing services, theories, and technologies within a new frame when it becomes necessary. Starting with an assessment of clients' needs is the most direct way to develop creative programs, provided that perception of need is not biased by a narrowly conceived theoretical framework (Drucker, 1973).

This philosophy of innovation agrees with the principles of social work practice. The philosophy places a central importance on assessment of need and emphasizes systematic, rather than haphazard or unplanned, goals. It creates the potential for action that can be initiated at the demand of client groups, by practitioners or administrators of social agencies, or by community leaders.

Fitting Theories to Client Needs

Adolescents become clients when their inner world, their sense of self, and their environment are not in harmony with each other and are under threat of disorganization. The complex and chaotic nature of their lives and problems can evoke two creative responses. One is the search for new combinations of theories that offer more effective means for understanding their needs. The other response is the search for a sufficiently flexible structure of practice that provides a method for applying these theories without abandoning the values of systematic practice.

Every profession draws on a certain range of theories in framing its practice. The complexity of practice is dependent not only on the number and compatibility of these theories, but also on the process or design that informs social workers of how theories are to be applied. Practice dominated by a single theory for analyzing problems is likely to be rigid and defensive. Theoretical purity restricts vision and overlooks important variables. On the other hand, practice that is open to many theories, but does not sufficiently examine how they should be applied, runs the risk of having no systematic basis for approaching problems of a similar kind, or of defining effectiveness. It fosters the selection of theories and techniques based on practitioners' subjective preferences.

In a recent study, of 267 clinical social workers, 54 percent ($n = 144$) identified their practices as eclectic (Jayaratne, 1978). Yet, eclecticism still is regarded with disfavor by many social work educators and leaders, partially because it is an ambiguous term. It often is confused with being atheoretical, or having no explicit group of theories that informs practice. There is also confusion between theoretical and technical eclecticism.

Theoretical eclecticism attempts to use or integrate a number of diverse, but compatible, theories. Proponents suggest that, although many of the theories and practice approaches use their own particular frames of reference and terminology, they actually are not as different as they appear. Theoretical eclectics seek commonalities among these theories, and stress those basic processes that are shared by all of them (Garfield, 1986). Their approach emphasizes the importance of choosing a theory that best explains the particular problem of the client, or yields the most effective practice outcomes. Opponents point out that, although there may be some superficial similarities among the theories, there are fundamental and irreconcilable differences that make integration unrealistic (Lazarus, 1986). These include essentially different values and practice assumptions, inconsistent views of human nature and how people change, and thus divergent processes of treatment.

Technical eclecticism abandons the search for a frame of reference that reconciles these differences at some level of generality. Instead, it draws on techniques derived from a variety of theories without regard for their compatibility (Lazarus, 1986). Proponents suggest that technical eclecticism allows for the use of a wide range of techniques not available to theoretical purists. They point out that the quest to understand why a technique works, or what theory it is derived from, never should supplant the need to apply what actually works in practice. They consider it unprofessional for the practitioner not to use techniques that have been found to be highly effective in the treatment of certain problems (Lazarus, 1986). Opponents do not suggest withholding potentially helpful treatment techniques. However, they point out that a focus on technique deters the development of an organized system of treatment and limits the potential for research and verification. They also question whether effective technical interventions can be carried out, if they are unconnected to their originating theory. Because few practitioners have the capacity to be fully conversant with the newest developments in all theoretical approaches, they risk using a technique out of context or applying it inappropriately.

The nature of clinical work with adolescents demands a broad range of orienting theories. Most practicing social workers draw from at least several of these theories, combining them in informal ways. Theorists recognize this necessity for technical eclecticism. However, they continue to search for an organizing and integrative framework (Germain, 1979). Both efforts are important and can be pursued concurrently. What is crucial is that practitioners and theorists contribute to each other's endeavors. Practitioners are, of necessity, pragmatic in their orientation. Their wisdom is made vital by rich and varied contact with clients. They use theories that have the greatest clinical potential, organizing them into informal frameworks that are useful professionally. Once developed, they are used almost automatically and seldom are formally conceptualized. Social work educators and theorists struggle to develop frameworks that synchronize groups of theories that are consistent in terms of major professional values, goals, perceptions, and underlying assumptions. To be useful, guides for innovation must be offered at levels of generalization that give practitioners different perspectives of their clients.

Practitioners and theorists who want to avoid theoretical straitjackets can seek to seriously critique the theories they find most conducive, rather than simply defend them, and study at least one other competing theory in depth, focusing on its strengths rather than its weaknesses. There is nothing so practical as a good theoretical approach to theory.

References

Chilman, C. S. (1983). *Adolescent sexuality in a changing American society.* New York: John Wiley & Sons.

Coppollilo, H. P. (1980). The tides of change in adolescence. In S. I. Greenspan & G. H. Pollock (Eds.), *The course of life: Psychoanalytic contributions toward understanding personality development: Vol. Two—Latency, adolescence and youth* (DHHS Publication No. ADM 80–999, pp. 397–410). Washington, DC: U.S. Government Printing Office.

deAnda, D. (1985). The Hispanic adolescent mother: Assessing risk in relation to stress and social support. In W. I. Vega & M. R. Miranda (Eds.), *Stress and Hispanic mental health: Relating research to practice* (DHHS Publication No. ADM 85–1410, pp. 267–287). Washington, DC: U.S. Government Printing Office.

Drucker, P. (1973). *Management: Tasks, responsibilities and practices.* New York: Harper & Row.

Elkind, D. (1975). Recent research on cognitive development in adolescence. In S. E. Dragastin & G. H. Elder (Eds.), *Adolescence in the Life Cycle: Psychological Change and Social Context* (pp. 49–61). New York: John Wiley & Sons.

Garfield, S. L. (1986). An eclectic psychotherapy. In J. Norcross (Ed.), *Handbook of eclectic psychotherapy* (pp. 132–162). New York: Brunner/Mazel.

Germain, C. (1979). *Social work practice: People and environments.* New York: Columbia University Press.

Ginsberg, L. H. (1975). Normative life crises: Applied perspectives. In N. Datan & L. H. Ginsberg (Eds.), *Life-Span Developmental Psychology* (pp. 11–16). New York: Academic Press.

Gribbin, J. (1984). *In search of Schrodinger's cat: Quantum physics and reality.* New York: Bantam Books.

Group for the Advancement of Psychiatry, Committee on Adolescence. (1986). *Crisis of adolescence, teen-age pregnancy: Impact of adolescent development.* New York: Brunner/Mazel.

Jayaratne, S. (1978). A study of clinical eclecticism. *Journal of Social Service Review, 52,* 621–631.

Lamb, D. (1978). *Psychotherapy with adolescent girls.* San Francisco: Jossey–Bass.

Lazarus, A. (1986). Multimodal therapy. In J. Norcross (Ed.), *Handbook of eclectic psychotherapy* (pp. 65–93). New York: Brunner/Mazel.

Lewis, H. (1972). Developing a program responsive to new knowledge and values. In E. Mullen, J. Dumpson, & Associates (Eds.), *Evaluation of social work intervention* (pp. 71–89). San Francisco: Jossey–Bass.

Lewis, H. (1982). *The intellectual base of social work practice: Tools for thought in a helping profession.* New York: Haworth Press.

Luker, K. (1975). *Taking chances: Abortion and the decision not to contracept.* Berkeley: University of California Press.

Marcia, J. (1980). Identity in adolescence. (1980). In J. Adelson (Ed.), *Handbook of adolescent psychology* (pp. 159–187). New York: John Wiley & Sons.

Masterson, J. (1985). *The real self: A developmental, self and object relations approach.* New York: Brunner/Mazel.

Needle, R. H., Glynn, T. J., & Needle, M. P. (1983). Drug abuse: Adolescent addictions and the family. In C. R. Figley & H. I. McCubin (Eds.), *Stress and the family, Volume II: Coping with catastrophe* (pp. 37–52). New York: Brunner/ Mazel.

Neufeldt, V. (Ed.). (1988). *Webster's new world dictionary* (3rd college ed.). New York: Simon & Schuster.

Norcross, J. (1986). Eclectic psychotherapy: An introduction and overview. In J. Norcross (Ed.), *Handbook of eclectic psychotherapy* (pp. 3–24). New York: Brunner/Mazel.

Rickloff, J., & Klemanski, C. (1979). Depression and suicide. In W. Hall & C. Young (Eds.), *Proceedings, health and social needs of the adolescent: Professional responsibilities* (pp. 46–50). Pittsburgh, PA: University of Pittsburgh.

Rosenberg, M. (1975). The dissonant context and the adolescent self-concept. In S. Dragastin & G. Elder (Eds.), *Adolescence in the life cycle: Psychological change and social context* (pp. 97–116). New York: John Wiley & Sons.

Rychlak, J. F. (1981). *A philosophy of science for personality theory.* Melbourne, FL: Robert Krieger.

Young, A., Berkman, B., & Rehr, H. (1975). Parental influence on pregnant adolescents. *Social Work, 20,* 387–392.

Keeping an Open Mind

To think creatively, a person's mind must be open to new ideas and interpretations. In fact, one of the greatest barriers to creative thinking is premature closure—a mind that is closed too soon. Our minds tend to want to fill in the gaps and resolve a problem. As Edwards (1987) explained, "A prime requirement for the Saturation stage . . . is to keep an open mind, to go on seeing information and ideas without ever satisfying the brain's longing for closure. . . . You must go on 'seeing' without giving in to premature knowing" (p. 175).

Ideology and ethics are two of the major factors that can lead to closure. The function of ideology is to provide a coherent picture. Certain aspects of reality are emphasized, and others are ignored. At the same time, competing ideologies are overtly or covertly denigrated. It is difficult to be skeptical about one's deepest beliefs.

Similarly, thinking critically about one's ethics is difficult. What could be more disorienting than to discover what one thought to be good really was bad? Adams (1979) gave a dynamic interpretation of how this is kept from happening, thereby maintaining stability and equilibrium.

He noted that information is usually remembered in context, and the context is remembered along with the information. When the information is later recalled for use in problem solving, residual information and feelings from the original context tend to accompany it. This complicates the conceptual process, because the residual material also must be dealt with.

For example, if a social worker's first introduction to the importance of client self-determination was through an admired supervisor, it may be difficult later to think of client self-determination as limited to Western cultures. In a sense, this technique has been stereotyped. Adams noted that

information is also filed in memory in a structured way. It is arranged in categories according to likely associations. The structured information in one's memory is so important that one may dismiss information that is inconsistent with that which is already there. Psychologists write about an unpleasant internal state called cognitive dissonance that results from an inconsistency among a person's knowledge, feelings and behavior. The individual attempts to minimize the dissonance. One way to do this is to devalue information that does not fit one's stereotype. (p. 18)

Changes in paradigms, or worldviews, have been called sea changes. Few people are going to make many intellectual sea changes on their own, especially in a value-based profession such as social work, where practitioners' commitments often have an ideological base. For example, when people oppose racism and sexism, certain ideas and programs are accepted because of their good intentions. It is difficult in such situations to suggest, or even think, that some of these programs may be shortsighted, wasteful, or counterproductive. Who wants to be thought of as racist or sexist?

The quiet intimidation that occurs in such charged situations stifles communication and limits the generation of ideas. One's values are not easily questioned. Nothing is more threatening or unsettling than the suggestion that one's beliefs and values are wrong.

The following chapter illustrates how important it is for those who wish to be innovative to be able to look at their values and entertain the possibility that what is unpalatable also may be true. Starr's chapter challenges some of the more central values of social work and provides a startling view of how practice concepts are rooted in time and place. The chapter clearly illustrates the dangers of blind adherence to what was previously thought to be sacrosanct.

The chapter also illustrates two more heuristics of the saturation phase of creativity, defined by Edwards (1987):

[1.] Perceive the lights and shadows of a problem. What is visible—in the light—and what is in shadow? What parts can't be "seen into" at this moment?

[2.] And finally, perceive the Gestalt of the problem. What is the unique set of qualities, the "thingness of the thing"—the quidditas of Aquinas—that makes the problem what it is and none other? (p. 127)

Harold H. Weissman
Editor/Senior Author

References

Adams, J. (1979). *Conceptual blockbusting.* New York: W. W. Norton.
Edwards, B. (1987). *Drawing on the artist within: A guide to innovation, invention, imagination, and creativity* (Fireside ed.). New York: Simon & Schuster.

Questioning Basic Values: Working with New Immigrants and Refugees

Rose Starr

Like all professions, social work is value-based. These value preferences are the foundation of ethical principles that provide guidelines for social workers' obligations and prohibitions with clients, colleagues, employers, and society at large (Levy, 1976; Lewis, 1982). Do the profession's strongly-held values and related ethical imperatives operate as a prod, or as a constraint, to practice creativity and innovation? Do shifts in practice that reflect new client needs and conditions influence the basic values of the profession?

Do social workers' values and ethics, rooted in Western culture, protect or deflect the interests of clients who do not share those same values and ethics? There is a dynamic interplay between the basic professional values of client self-determination and confidentiality and social workers' efforts to understand and meet the changed needs and cultural norms of new immigrant populations. First, social workers must understand the important roles that the experiences and stress of immigration play in clients' lives. According to Rhindress (1985), a social work specialist with Vietnamese and Cambodian refugees, "The circumstances of flight, the

Several authors cited in this chapter (P. Reubens, M. E. Rhindress, R. Brand, and S. Chan) presented papers at an institute for clinicians, "Helping Disadvantaged Clients: The Practice Wisdom of Clinical Social Workers" on May 16, 1985. The institute was sponsored by the Doctor of Social Welfare Program of the City University of New York and held at the Hunter College School of Social Work, New York. At the time of the presentation, they were social workers at Columbia Presbyterian Hospital, and the New York Association for New Americans.

length of time spent in a refugee holding center and the individual's particular experience prior to his/her flight have a direct impact on the nature of the adjustment upon resettlement in the country of final asylum" (p. 6).

Similarly, Reubens (1985) underscored the "psychologically wrenching experience" (p. 2) of immigration, the "narcissistic injuries" with "loss of status and of self-objects in the form of familiar neighborhoods, persons and customs" (p. 9), all of which may be exacerbated by racism in the receiving country (p. 3). Brand (1985) also identified the importance of recent stressful conditions in her summary of work with Vietnamese, Cambodian, and Ethiopian refugees:

> Theoretically speaking, I have two frames of reference, stress and culture. . . . Freud dealt with early history as the source of certain psychological problems and illnesses. I do not believe his work is generally helpful for refugees, because he did not deal with situational stress. Had he lived beyond 1939, perhaps he would have done so (p. 12).

Chan (1985) emphasized the impact of religion and philosophy on immigrants' attitudes towards health and mental health problems and services. For example, Asian people view mental illness "as a supernatural or neurological problem" or as "punishment for wrongdoing" (p. 3). As a result, the mentally ill are feared, avoided, and "often hidden by the family causing delays in seeking treatment" (p. 3). Similarly, the Asian view of the harmony of mind and body can account for the frequent "somatization and externalization of emotional problems" (p. 3) and consequent seeking of help from health care, rather than mental health, service systems.

The role and nature of the family is another facet of new immigrant culture crucial to understanding not only the newcomers' perceptions and adaptation, but also the need for new approaches in social work practice. The authority of the family unit and the relative unimportance of individual independence and autonomy—strikingly similar in both Latin American and Asian societies—have spurred a redefinition of key practice principles and their implementation.

As described by Reubens (1985),

> Social work teaches us that family and community are important supports for individuals, but I discovered that in traditional cultures, family and village are virtually extensions of the self. . . . The Hispanic family is an extended kinship network including *compadres* (godparents). Individual autonomy is not highly valued and thus clients may appear "passive" to social workers.

Operating from our training, we may misdiagnose families as "undifferentiated" or individuals as suffering from "separation problems." I learned to adjust my diagnostic thinking by appreciating that group strengths were an alternative to American culture's individualistic values. (p. 8)

Similarly, Rhindress (1983) pointed out that "in Khmer [Cambodian] culture, the family or authority figure makes a decision by which other members abide" (p. 7). Emphasizing the role the community plays in the client's world, she cautioned social workers against "alienate[ing] the client or the community by disregarding his culturally-conditioned method of problem-solving" in which elders and neighbors would naturally participate (p. 9).

Reinterpreting Basic Practice Values

Social workers' concepts must be adjusted to take into account the family and community values of many new immigrant populations. Client self-determination and confidentiality, as well as the social worker's nondirective approach, must be reexamined. The emphasis of social work on the right of individual clients to make their own choices and decisions, the obligation of social workers not to impose their own values and goals on clients, and the necessity for client privacy in personal matters all require reinterpretation in accordance with new immigrants' cultural norms.

For the most part, this reinterpretation moves social workers away from rigid definitions and polarities toward greater flexibility in their understanding and application of professional methods and principles. In the process, the dichotomies that have constrained professional conceptions of ethical practice—either one is rational or subjective, pro-individual or pro-society, for independence or dependence, in support of client self-determination or social worker authority—have been changed. The social worker is urged to consider a continuum of approaches and values. The selection of which of these to use should be determined by a full, individualized assessment of client needs and goals, within a cultural context. As the following case studies illustrate, it is impossible to consider client culture, to "start where the client is" and serve clients' interests without being open to the need for change in professional values and methods.

According to Chan (1985), the social worker must be "family-centered rather than individual-centered when formulating treatment goals and plans. The Asian family relationship is more interdependent than the Western family; therefore, the entire family has to be engaged for support"

(p. 7). Similarly, Reubens (1985) highlighted the implications of Hispanic family unity and gender-based role expectations in the assessment and treatment of female clients. "I had to learn," she stated, "that it is normative for these women to spend the day in [their] mother's company, to define themselves only via the family, and to refuse to assert individual needs" (p. 9).

However, as both Chan (1985) and Reubens (1985) suggested, the approach to the new immigrant family may require adaptation to rather strict generational and sex role expectations. Chan discovered that "the traditional concept of family therapy is not readily workable with the Asian family in which the generation line and sex line is strong" (p. 7). Chan found it useful to incorporate individual sessions within a family therapy concept. Recognizing that a social worker may represent a challenge to male authority, Reubens (1985) suggested that home visits are essential to an acceptable adaptation of family work with new Hispanic immigrants:

> [This allows] the head of the family . . . [to] be on his own turf. [He] . . . [may feel] compelled to stay for the meeting in order to be a good host. At the same time, [it is important that] the social worker . . . alter her/his expectations of change in family sex roles. [A] most difficult challenge, [this] reflects the need to "start where the client is" and offer our values as alternatives without imposing them. . . . (p. 14)

Rhindress's (1983) work with a pregnant Khmer orphan further illustrates the way in which the concept of self-determination and family work can be reshaped to be congruent with cultural values and helpful to the client.

> I received news from a Khmer paraprofessional that one of the orphan girls apparently was pregnant and deciding whether or not to abort the baby. . . . During the initial phase of this crisis, I was working from traditional Western values in which my primary goals were to offer support and clarify options. I was concerned that this girl make her own decisions as she was being inundated with advice from various sources. [However,] in attempting to help the girl make a decision, I was met with constant requests from her that *I* make decisions *for* her. . . . On the third interview the girl's 16-year-old brother joined her. During the session, the girl agreed that being the oldest male, her brother was now the head of the family and therefore would make all her decisions. He was insistent on her complying with his decisions, stating that, if she did not agree to listen to him, he and the other three siblings would disown her. As a good social worker I was rather shaken by this development and sought the advice of a wise priest who was well-versed in

Asian culture. Through him I learned that this arrangement was in keeping with the dictates of the culture.

In attempting to defend her right to self-determination, I was violating cultural norms. Rather than providing comfort, structure and support, I was causing confusion and anxiety in a young girl who was already quite anxious and frightened. In Khmer culture, the family or authority figure makes a decision by which other members abide. My work subsequently shifted to greater interaction with the brother who, feeling frightened and confused by this heavy responsibility, turned to our agency for guidance. (pp. 6–7)

The importance of developing innovative, culturally adapted definitions of confidentiality also is illustrated by Rhindress's work with Cambodian refugees. In that culture, an insistence on privacy in the helping process would artificially remove the client from the social influence and support of his or her community. Such an insistence also would be perceived as disrespectful to community and family elders, and thus would injure, rather than enhance, client trust. Flexibility in the application of a privacy principle is illustrated in the following example by Rhindress (1985):

A woman comes to a worker asking for help because her husband is unfaithful. He has recently hit her during an argument. The worker agrees to meet the husband and wife in the home where she finds the couple, an uncle, a mother-in-law, a few neighbors and several children. According to traditional social work practice theory, the worker should attempt to arrange for privacy. In this situation, however, the worker would lose credibility if she refused to conduct the interview. The client knows he must answer not only to his wife but also to his community and family elders. As he tells his story, various elders may chime in to clarify, confirm, or correct him or his wife. They may even take an active role in deciding what needs to be done to rectify the situation. The situation is viewed by the client and the community as a community problem. He will be forgiven as long as he tries to follow their advice and that of the worker. . . . From the client's perspective, if the worker is willing to [ask the elders to leave and] cause [them] to lose face, she may also mishandle the trust the client is investing in her.

If the worker feels that it is inappropriate to discuss the particular situation in the context of family or community, she may choose a middle ground approach. For example, she may say, "I am aware that there has been a problem in the family. I'm sure that you all want to help and I appreciate your being here. If [the client] wants to continue, we can talk a little about what has happened but tonight I was just stopping by to see how things are going. We can talk more about this in my office." This modification would achieve various goals. First, the worker is demonstrating her willingness to help as exhibited by the willingness to come to the apartment. Second, the worker is validating the role of the elders in giving them the opportunity to express themselves. Finally, the worker is allowing the client to see her sensitivity to both his culture and his possible desire for less public exposure. The door is open for more intensive discussion in another setting. Above all, face has been saved, thereby engendering trust. (pp. 8–9)

Protecting Client Rights

To enable clients to determine their own destiny in accordance with their own values and needs, social workers and other mental health professionals have consciously avoided imposing their values on the client through direct or indirect manipulation of their position of authority and expertise. The client's right to decide and to differ from the worker are historic ethical mandates—even more important to protect when worker and client perspectives on what is right and good stem from diverse cultural values. It is important for social workers to consider carefully their stance on giving advice, providing direction, and using the authority attached to their role as expert.

Rhindress (1985) addressed the relationship between client self-determination and worker authority with Indo-Chinese refugees:

> Social workers are, by design, wary of using authority, fearful of seeming coercive or of tampering with one's right to self-determination. The concept of self-determination, however, is a largely alien one to this population. They come from a value and belief system of clearly defined roles where decisions are made by those who have the right to make them. Parents decide for children, even when those children are married with offspring of their own. Husbands have the right to decide for wives. Social workers then, are at least expected to have an opinion on what a client ought best do in a given situation. The client comes seeking advice, not a discussion of how he feels about his situation. If the worker seems to not have an opinion he may feel let down and distrustful. It is possible to communicate that a client must take responsibility for his/her own actions while also giving clear direction as to the avenues open for action. (p. 10)

Understanding that the use of nondirective, open-ended questions with this population would be culturally alien and counterproductive, Rhindress (1985) suggested that professionals take an active, directive stance in exploring clients' feelings. In her experience, this approach enhances client control and growth in the helping process. The following examples show the connection between worker direction and client choice in individual and group modes of intervention.

> Another effective tool for specific intervention is verbalization of feelings for the client. Keeping in mind that they have not been raised in an atmosphere

which places value on talking out one's problems, one would do well to keep away from open-ended questions. Rather than asking "How do you feel about it?" one might try, "I imagine you might feel. . . ." Once again, our social work training has warned us against too frequent use of such a type of question. However, the Indo-Chinese are made to feel very uncomfortable with open-ended questions. They have learned to always try to determine the answer that the asker really is looking for and then to answer accordingly. Therefore, a question deliberately designed not to give clues as to the asker's thoughts on a subject puts the client in a bind. If the question is put in the latter fashion it puts the client at ease. If the worker has expressed a sentiment which is not consistent with the client's feeling and has created the right atmosphere of trust, he/she will correct you. Having given them a clear message as to what you are thinking about where their thoughts may be, they will be sure to set you straight if need be.

Open-ended statements are not effective in group settings either. For example, in an effort to get a group to express their feelings of culture shock or disappointment with America, a worker might try, "You learned a lot about America in cultural orientation. What did you think you got here? Is it what you expected?" The group would probably stare uncomfortably at the floor wondering what the worker wants. Of course it isn't what they expected. They expected a picture post card America, but how can they tell you that?

A more effective approach would be to relate a story: "I have a Cambodian friend who said that in cultural orientation they told him that one must never throw garbage in the street. When he got here he put the ashes from his cigarettes in his pockets. After being here a few days he saw that everyone threw his garbage in the street and he felt angry and foolish about his pocket full of ashes." The response is often laughter and a clamoring to tell their own versions of disappointment. Thus the process of beginning to deal with these feelings begins, and permission to express negative feelings is communicated in a humorous vein. To merely speak of one's disillusionment with America would be disrespectful to the American worker as she might feel hurt or angry. (pp. 12–13)

Shifting notions and adaptations of client self-determination, confidentiality, and social worker authority result from the efforts of professionals to forge new, culturally-compatible methods of helping. Their work clarifies important ingredients in the practice innovation process and the relationship of means and ends in professional work.

Meeting Client Needs

The practice innovations described are successful modes of engaging and retaining new immigrants as clients. Finding better methods of establishing a client relationship and generating continuity and trust have influenced the ways these social workers understood and implemented practice principles. The need for change was obvious when they discovered that use of basic social work principles without appropriate adaptations was not only ineffective, but also potentially harmful— creating client conflicts, anxiety, and the dilemma of choice between professional service and family values.

From this perspective, client self-determination, confidentiality, and social worker nondirection are not immutable mandates with singular definitions, but general prescriptions in the service of far more important ends. Thus, the question for professionals with new immigrants, and perhaps with other populations, is not whether important professional values should be adhered to, but how they should be interpreted to meet client needs and interests. This distinguishing of means and ends in the helping process reaffirms the centrality of assessment and purpose in professional function. Innovation in method, change, and adaptation in the operationalization of value preferences should be the norm. As Germain (1983) noted,

> It is inevitable that practitioners and educators will reach the conclusion . . . that people's needs must define the method, and not the other way around. (p. 50)

References

Brand, R. (1985, May). *Depression and loss in Third World immigrants*. Paper presented at the doctoral program conference of the Hunter College School of Social Work, City University of New York.

Chan, S. (1985, May). *An Eastern view of mental health—the practice wisdom of clinical social workers*. Paper presented at the doctoral program conference of the Hunter College School of Social Work, City University of New York.

Germain, C. B. (1983). Technological advances. In A. Rosenblatt & D. Waldfogel (Eds.), *Handbook of clinical social work* (pp. 26–57). San Francisco: Jossey–Bass.

Levy, C. S. (1976). *Social work ethics*. New York: Human Sciences Press.

Lewis, H. (1982). *The intellectual base of social work practice*. New York: Haworth Press.

Rhindress, M. E. (1983, November). *Field practice in international social work: The Thailand experience*. Paper presented at the symposium of the National Association of Social Workers, Washington, DC.

Rhindress, M. E. (1985, May). *Approaches to social work with Vietnamese and Cambodian families*. Paper presented at the doctoral program conference of the Hunter College School of Social Work, City University of New York.

Reubens, P. (1985, May). *Developing practice wisdom to help recent Hispanic immigrants*. Paper presented at the doctoral program conference of the Hunter College School of Social Work, City University of New York.

Creativity and Professionalism

Social work is a relatively new profession, and it is not completely accepted or understood by the public. The push for credentialing, licensing, and scientific legitimacy are only a limited response to this situation. A great deal of creativity and innovation is needed before social work can fulfill society's needs and become more fully accepted as a profession.

If saturation is indeed a key phase of the creative process, then the organized profession should provide its members with the information they need to reach saturation. One of the main purposes of a profession is to keep track of its members' failures and successes, so that professional knowledge and skill are increased. When this tracking is not done or is done poorly, there not only is a loss in what might be learned and passed on but a good chance that the same errors are repeated. Fine (1981) noted that a profession must promote the diffusion, transfer, and refinement of ideas. This occurs through a social process, where people exchange and change ideas, and a cultural process, where criteria of acceptability and choice are professionally promulgated.

In the next chapter, Rothman and Ayala note that the diffusion of knowledge about program and techniques is as professionally important as the creation of such knowledge. New ideas must be tried out in many places if they are to be developed and improved on.

Much of the practice knowledge of the social work profession is borrowed from other disciplines. Certainly, there is creativity involved in adapting, transforming, and putting this knowledge to use. However, a unique body of practice knowledge must be developed for the social work profession by its creative practitioners. There simply is no source from which to borrow much of this knowledge.

Harold H. Weissman
Editor/Senior Author

Reference

Fine, S. (1981). *The marketing of ideas and social issues.* New York: Praeger.

Linking Knowledge Saturation to Innovation

Jack Rothman and Frank Ayala, Jr.

Social workers use many arguments to defend the lack of use of social work research in developing new policies and practices. Findings are too abstract, or not timely, they say. Social research is not precise enough. For whatever reason, practitioners and policymakers use other means and sources for making innovative decisions. There are indeed gaps between research findings and their application, and these gaps are pronounced (Rothman, 1979). However, there are also ways to build and strengthen the links between research knowledge and innovation planners.

Once an innovative policy or practice is created, whether by researchers or practitioners, there also are gaps in getting information about it to those who should know about it. The process of information diffusion typically is slow, halting, and inefficient (Rogers, 1983).

Currently, there is no well-established mechanism that facilitates communication about new innovations. The kinds of structures, roles, and procedures needed to accomplish this linkage are almost totally missing in social work (Guba, 1968). This crippling void has gone unrecognized by social workers.

Linking Innovations with Practitioners

The social work profession could benefit greatly from linking networks similar to those available in the field of education. Through the Educational Resources Information Center (ERIC), educators have a national computerized information system that facilitates broad and rapid retrieval of professional knowledge by educators. There is no similar network for social workers.

In existence since 1966, ERIC currently is sponsored by the U.S. Department of Education, Office of Educational Research and Improvement. ERIC links practitioners with tested innovations using the following four components:

1. It provides an online retrieval capability for those wishing to access information via computer.

2. Through ERIC, users may obtain microfiche or paper copies of documents from the database.

3. "ERIC serves as a permanent archive for significant education documents that might otherwise be lost to the profession" (Bell, Senese, & Sweet, 1982, p. 2).

4. ERIC is a network of organizations including 16 subject-oriented clearinghouses and several commercial organizations linking educators and scholars with specialized content areas.

The ERIC clearinghouses are located at universities or professional organizations. Each clearinghouse emphasizes a different multidisciplinary area. "Each is responsible for searching out and acquiring the significant educational literature within its . . . area" (Bell, Senese, & Sweet, 1982, p. 4), with the subsequent screening, selection, and processing of items for entry into the database. Clearinghouses also produce analyses of the information acquired and help users retrieve information from the database. Some examples of ERIC clearinghouse specialties are adult, career, and vocational education; counseling and personnel services; educational management; handicapped and gifted children; higher education; and social studies/social services education. Several of these specialties are relevant to social work.

The knowledge base compiled by these various clearinghouses provides access to information of interest to practitioners, researchers, students, and other users. After 20 years of operation, ERIC has become the repository of countless documents that describe "innovative curriculum materials, new technological advances, and effective teaching methods . . . developed and tested in education laboratories, research and development centers, and classrooms throughout the country" (Bell, Senese, & Sweet, p. 1). Without this system of clearinghouses, much of this type of information might not have been accumulated. Practitioners would not have had a designated place and procedure for gaining this knowledge.

Identifying Diffusing Innovation Information

The federally funded National Diffusion Network (NDN), started in 1974 by the U.S. Office of Education, links practitioners to innovation by making locally developed exemplary programs available for adoption by schools, colleges, and other institutions throughout the United States. By providing programs with funding for dissemination and supporting the work of regional facilitators, NDN promotes awareness of effective program innovations and assists with their adoption.

However, before programs can become part of NDN, they first must be evaluated for their effectiveness and worth for replication in other schools. Each program is reviewed by the Joint Dissemination Review Panel (JDRP) of the Department of Education and the National Institute of Education. Program developers seeking funds must give convincing evidence of the positive impact of their programs. Additionally, these program developers must demonstrate the feasibility of reproducing the programs elsewhere. According to LoGuidice (1985), effectiveness is the main criterion for acceptance. Although approval by JDRP may bestow public and professional recognition on innovative programs, the essential benefit is entry into a federal diffusion system for dissemination funds. If funded, such program innovations may be adopted by schools throughout the country and the world.

This diffusion effort involves a variety of personnel and activities. NDN offers program leaders as linking agents, or developer/demonstrators, whose only job is to help interested organizations with the adoption and adaptation of educational program innovations. This is accomplished largely through in-service training for staff members of the adopting school, and varied follow-up help, such as visits, additional training, and communication via newsletters and the telephone. There are also NDN state facilitators, who may sponsor state or regional conferences on innovations, or arrange awareness sessions focusing on one or more NDN programs. They also may work with practitioners to review NDN innovations that may meet the needs of their particular school or organization.

The kinds of program innovations that receive dissemination funds cover a broad range of educational needs. Many are concerned with the basic skills area. Other programs address career and adult education, organization and administration, bilingual and migrant education, and special interests such as communication, technology, health, and human behavior. With dissemination support, each NDN program maintains a demonstration project that advises interested visitors about program details. In addition, NDN helps potential adopters gain access to information about programs that they are unable to visit.

Costs have been minimal to those adopting NDN program innovations. Typically, the services of NDN's facilitators are free, so any costs associated with adopting a program usually involve only required materials or the compensation due staff for participating in training. There also are expenses associated with the basic conditions that NDN requires adopters to meet. For example, the signed adoption agreement might require the implementation of a pretest and posttest assessment, with the results submitted to NDN for evaluation of the program's impact. In fact, cost effectiveness is one reason NDN was founded (Neill, 1980). According to Neill, making effective program innovation available for adoption at low cost saves adopting institutions "the time and expense of looking for a solution that already exists—reinventing the wheel" (p. 45). It is common knowledge that social workers spend much time reinventing practices and policies, without having the means to find already existing programs.

Since NDN began, tens of thousands of education practitioners have received in-service training in the use of NDN programs, and hundreds of thousands of student clients have benefited from those programs. Some NDN projects were the result of research. Others came about because a teacher could not find a solution to a problem but had an idea worth trying (Neill, 1980). Research knowledge is, indeed, a significant stimulus for innovative practice, but it is not the only source. Creative social work practitioners could benefit greatly from linkage networks like ERIC and NDN to advance practice and program development.

Too often in social work, the innovation process is thought of only as the inspired stirrings of an individual. However, innovation more often is a social phenomenon. It requires the profession to take responsibility for building mechanisms to facilitate communication about innovations.

As Kadushin (1971) so aptly stated, "Research may never be able to give us as much as we want. But . . . [it] may be able to give us some increasingly modest increment of what we need" (p. 64). Learning about the research and innovation of others can help social workers offer more informed and more effective help to the clients they serve. Facilitating this knowledge should be a major goal of the social work profession.

References

Bell, T. H., Senese, D. J., & Sweet, Jr., R. W. (1982). *All about ERIC: Educational Resources Information Center.* Washington, DC: National Institute of Education.

Guba, E. G. (1968). Development, diffusion and evaluation. In T. L. Eiddell & J. M. Kitchel (Eds.), *Knowledge production and utilization* (Vol. 1; pp. 37–63). Columbus, Ohio: University Council for Educational Administration and Center for the Advanced Study of Educational Administration (University of Oregon).

Kadushin, A. (1971). Child welfare. In H. S. Maas (Ed.), *Research in the social services: A five-year review* (pp. 13–69). New York: National Association of Social Workers.

LoGuidice, T. (1985). The National Diffusion Network: A report on a resource for America's elementary and secondary schools. *The Clearing House, 59*(1), 33–34.

Neill, S. B. (1980, June). The National Diffusion Network. *The National Elementary Principal*, 45–48.

Rogers, E. M. (1983). *Diffusion of innovations* (3rd ed.). New York: Free Press–Macmillan.

Rothman, J. (1979). Gaps and linkages in research utilization: Enhancing utilization through a research and development approach. In A. Rubin & A. Rosenblatt (Eds.), *Sourcebook on research utilization* (pp. 81–109). New York: Council on Social Work Education.

Summation of Part Two

A profession molds what its practitioners think in terms of priority of problems to be solved and appropriate ways to solve them, as well as how to perceive those who seek the services of the profession.

The aspiring innovator, whether teacher or practitioner, must help to create a professional environment that supports and promotes a creative approach to professionalism.

Von Maanen and Schein (1979) suggested that the surest way to develop conformists is to involve new recruits "in a definite series of cumulative stages . . . involving role models who set the 'correct' example for the recruit; and processes which through various means, involve the recruits' redefinition of self around certain recognized organizational variables" (p. 253).

If Von Maanen and Schein are correct, graduate school officials need to rethink some of their socialization processes. For example, one graduate school instructor asked her students to write a paper on all the clichés they had learned in two years. "Start where the client is," "partialize the problem," and "work it through" indeed are important ideas. Yet, in a playful way the instructor got her students to realize that these clichés masked as much as they revealed, and sounded much more meaningful than they actually were.

The concept of structuring playfulness into the profession offers practitioners a way to saturate themselves with ideas and information about a particular problem. As March and Olsen (1979) suggested:

> If we had a good technology of foolishness, it might (in combination with the technology of reason) help in a small way to develop the unusual combinations of attitudes and behaviors that describe the interesting (social workers), interesting (agencies), and (one of the more) interesting (professions) of the world. (p. 81)

This is particularly important because playfulness offers a way of seeing things differently, of slipping the boundaries of sequential, logical, and analytical thinking. Simply gathering a great deal of information is necessary, but certainly not sufficient to fulfill the saturation stage of creative thinking. Information has to be reworked and recombined. One has to *play* with it.

Saturation: Exhausting the Possibilities

During saturation, one should try both to learn everything possible about a problem and to look at this information from as many different angles as possible. The trick is not to jump to conclusions. To achieve this, often we need "glitches"—mental devices that help the mind accept information that may contradict long-standing beliefs and preconceptions. Playfulness, in one sense, serves as a glitch.

For example, nothing could be more salutory for furthering creativity than exposing the difference between theory and practice. One method of doing this would be for the major social work journals to print practitioner critiques of articles written by professors. Each critique could conclude by assigning the professor a grade! Something is unhealthy in a profession where one group does the work and the other group—with only a peripheral connection to practice—does most of the writing.

Similarly, to get a first insight into a problem, there are approaches to information and problem solution that can promote saturation, and ultimately insight, into a problem. Saturation occurs when all the ways to solve a problem are exhausted. In Part Two, the following four techniques were discussed:

1. Resist the premature naming of data or observations as words include and exclude, and what is excluded may be a crucial part of the sought-for solution.

2. Look closely at the way values and ideology affect the sense of what is part of the problem and what is part of the solution as well as what can be and what cannot be questioned.

3. Broaden perspective by trying to reverse the figure and ground of the problem—focus on the background rather than the foreground.

4. Express the problem in a nonverbal way if it seems as though all of the ways of looking at the problem have been exhausted.

Imaging and visualization are particularly useful when trying the fourth technique. "Einstein was famous for his thought experiments, fantastic flights of fancy that led him to imagine, for example, what it would be like to ride on a light beam, a cerebral magical mystery tour that offered him the insights he needed to produce the special theory of relativity (Cole, 1988, p. C16).

Finally, to truly be saturated, it probably is necessary to break some rules and take risks. Echoing March and Olsen (1979), Cole (1988) suggested a certain amount of playing at problem solution.

In real play, we try things just to see what happens. In other words we take risks. What we risk, above all, is making a fool of ourselves. . . . Only by risking ridicule can we come out from the covers of conventional wisdom. Without breaking rules, it is impossible to come up with truly new solutions. (p. C16)

An organized profession, such as social work, should help its practitioners with the above suggestions for achieving creative saturation. There is a cumulative and historical importance to the development of new ideas. As Einstein said, "We stand on the shoulders of giants." Most professions offer their members a limited set of concepts that explains the interrelationships of the phenomena with which they deal. These concepts then determine what practitioners see in a situation, and can result in premature closure in thinking. Creative journal editorial policies and structuring of professional meetings, dissemination and evaluation of new ideas, and legitimization of questioning cherished ideas and ideals through professional playfulness (temporarily relaxing the structures of logic and professional norms) are all ways an organized profession could support creativity. For example, the concepts of system and ecology have penetrated social work thinking in the past decade. Although they have been useful, little attention has been given to their potential limitations. In their attempt at systemic and ecological inclusiveness, what do those concepts blur— do they create the illusion of a gestalt where only chaos exists?

Much of the professional thinking is embedded in metaphors and analogies. Saturation should bring to light the implicit and explicit metaphors and analogies. Then, information is looked at from the point of view of different metaphors and analogies, and, as Morton Hunt stated, "Metaphorical–analogical thinking opens new pathways of thought and thus of creative problem solving" (as cited in Edwards, 1985, p. 150).

Hunt continued,

If the unlike things are really alike in some ways, perhaps they are so in others; that is the meaning of analogy. We pursue the thought, and find new meanings, new understanding, and often, new solutions to old problems. (as cited in Edwards, 1985, p. 150)

The Role of Memory

Some researchers see saturation as concerned with the storage and retrieval of information and algorithms, or formulas for solving problems. Memory plays a key role in this process.

Creative artists have been shown to have great recall not only of people or events, but also of smells, feelings, colors, and other associations related to the person or event. The creative person is able to fully saturate himself or herself in all dimensions of a problem. He or she remembers

119

facts, feelings, ideas, people, sensations, cues, and problem-solving techniques that went along with events, interactions, and situations. The greater the recall, the greater the detail in our cognitive maps—the more likely the connections between the seemingly unconnected. One-dimensional recall may represent a thinness of material, a lack of anything to grab onto to make a connection. Those interested in maximizing their creative possibilities should consider the questions: What is my memory like? What do I ordinarily perceive and remember? Do I remember how and why I did something as well as what I did? Is the problem my memory or my powers of observation and perception? It is possible to starve, rather than saturate, one's creativity by lack of material.

How does one know when one is saturated? One practical answer drawn from countless experiences and creative anecdotes is simply to put the problem aside for a time. The next two chapters look further at the role of relaxation in creativity.

Harold H. Weissman
Editor/Senior Author

References

Cole, K. C. (1988, November 30). Play by definition suspends the rules. *New York Times*, p. C16.

Edwards, B. (1985). *Drawing on the artist within: A guide to innovation, invention, imagination and creativity* (Fireside ed.). New York: Simon & Schuster.

March, J., & Olsen, J. (1979). *Ambiguity and choice in organizations*. Bergen, Norway: Universitetsforlaget.

Von Maanen, J., & Schein, E. (1979). Toward a theory of organizational socialization. In B. Staw (Ed.), *Research in organizational behavior* (pp. 209–264). Greenwich, CT: JAI Press.

PART THREE
Creativity and Innovation in Organizational Contexts

Illumination

There are two kinds of truth, small truth and great truth. You can recognize a small truth because its opposite is a falsehood. The opposite of a great truth is another truth.

—Niels Bohr

An invention or a discovery does not become an innovation until others accept it. Sometimes innovators first have to adapt what others have invented or discovered, and then "sell" the adaptations to others. At other times, they must get their own inventions accepted.

In addition to the generation of ideas, innovation as a process includes the initiation, implementation, and adoption or institutionalization of an innovation. It is not a process one carries out alone. *Initiation* refers to getting the authority and resources to innovate. *Implementation* refers to creating procedures for use of an innovation, then operating or testing it. *Institutionalization* is the validation and acceptance of an innovation as a permanent part of organizational structures or professional practice.

In each of its phases, innovation may require all of the stages of creativity. Thinking about how to get a project initiated, implemented, or institutionalized all, in turn, may require first insight, saturation, incubation, illumination, and verification. In Part Three, the roles that illumination and verification play in the process of innovation are examined.

Illumination: Hitting the Jackpot

Illumination refers to the moment of insight when a person first becomes conscious of the solution to a problem. It is not necessarily an instantaneous revelation. There could be a number of small incremental revelations that ultimately add up to something larger.

No one has been able yet to adequately describe what occurs during incubation and at the moment of insight. There is no operational statement for programming an insight—do *x* and *y* and then incubate *z* for 2 weeks and the result will be "illumination."[1]

The best theory is that, during the saturation phase, the mind is "programmed" with different ways of looking at a problem, information related to it, and the requirements a solution would have to satisfy to be acceptable. Illumination can be compared with the jackpot in the slot

---

[1] In keeping with the possibility that stages of creativity, in real situations, may be out of order or omitted, incubation is discussed in the next chapter.

machine. The winning combination, or pattern of connections, suddenly is lined up.

It is possible that the problem-solving techniques ordinarily used during saturation give only a limited angle or view of a problem, thereby raising the odds against finding the winning combination. For example, reasoning techniques include Trial-and-Error, Hill Climbing (that is, do whatever seems best at the time), and Means–End analysis (Waldrop, 1988, p. 27).

A certain amount of adeptness at different problem-solving techniques during saturation should increase the number of permutations that can be considered during incubation. Different techniques highlight different aspects of a problem, and thereby magnify both the quantity and quality of information on the problem. Gardner (1983) suggested that

> faced with a problem too complex or unwieldy to solve, the [person] . . . is counseled to find a simple problem within the larger one, to seek a solution to the simpler component, and then to build upon that solution. The student is also advised to propose a possible solution and to work backward to the problem: or to describe the characteristics that a solution should have and then, in turn, to try to attain each of them. Another popular method is indirect proof: one assumes the opposite of what one is trying to prove and ascertains the consequences of that assumption. (p. 144)

Memory can include both data and ways to manipulate that data. The mind needs access to both for illumination to occur. Ideas must be sifted and judged both consciously and unconsciously. Pauling (as cited in John-Steiner, 1985) has suggested that to be a creative thinker, "one has to have many, many ideas and know how to choose from them" (p. 202).

Incubation probably is a type of rumination. The many reports of people getting insight into a problem while doing something totally disconnected to it probably can be traced to a preconscious musing about the problem.

Right Solution: Harmony, Elegance, and Beauty

Although there is no consensus about the means to attain illumination, there is considerable anecdotal material to suggest that the solution, however determined, feels "right" to the creator. As Edwards (1987) stated,

> Because it fits and reconciles all parts of the problem, the solution is joyfully embraced without intervening doubts or questions. . . . And while truly creative solutions . . . often take additional time, the idea, the strategy, the guiding principle does often arrive in a luminous moment. (p. 227)

Part of the pleasure of illumination is aesthetic. Creators report their solution to be harmonious, because disparate parts suddenly fit together; elegant, because it embodies a sense of proportion; and beautiful, because the problem and solution are united in one whole picture (Heus & Pincus, 1986, pp. 394–398). The sense of rightness and beauty and integrity has ramifications beyond aesthetic pleasure. This sense supplies the courage and conviction to complete the project. The illumination may have provided the clue or the guide, but the idea has to be developed, the innovation operationalized and tried out, and the new program begun.

In the following chapter, Young provides an interesting look at how acknowledged innovators achieved their reputations—what skills they possessed, how they interacted with their environments, and most importantly, how they carried through on their insights. He also describes how the innovators' belief in the "rightness" of the innovation supplied the confidence to persevere and prove that the idea worked.

Other professionals must accept an invention or discovery if it is to become an innovation. This verification process can take many years. Young gives a clear picture of what a creative social entrepreneur does. As Kingdon (1984) noted,

> Policy entrepreneurs do not leave consideration of their pet proposals to accident. Instead, they push for consideration in many ways and in many forums. In the process of policy development recombination (the coupling of already-familiar elements) is more important than mutation (the appearance of wholly new forms). Thus entrepreneurs, who broker people and ideas, are more important than inventors. Because recombination is more important than invention, there may be "no new thing under the sun" at the same time that there may be dramatic change and innovation. There is change, but it involves the recombination of already-familiar elements. (p. 210)

Harold H. Weissman
Editor/Senior Author

References

Edwards, B. (1987). *Drawing on the artist within: A guide to innovation, invention, imagination, and creativity.* (Fireside ed.). New York: Simon & Schuster.

Gardner, H. (1983). *Frames of mind.* New York: Basic Books.

Heus, M., & Pincus, A. (1986). *The creative generalist: A guide to social work practice.* Barneveld, WI: Micamar.

John-Steiner, V. (1985). *Notebooks of the mind.* Albuquerque: University of New Mexico Press.

Kingdon, J. (1984). *Agendas, alternatives and public policy.* Boston: Little, Brown.

Waldrop, M. M. (1988, July). Toward a unified theory of cognition. *Science, 242,* 27.

Champions of Change: Entrepreneurs in Social Work

Dennis R. Young

Until recently "entrepreneurship" was a word essentially foreign to social work. When entrepreneurship was mentioned, it carried the negative connotations of individualism and moneymaking—values contrary to the community-oriented, self-sacrificing, and helping orientation of the social work profession. In the 1980s, this view seemed to change. As government began to withdraw its support of social programs, people in human service agencies realized they needed to be enterprising to survive. Moreover, profitmaking ventures supporting social objectives became legitimate, even glamorous undertakings.

The historical antagonism toward entrepreneurship in social work was based on a misunderstanding of this process and its role in providing effective social services. Interestingly enough, the present glamorization of entrepreneurship also is based on a narrow and possibly misguided interpretation. Although entrepreneurship clearly is a process that centers on individual initiative, action for profit is not its essence. Rather, *entrepreneurship* is individual initiative taken to bring about change in the delivery of a good or service. Profit is only one possible motivation for this initiative. Indeed, in social work as opposed to other areas of economic activity, monetary reward is less important than other sources of motivation.

Invention, Innovation, and Entrepreneurship

Entrepreneurship is an essential element in bringing about constructive change in social work. However, it is important to understand what is meant by "change" and how an entrepreneur brings change about. First, the distinction must be made between invention and innovation. An *invention* is a new idea, either a new service or product, a better method of producing that service or product, or a more efficient way of organizing the markets for purchasing inputs to production or distributing output services or products. Until an invention is implemented, however, there is no change. An *innovation*, therefore, is an invention put into practice.

An entrepreneur innovates, or puts a new invention or idea into practice. Entrepreneurs need not be the inventors—usually they are not. Also, the idea itself need not be "new" but only new to the context in which the entrepreneur applies it. The entrepreneur is the individual who is able to bring all the pieces together—the idea, the resources, the organization, and so forth—to make the idea work where it has not been tried successfully before.

One example illustrates invention, innovation, and entrepreneurship. In the late 1960s, pressure was building on the New York City foster care system to accommodate new and difficult populations of neglected and dependent children. The idea of a "diagnostic center" was suggested to provide a complete psychological, physical, and social analysis of a child's problem before his or her placement into foster care. This idea may have been borrowed from the field of medicine, where the concept of a central intensive diagnostic facility is embodied in such institutions as the Mayo Clinic. The diagnostic center concept was first introduced into the New York City foster care system in 1969 by Sister Mary Paul Janchill at the Euphrasian Residence of the Sisters of the Good Shepherd Residences, Inc. (Young, 1980). Although Janchill indeed may have been the inventor of the diagnostic center concept, she did not become the entrepreneur of this invention until she successfully incorporated it (as an innovation) into the operations of the Euphrasian Residence. Soon after this success, other agencies developed their own diagnostic centers; for instance, the Jewish Child Care Agency created its Pleasantville (NY) Diagnostic Center. This project was not simply an imitation. It represented a real innovation within its own agency contexts, and it was pioneered by entrepreneurs just as worthy of that description as Janchill (Young, 1985).

Necessary and Sufficient Conditions

Entrepreneurship is integral to innovation in social work. However, it also is important to understand that it is just one key element in the process of bringing about change. In mathematicians' terms, entrepreneurship is a necessary, but not a sufficient, condition for change. For example, in the Euphrasian case, the diagnostic center would not have existed without the entrepreneurial work of Janchill. However, this development was not inevitable, at least in the time and place in which it occurred. The point may be generalized beyond this one example. Innovations require champions; they do not come about by themselves. Those champions are the social entrepreneurs.

Although entrepreneurs are necessary for social work innovation, without conducive conditions in which to work, they will not succeed, and may not even try. Here, the "sufficient conditions" necessary for innovation include the appropriate social context, the state of knowledge and professional thinking in social work, and the receptivity of organizations through which the entrepreneurs may work.

Compare the Pleasantville experience with another case where the innovation was stunted by unfavorable circumstances. In the Pleasantville case, external developments called for change, the organization was under pressure to create this change, and the idea of a diagnostic center was already accepted in professional circles. The entrepreneurs put the pieces together and succeeded. Contrast this with the case of the Sagamore Children's Center, a New York state inpatient psychiatric facility for children (Young, 1985). In the mid-1970s, the director of the center tried to shift the program emphasis from inpatient residential services to an outpatient diagnosis and treatment program, which included an innovative training component for parents of autistic children. The new program was inspired by state-of-the-art thinking about preventive and early intervention services.

At first, the innovation seemed to "take." With the help of a federal grant and the force of her own personality and professional stature, the director implemented her program for a 3-year period. However, the program was not accepted by state officials, who thought in terms of conventional "patient-bed" service measures and who coveted Sagamore's institutional space to accommodate growing demands for adolescent inpatient care. Morale problems of the residual inpatient staff also tarnished the image of the facility. When the federal grant ran out, the director left and her program was disassembled (Young, 1985). Her entrepreneurial work was insufficient to ensure innovation. There was a failure to institutionalize the program, an important concern for successful social entrepreneurs.

Even in failure, however, the Sagamore case demonstrates the role of entrepreneurship in innovation. Programs like the parent training begun at Sagamore were adopted elsewhere within the local children's mental health system, and served to improve the range of services available to families of autistic children.

Impetus for Entrepreneurship

Entrepreneurs are innovators, but they rarely take initiative simply for the sake of innovation. Entrepreneurs usually are spurred into action by problems, and much of their activity may be described as a process of solving a problem. In addition, part of what defines a receptive environment in which an innovation will be accepted is the widely held belief that the problem must be solved.

Problem-solving activity at the program and policy level goes in two directions. Entrepreneurs demonstrate innovations that ultimately may be adopted as program responses to public problems. Alternatively, public agencies define problems and create grant opportunities to which social entrepreneurs may respond with innovative proposals. Often the processes are intertwined. For example, entrepreneurs may lobby for the legislation that creates the opportunities for innovative program responses.

A close examination of most entrepreneurial ventures reveals problem solving at three simultaneous levels—(1) program, (2) organizational, and (3) personal. For example, in one case, a new agency was an explicit response to the problem of inadequate care for older minority children; it also solved the organization's problem of extricating itself from the burden of an overbearing internal foster care service (Young, 1985). Finally, it addressed the personal problem of a new executive director who had a special feeling of obligation to minority groups. The rare person who combines idealism with social entrepreneurship may operate alone at the program and policy level, seeking social reform without an impetus from organizational or personal problems. However, most social service entrepreneurship represents a more complex mix of motives and circumstances.

Who Are the Social Entrepreneurs?

If social service entrepreneurs are essential to the accomplishment of constructive change, is it possible to identify their distinctive traits and then encourage others with those traits to engage in social work? What do these entrepreneurs have in common that differentiates them from nonentrepreneurs?

Personal Backgrounds

Based on a review of 21 case studies (Young, 1985), there seems to be nothing either unique or similar about social entrepreneurs in terms of ordinary demographic characteristics. In social services, at least, there is a mix of male and female entrepreneurs (Young, 1980, 1985). Most seem to come from middle-class or blue-collar backgrounds. Professionally, there also is an interesting mix. As expected, many are professional social workers. However, other professions such as education, mental health, and the clergy also are common in this group. In a few cases, social service entrepreneurs are not professionally credentialed. This is worth a second look. "Mavericks" whose ideas or approaches fall outside orthodox professional practice can be the source of substantial innovation. Unfortunately, these individuals have a difficult time having their work accepted by others.

Consider the case of Adelio Montanari (Young, 1980). In the 1960s and 1970s, he developed a reputation for receiving into his proprietary child care agency in Florida children that social service agencies in the North found too difficult to deal with. His innovation was the implementation of an almost old-fashioned style of care, in which he and his staff emulated strict parents trying to teach respect for others, insisting on good behavior, and demonstrating that they cared about and would try to help those in their charge.

Montanari's agency prospered but was always under attack. Montanari was accused of profiteering and violating professional standards because he allegedly paid no attention to formal staff qualifications. Some experts thought his methods were effective. However, their acceptance was severely limited by the walls of professional legitimacy Montanari could not penetrate.

Leadership Styles

Social entrepreneurs also have considerable variation in leadership style. Sister Lorraine Reilly of the Group-Live-in-Experience in the South Bronx or Bert Beck, who among other ventures galvanized the development of the Lower East Side Union in the early 1970s, are examples of "out-front" leaders with considerable public charisma who get things done by force of their personal charm and dynamism. Others, such as Joseph Gavrin, who nurtured the development of the Child Welfare Information Service in New York in the early 1970s, have an "indirect" leadership style, getting things done in a quiet way behind the scenes (Young, 1985).

Motives

Social entrepreneurs have a wide variety of motivations. They are not, as in the stereotypical view of business entrepreneurs, driven solely by money. In the social services, other motivations such as strong beliefs in particular causes or ideas, professional prestige, power, and autonomy are usually more important than monetary rewards, though none of these other motivations appears to dominate.

Taking Risks

However, most entrepreneurs seem to share certain personality traits and abilities. One of these traits is the willingness to bear risk. By definition, entrepreneurs are unsatisfied with the status quo, yet the advocacy of innovation involves uncertainty of outcome and often engenders skepticism by colleagues and constituents. If ventures do not work out, social entrepreneurs risk derision and loss of professional esteem. In addition, they often jeopardize their own personal well-being by risking their jobs or by devoting themselves to a risky venture, rather than accepting more secure employment. For example, the founders of the Melville House in Long Island, New York, left safe employment at a state institution to establish their own residential agency for teenaged boys (Young, 1985). Virtually all social service ventures involved risk-taking, although the direct risks are not necessarily financial. Often, the risks taken are attractive because the alternative of "doing nothing" may be even more risky in the long run. Again, entrepreneurship usually occurs as a response to solving a problem, and solution may require a bold response.

Political Skills

Case studies reveal that social entrepreneurs also have in common skills in dealing with people (Young, 1985). Much entrepreneurial activity consists of "making deals." In the political arena, this activity may involve getting grants or contracts, obtaining sponsorship of key supporters, working for passage of enabling legislation, or satisfying regulatory authorities. Within organizations, entrepreneurs may get officers to authorize projects and allocate staff and resources, reach agreements with other program managers, and so forth. In the business world, entre-

131

preneurs may negotiate labor and supply contracts, service contracts, or facility purchases and rentals. While all entrepreneurs need interpersonal skills, the social entrepreneur is probably more dependent on such skills than his counterpart in business. Although both business and social entrepreneurs must be adept in dealing with people, the social entrepreneur needs to be especially well-versed in organizational and governmental politics and processes.

Dedication

Two characteristics that all entrepreneurs appear to share are exceptionally high levels of energy and a single-minded dedication to purpose. They have substantial energy and they focus it intensely on the project at hand. When they do not have these attributes, their projects tend to founder (Young, 1985). In addition, entrepreneurs tell horror stories about trying to get new programs or agencies off the ground. The financial, regulatory, political, and bureaucratic barriers often seem endless, frustrating, and sometimes insurmountable, particularly for social service ventures in or dependent on the public sector. Only the most dedicated social entrepreneurs can stay the course.

Encouraging Social Entrepreneurship

Given the crucial role that entrepreneurship plays in creating social work innovations, it is logical to ask if the process of entrepreneurship is intrinsically haphazard in its incidence and success or whether anything can be done to make this process more reliable in bringing about constructive change. Although McClelland of Harvard University has done considerable research on identifying the characteristics of potential entrepreneurs and in training them for work in the private sector in less developed countries (McClelland & Steele, 1973), the early selection and training of social entrepreneurs is probably beyond the present state of understanding.

These individuals will select their opportunities for venture activity at strategic times in their personal careers, in the organization's history, or in the field's development. They become identified as entrepreneurs only after the fact. This does not mean, however, that nothing can be done to foster social entrepreneurship. The two areas where progress may be possible are (1) education of social service professionals and (2) structuring of the organizational environment of social services.

Education

It is doubtful if entrepreneurship itself can be taught—that is, if university training alone can make someone into an entrepreneur, even if that person possesses the necessary personal traits. However, if entrepreneurship essentially is an active problem-solving process, then certain skills and areas of knowledge useful in this process can be transmitted in college curricula. Such subjects would include analytic and strategic thinking, understanding of politics and organizational processes, and principles of negotiation, marketing, and grantsmanship. A liberal education in the social sciences and humanities also would help give the would-be social service entrepreneur a general perspective with which to understand the social problems and policies that need innovation. To the extent that knowledge needed for entrepreneurship cannot be codified but may be learned by example, discussion and analysis of case studies of successful and unsuccessful social service ventures, and the development of mentoring arrangements in which successful social entrepreneurs take students under their wing in field work practicums, also may be useful.

Changing the Organizational Environment

There are two levels at which the environment of a social service organization can encourage or discourage entrepreneurial activity: (1) the managerial atmosphere within the agency and (2) the economic and regulatory setting of the agency. In an organization, the top management sets a tone which may encourage entrepreneurship or stifle it. Entrepreneurs are willing to take risks, but the level of risk taken will depend on what is tolerated by management. In the case of a Sanctuary program, for example, the chief of the Huntington, New York, Youth Bureau supported his social workers whom he knew were flirting with code infractions by boarding runaway youths in unauthorized homes (Young, 1985). Rather than stifle their initiative, he worked with these caseworkers to seek legitimation and funding for their activity (Young, 1985). The chief encouraged an entrepreneurial environment in his agency in a number of ways: by encouraging grantseeking and creative responses to grant opportunities, by providing overhead support for promising new programs, and by delegating responsibility so that potential entrepreneurs could develop their own approaches to problems and could maintain a sense of ownership for their initiatives.

Finally, a managerial regime that encourages entrepreneurial activity should evaluate its personnel and programs on the basis of results—whether the approach solves the problem, rather than whether it conforms to accepted practice modes. The same managerial attitude that judges by results also would tend to seek out the best, most creative, and dedicated people from a variety of backgrounds rather than form a staff from a single field of practice.

Certain external factors also may affect entrepreneurial initiative. If the characterization of entrepreneurship as a problem-solving activity is accepted, then it follows that entrepreneurship may be encouraged by funding and regulating social services in a manner that encourages this problem solving. For instance, rather than categorical funding of particular service designs, such as residential foster care, Meals-on-Wheels, and so forth, agencies might be funded by block grants addressed to solving the problems faced by particular client groups, such as pregnant teenagers or drug abusers, or by per capita grants for individual clients, such as the homebound elderly. In this way, the funds could support whatever solutions or service packages the providing agency found most effective in dealing with the problems at hand, even if those solutions involved approaches to counseling, health services, education, job training, income assistance, or other forms of assistance outside the boundaries of conventional prescription.

If these approaches were accepted, evaluation and regulation of services should focus on results, rather than conformity with codes of practice. Thus, a premium could be put on defining client problems and developing measurable indicators of success. Because of measurement problems and potential abuses, such methods of funding and regulation might be limited in their potential applications. Still, if entrepreneurship is to be encouraged, this seems to be the direction in which to experiment.

Risks in Encouraging Entrepreneurship

Just as entrepreneurship itself entails risk-taking, so does offering recommendations for encouraging social entrepreneurship. There is a certain paradox in suggesting changes that would reduce the barriers that entrepreneurs now face. Although more tolerant organizational environments would make the entrepreneur's work easier, such improvement might also remove some of the challenge. It is possible that making life easier for entrepreneurs could reduce, rather than stimulate, entrepreneurial behavior. Entrepreneurship may be encouraged more by adversity than by acceptance. If so, our policy prescriptions would have to be reversed.

Perhaps a more serious risk is that entrepreneurial behavior left unchecked eventually may become counterproductive. Entrepreneurs tend to be lone rangers who singlemindedly and vigorously pursue certain clear and narrow objectives. They can become so enamored of their projects that they sometimes fail to see the big picture. They may head in a direction that is wasteful or in conflict with the productive work of others. They sometimes support their ventures after they have outlived their usefulness. Other entrepreneurs, more enamored with the process than the long-term prospects of managing their ventures, leave their projects too early, before they can be stabilized under other management.

Finally, there are potential risks in creating an environment encouraging entrepreneurship. For instance, a regulatory and managerial environment tolerant of creativity, diversity of personnel backgrounds, and widely different approaches to problem-solving, may not provide enough protection against shysters and quacks. An educational program accepting a variety of approaches to social work may dilute the effectiveness of clinical practice or undermine professional morale.

Clearly, entrepreneurship is an integral element in the accomplishment of constructive change in social work. Social entrepreneurs are the catalysts for transforming a promising idea, a potential solution to an important problem, into an innovation that can eventually reach general practice. Given the myriad and increasing social service problems of today, the relative slowness with which effective solutions to these problems currently are developed, and the recentness of any recognition, entrepreneurship appears to be a scarce resource that should be developed and nurtured.

References

McClelland, D. C., & Steele, R. S. (Eds.). (1973). *Human motivation*. Morris, NJ: General Learning Press.

Young, D. R. (1980). Euphrasian Residence, North Town, Inc., and Paisano Maximum Care Unit: Montanari Clinical School. In *Human service enterprise: Case studies of entrepreneurship in child welfare*. Unpublished manuscript, Program on Non-Profit Organizations, Yale University.

Young, D. R. (1985). *Casebook of management for nonprofit organizations: Entrepreneurship and organizational change in the human services*. New York: Haworth Press.

Verification

Some ideas or innovations are verified simply by being put to use. For example, a new form is used. It requires less time to fill out, and the staff fills it out more promptly and accurately. Other innovations are more complex, and the verification process may take several years.

The final stage of the creative process, *verification*, refers to proving the validity and usefulness of an idea. According to Biondi (as cited in Gordon & Zemke, 1986), a schizophrenic generates three million ideas a day, and a great many of these ideas are novel. Yet, beyond their use for treatment, the ideas are useless.

Verification involves clarity about what is to be verified, the means that will be used to validate the innovation, the type of data to be collected, how the data will be analyzed, and standards of verification. Verification should be part of the working out of every innovation. Analytical, logical (L-mode) thinking usually dominates in verification.

Verification begins with specificity and clarity. Few ideas emerge fully formed. More often they need explanation, correction, additions, and revisions to accommodate a variety of interests and concerns.

Thomas (1984) referred to design as a systematic, disciplined activity to create a working model. Design calls for orderly analysis and solution of a series of problems, which culminate in proceduralization (p. 152). A "great idea" usually has to be transformed into a working model, or in social work, into appropriate practice guidelines. Often this step is not carried out fully, making verification difficult. Some ideas are accepted on the basis of the prestige of the innovator—thus circumventing verification.

In the following chapter, Turner makes the point that innovations seldom can be developed fully in isolation. In the verification stage, ideas must be talked over with others, and criticism needs to be invited.

The profession plays a role in fostering the systematic development of ideas. Here, Turner suggests some strategies for accomplishing this. He echoes Bloom's (1975) apt comment:

> I believe that the issue of systematic formulation of practice wisdom is one of the unrecognized critical issues of the helping professions. Vast numbers

of individual and agency innovations are effectively lost to others who might profit from this knowledge. . . . Reports of case illustrations without the accompanying conceptual analysis—abstracting beyond a particular case to derive the intervention ideas applicable to other situations—have little value beyond their human interest descriptions. Is there no way to make use of this reservoir of experience? (p. 66)

Harold H. Weissman
Editor/Senior Author

References

Bloom, M. (1975). *The paradox of helping: Introduction of the philosophy of scientific practice.* New York: John Wiley & Sons.

Gordon, J., & Zemke, R. (1986). Making them more creative. *Training, 23*(5), 30–35.

Thomas, E. (1984). *Designing interventions for the helping professions.* Beverly Hills: Sage Publications.

Operationalizing Practice Wisdom: An Administrative Challenge

Francis J. Turner

One of the enduring myths in the helping professions is that theory informs practice. However, as Berger (1985) noted,

> When one examines the theoretical works of, say, Freud, Kernberg, Kohut, Guntrip, Fairbairn, Matte Blance, Hartmann, or Rapaport with an eye to extracting specific technical recommendations, one must conclude that the great bulk of theorizing has generated comparatively few clinical principles or recommendations. This holds even in those works that specifically claim to consider the clinical implications of a particular body of theory, and further supports my premise that practice is not logically entailed in theory. (p. 25)

There has been and continues to be a need for practitioners to think creatively about the connection between theory and therapy. Most clinical or practice techniques have resulted from the trial and error experiences of social work practitioners. Once these techniques, or wisdom, have been created, there must be a systematic professional validation of them. The wisdom must be converted into knowledge. Thomas (1984) explained this conversion:

> Proceduralization is the process by which desired activities of the helping process are described, explicated, and made into procedures that helping persons and others involved in the helping process may follow. Such procedures prescribe desired intervention activities in terms of who does what, where, when, how, for whom, and under what conditions. They often take the form of practice principles, practice guidelines, and ethical codes. (p. 163)

Factors that prevent social work proceduralization include the diversity of cases; time and effort required; lack of a tradition to develop procedures; rapid change of some helping methods; lack of required analytical skills; and the sense that there is something impersonal, inflexible, constraining, and mechanical about procedures. These factors can be real impediments. However, as Thomas (1984) pointed out, the long-term effect of failure to formulate helping methods into suitable procedures is that the field has less to show for its prior effort, there have been few cumulative advances, and the development of intervention theories and helping methodology has been retarded (pp. 163–164).

Developing Practice Wisdom

Practice wisdom is the result of a process in which experienced practitioners develop a rich, diverse, and almost intuitive style of using their knowledge, experience, and skills effectively in practice. The methods they develop apparently are not precisely formulated or consciously built on theory, or a direct consequence of research. Rather, they appear to be a combination of acquired skills, established routines, intuition, experience, and an acceptance of their own competence.

The creation of practice wisdom involves the following eight discrete but interrelated abilities as part of a practitioner's mental modeling of clinical action and response:

1. the ability to involve and retain persons appropriately into the helping situation

2. the ability to understand and assess the strengths in clients and situations

3. the ability to understand and assess the limitations and problems in clients and situations

4. the ability to understand the areas where change is sought

5. the ability to understand the areas where change is possible

6. the ability to assess what combinations of interventions and resources will bring about the desired change

7. the knowledge of existing resources and the ability to make skillful use of them

8. the ability to recognize one's level of competence in individual situations

As social workers become more comfortable with their competence the process of using these abilities in working with clients almost becomes intuitive, even though to the outsider the practitioner may appear to be functioning without a diagnosis or treatment plan. Practice wisdom is not only the skillful use of knowledge without a tested knowledge base. Rather, practice wisdom is a subtle and effective use of both knowledge and theory. If this is true, then there is an ongoing development of common knowledge and competence taking place in social work, which has not been tapped effectively as a source of new knowledge and skill. Social workers have a responsibility to further develop and codify their knowledge.

Limitations on Developing Practice Wisdom

The concept of practice wisdom implies idiosyncrasy. Each person uses his or her knowledge, skill, and selves in an individualized way. However, there are similarities in how practitioners acquire their knowledge and skill.

The formal acquisition of knowledge begins with professional education and continues to be developed through professional education and experience. However, some professional experiences limit the ability to build on practice wisdom.

Sharing Practice Wisdom

In the past, social workers at times have viewed supervision as a symbol of dependency and the mark of the nonautonomous practitioner. However, supervision also can be seen as a means of building and sharing practice knowledge. This process provides an opportunity to think about situations in a different way. The perspective of knowledge, levels of certainty, gaps in knowledge, and other ways to assess one's knowledge all can be examined. This process provides a rich opportunity to take a more objective, conscious look at the knowledge on which one's practice is based. Self-evaluation also can enhance practice wisdom.

Previously, social work supervision has emphasized the minimizing of inappropriate subjectivity in practice. Because of this emphasis, the potential of self-learning to enhance the profession's practice wisdom has been underestimated greatly.

This underestimation has been reinforced further by the tradition of seeing practitioners, researchers, and administrators as separate groups. A more fruitful concept would be for the administrator to see the practitioner as a practicing scientist and the researcher as the scientific practitioner. In this way, clinicians could learn better how the periodic, structured examination of single cases or a group of cases in one's caseload not only can improve individual competence but also can be a rich resource in the development of the profession's body of practice knowledge. Similarly, administrators need to put more efforts and resources into assisting clinicians in doing formal research, including the operationalization of concepts.

The development of practice knowledge will advance not by one or two dramatic research projects, but from the gradual accumulation of knowledge derived from hundreds of research projects dealing with minute aspects of practice. Social work is a highly complex field. Thus, social work research also must be painstakingly slow and complex. A greater appreciation must be developed for the complexities of practice and the problems this creates for the systematic development and testing of knowledge.

Another variable that makes it difficult to tap practitioners' practice wisdom effectively is the rich and complex theory base of social work. In clinical practice, there currently are 25 or more theories that can be drawn on as a basis for intervention. Most social workers combine concepts from a range of interlocking theoretical approaches, which makes it difficult to isolate and correlate concepts to create a change in practice wisdom.

There are two more characteristics of social work that make research into practice even more difficult. The first is the long-standing commitment to individualizing clients and the practitioners' intervention with them. Because of this attitude, social workers tend to avoid a prescriptive type of intervention based on a closed system of differential diagnosis. They avoid an attempt to classify the client by paradigm, and then respond predictably based on this diagnosis.

Also, the social work profession has not stressed using the written word, such as articles, books, and reports, to teach practitioners. Instead, social workers have depended on the transmission of wisdom through conferences, supervision, and consultation. Case records have been used extensively as a part of practice, but not in the process of codifying practice wisdom. Fortunately, this situation has begun to change in the past few years. Now, a rich, complex, and extensive body of written literature is being developed.

Strategies for Sharing Practice Wisdom

As a profession, social work has done well in fostering autonomous clinical practice. This has resulted in a highly effective structure of imaginative interventions, use of a wide spectrum of interlocking theories, and adjustment to a scarcity of resources.

What the profession has not done well is learning to gather, examine, describe, compare, and measure this practice wisdom in a way that permits us to learn from it. As seekers of knowledge, effectiveness, and excellence, social workers have a responsibility to pursue this goal.

Researchers and administrators need to find methods to help practitioners make their interventions and their thoughts on interventions available for study and analysis. These methods cannot be intrusive, time-consuming, or inconvenient. Also, much more effort must be put into providing practitioners with useful research results.

Methods to gather data in a wide range and large number of settings also are needed. Because of the complexity of the situations and the number of significant variables in them, researchers need a timely way to gather common information from hundreds of practitioners about thousands of cases in a wide range of settings.

Once developed, this research tool should permit the identification of patterns in interventions and outcomes. Effective practitioners probably deal with similar situations in similar ways. When sufficient data is gathered, it probably will be evident that social work practice is much more patterned than practitioners have realized.

The tremendous range, power, and availability of existing and developing communications technology also must be used more fully. This technology permits quick access, analysis, and feedback from large amounts of intervention data. These data also will have an important and exciting use for the practitioner. It should be possible for social workers to easily access large banks of accumulated case data for information that can be helpful to their own practices. This has been done in other disciplines. There is no reason it cannot be done in social work.

However, to accomplish this goal, there must be increased precision in social work terminology. Because of social workers' range of theoretical concepts, reliance on oral transmission of practice knowledge, and emphasis on individual autonomy, sufficient stress has not been put on the need for precision in concepts.

As computer programs are developed to gather and store knowledge, the commonality of concepts and the weighing of phenomena must be emphasized. This increase in precision also will assist practitioners by making intervention more precise and accountable.

Finally, administrators need to encourage a different, less time-consuming, kind of professional writing. Many practitioners do not have time to expend the effort required for journal articles. Publishing brief half-page vignettes of interesting cases would give practitioners a medium for sharing successes, problems, and failures with other colleagues. In addition, existing computer networks could be used to share quickly, and over a vast area, various kinds of social work practice information. A series of these networks would provide practitioners with a way to share brief information on practice and specific practice patterns. The existing body of practice wisdom must be made available in a manner that permits social workers to learn from it and expand on it.

Role of the Profession

It is foolhardy to put this responsibility solely on the individual practitioner. Administrators need to collectively consider how best to structure the profession to promote the development of practice ideas. Too many good ideas literally die aborning because structures are not in place to nurture and develop them. Practitioners need to be rewarded for improvising.

More important, the profession must consider organized ways to verify new ideas and programs. Waiting for government or foundation grants simply will not do. Leaving this organized verification up to the personal interests and predilections of researchers and scholars also will not do.

Without discounting the methodological difficulties of evaluation, a collective agenda for verification must be created. Then, novel ways of implementing the verifications have to be developed. For example, specific topics could be selected and urged on specific doctoral programs for dissertations that their students would carry out. If there is anything to be learned from the past, it is that the profession and its collective agencies must be creative about verification of new ideas and techniques—otherwise there will be little systematic verification.

References

Berger, L. (1985). *Psychoanalytic theory and clinical relevance.* Hillsdale, NJ: Analytic Press.

Thomas, E. (1984). *Designing interventions for the helping professions.* Beverly Hills, CA: Sage Publications.

Initiating Innovative Ideas

Von Oech (1988) pointed out that there are two phases in the development of new ideas: (1) a germinal phase and (2) a practical one. "In the germinal phase, ideas are generated and manipulated; in the practical phase, they are evaluated and executed" (p. 31).

One of the more unfortunate occurrences in social work is the widespread acceptance of an innovation before it has been evaluated and verified. The results often are disillusionment when the innovation fails and a concomitant loss of faith in the capacity to find new solutions or keep on trying.

In fact, it is quite difficult to transfer ideas into innovations in established organizations. How is it that some unverified ideas are accepted, but other, better formulated ideas are not?

Bromberg's chapter, which follows, offers some clues. She suggests that novel problem formulations are not the same as novel solutions. She also suggests that the salvaging of ill-formed ideas is crucial, because these ideas often contain important germs of truth. She implies that the acceptance of unverified ideas is more the norm than the exception and that this probably will continue.

Rogers and Shoemaker (as cited in Fine, 1981) suggested why ideas, even ill-formed ones, are accepted:

> Relative advantage is the degree to which an innovation is perceived as better than the idea it supersedes. The degree of relative advantage may be measured in economic terms, but often social prestige factors, convenience and satisfaction, are also important components. . . . The greater the perceived relative advantage of innovation, the more rapid its rate of adoption. . . .
>
> Compatibility is the degree to which innovation is perceived as being consistent with the existing values, past experiences and needs of the receivers. An idea that is not compatible with the prevalent values and rules of the social system will not be adopted as readily as an innovation that is compatible. . . .

Complexity is the degree to which an innovation is perceived as difficult to understand and use. Some innovations are readily understood by most members of social systems; others are not and will be adopted more slowly. Trialability is the degree to which an innovation may be experimented with on a limited basis. More ideas that can be tried on the installment plan will generally be adopted more quickly than innovations that are not divisible. . . . Essentially an innovation that is "try-able" represents less risk to the individual who is considering it. . . . Observability is the degree to which the results of an innovation are visible by others. The easier it is for an individual to see the result of an innovation the more likely he is to adopt it. (p. 12)

Harold H. Weissman
Editor/Senior Author

References

Fine, S. (1981). *The marketing of ideas and social issues.* New York: Praeger.
Von Oech, R. (1988). *Whack on the side of the head: How to unlock your mind for innovation.* New York: Warner Books.

Deinstitutionalization: The Untoward Effects of Innovation

Eleanor Mallach Bromberg

How is it possible for deinstitutionalization, a creatively conceived revolution in mental health that is, with apparent consensual agreement supported by professionals, the community and the community's fiscal and legal guardians, to be destroyed by those who gave it life?

Seeds of Revolution: The Historical Context

During the 1950s, several factors acted to bring about a revolution in mental health—the opening of barricades to allow deinstitutionalization. Until that time, the procedures for the care of mentally ill people were relatively straightforward. Those needing treatment were placed in the custodial care of state mental hospitals, where they often spent the remainder of their lives. However, with the introduction of psychotropic drugs, the effective treatment and sympathetic management of severely psychotic patients was achieved (Klerman, 1980). Constant hospital care and supervision now was seen as obsolete for the majority of inpatients. Pharmacological psychiatry was perceived as the long-awaited cure. Its development did lead to reduced hospital stays and to the discharge of more patients (Okin, 1985).

Redefining the Therapeutic Environment

The discovery of a means to control hallucinations and delusions came at a time when overcrowding of state facilities was perceived as the

The author acknowledges Emily Bromberg, who assisted in the preparation of this chapter.

146

fundamental obstacle to the effective and humanitarian treatment of mentally ill people. Then, it was widely believed that state hospitals were stigmatizing and depersonalizing to patients and that these hospitals promoted chronic mental illness (Glick, 1979; Szasz, 1984). Exposés of the horrors of neglected and abused patients in institutions produced a society that was antiinstitutional (Klerman, 1979). The search for alternatives to institutionalization led to the migration of patients from the hospital into the community, where it was assumed that treatment would be better for the patient.

The early 1960s brought exploration of a range of alternatives to mental hospital care, culminating with the passing into law of the Community Mental Health Center Act in 1963. This act was intended to establish a range of community care settings that were appropriate to patient need, essentially redefining what was meant by a therapeutic environment. Unfortunately, the needs of deinstitutionalized patients quickly outstripped the development of treatment alternatives. Money could not follow the patient from the hospital into the community as planned. Despite reduced reliance on inpatient care, increased hospital costs continued to use more than half of all mental health funding (U.S. Department of Health and Human Services, 1980).

Changes in federal regulations permitted welfare assistance to patients described as permanently disabled. The development of Medicare and Medicaid encouraged patient care in locations where it would be reimbursable under these federal programs. Federal grant-in-aid programs, such as Old Age Assistance and Supplemental Security Income, provided financial support for transfer from hospital to community care. The new emphasis on community programs shifted the focus from the kind of patient served to the location of care. It had to be given in a place reimbursable under federal guidelines.

The federal government did not mandate that categorical grant-in-aid programs be used to depopulate mental hospitals (Lerman, 1980). State officials, whose budgets were reeling with the costs of running a two-tier Medicaid reimbursement system, discovered this discretionary option. After state claims for federal reimbursement topped $746 million in 1971, a funding cap of $2.5 billion was imposed.

Social reformers now were joined by conservative budget advisors and the federal government in supporting deinstitutionalization in state and local mental health programs. Although their theoretical rationales differed, the groups shared common goals.

Pressed by strong economic factors, conservative budget advisors joined the push for deinstitutionalization because it provided the opportunity to shift the burden of financing from the state to the federal level. State mental health administrators and legislators were eager to save money by reducing the state hospital census, shifting funds into the community, and closing state hospitals (Macht & Scherl, 1979). These normally divergent groups provided support and rationales for each other's goals. Releasing patients to the community would bring savings for state budgets and would satisfy the new treatment philosophy at the same time.

The social policies of deinstitutionalization also were supported by the legal system. Lawyers and state legislators argued that institutions deprived patients of their health and civil rights, and that patients were entitled to the least restrictive care possible. Deinstitutionalization was supported regardless of the fact that its implementation was complex and controversial, that the practical problems of designing and finding acceptance for treatment alternatives had not been solved, and that there was no clear consensus about who should be held responsible for ensuring access to care. Those arguments still could be made today.

Implementation: Revolution Meets Reality

The confusion over implementing deinstitutionalization began at the federal level. Fragmentation in service delivery was passed on at local and state levels. There was a lack of understanding of the complexity of the issues at the federal level. Federal officials offered grand rhetoric about the deinstitutionalization process, but left its implementation to state administrators to deal with in the best way they could.

For example, in the state of New York, chronically ill patients were moved into unprepared communities because of a policy that reflected fiscal concerns, interest group pressures, and vague ideals that only some leaders were willing to call deinstitutionalization. There was little trouble in emptying state hospital beds, and officials gave little forethought to the range of community alternatives that courts, legislatures, and federal agencies thought they were prescribing. The failure of deinstitutionalization resulted from the lack of a coordinated, comprehensive, and integrated plan for patient release, and of an effective service delivery system in the community. Selective use of psychiatric hospital care depends on the availability of other treatment alternatives. Community mental health facilities were not even conceived of in 1955, when the hospital release rates accelerated. In its extreme, deinstitutionalization has resulted in what has been labeled as the "dumping" of patients from state hospitals into dilapidated quarters in neighborhoods that are unprepared and reluctant to accept them.

Obviously, a misunderstanding existed about the role local communities would play. Deinstitutionalization was based on the assumption that communities were willing to assume responsibility for the care of the mentally ill in their own neighborhoods.

The public's response to deinstitutionalization was, and continues to be, a substantial barrier to the integration of mentally ill people into the community. Public opposition was widespread and intense. Many people were frightened of danger—they were concerned that former patients would be abandoned to inadequate community care systems, and worried that property values would decline (Barron, 1963). Zoning ordinances forced patient services into ghettos. Employers resisted hiring those people with mental hospital records. Local politicians began to reflect the fears of their constituency. Public opposition deterred the development of local services and the implementation of community mental health plans.

Where pressure for deinstitutionalization stemmed from concern over fiscal rather than treatment issues, community services were not planned or developed soon enough or fast enough. There were few provisions to give patients the broad range of services provided for them under one roof in the mental hospital (Feldman & Stadler, 1979). Patients now had to seek out medical and psychiatric care, social services, food, shelter, income, appropriate employment, and vocational rehabilitation. Inadequate planning for patient release, referral, and follow-up added to the problem.

Deinstitutionalization was superimposed on an established pattern of service delivery in which social service agencies and federal and local welfare benefit programs did not meet the needs of discharged mentally ill people. A perspective was developed around two levels of care, (1) inpatient versus (2) outpatient, that pitted the needs of community care facilities against the needs of the hospitals. There was an accompanying shift in fiscal and administrative authority as patients moved out of state hospitals and into the community. This has resulted in serious deficiencies in service integration in both the mental health system and the general human services system (New York State Mental Health Committee, 1982).

Backlash: The Revolution Falters

The deinstitutionalization process produced mental health systems that offered fragmented and inadequate services, with different levels of government responsible for the same kind of planning, funding, implementation, and monitoring. All were contracting for and providing their own services, and nobody was in charge.

It is the linkage among the component agencies of a mental health system, rather than the agencies themselves, that determines the community's ability to meet the needs of severely disturbed patients. The lack of agency interconnections prevents the reallocation of resources and debilitates community care. One psychiatrist stated, "Sometimes it seems as if the mental health care system has become so complex that one needs a college degree just to be a patient" (Feldman & Stadler, 1979, p. 335).

The absence of community services cannot be blamed solely on poor interagency implementation, or on lack of public acceptance. Community mental health systems were not granted the funding increases needed to provide a range of clinical and social supports (Kirschner & Pepper, 1981). For example, in New York intensive day treatment programs designed to maintain patients in the community were approved, but state funding for start-up of these programs was inadequate. The expectation that fewer hospital patients would result in a surplus of hospital funds and staff that could then be directed to patient care in the community did not materialize. Hospitals, especially those serving urban residents, continued to be filled with psychiatric emergencies. Hospital costs were kept high by increasing personnel costs and by the requirement of higher standards of care by national accrediting agencies.

For the most part, deinstitutionalization over the past 30 years has occurred through shorter hospital stays after admission, and through the diversion of many potential admissions to other programs (Kirschner & Pepper, 1981). The pressure for brief hospitalization should not be underestimated. With this pressure come cutbacks on inpatient psychotherapeutic care and an over-dependency on the use of patient medication. The result of this ineffective treatment was a readmission record that demolished any theory of the benefits of deinstitutionalization. The readmission rate is 50 percent within 1 year of discharge and 75 percent within 5 years (Lamb, 1981).

The situation is exacerbated by overrestrictive admission criteria. In a "Catch-22" process, deinstitutionalization produces clinicians who are encouraged to refuse admissions to many applicants. In most state hospitals, screening procedures tend to lead to a refusal of individuals who request services, and admission of those who resist them. The more amenable patient often is refused admission. Those rejected generally are people who require shelter, are difficult to treat, have problems with the law, or do not fit the age criteria (Shapiro, 1983). This attempt at reducing inappropriate admissions, while forcing brief hospitalization, appears to increase incidence of chronic illness in patients (Greenhill, 1979).

The result is the emergence of a population of young adult chronic patients who have been in and out of hospitals but have spent relatively little time there. Many of these patients represent a group of individuals who would have been permanently hospitalized 30 years ago. From the onset of their illness, they have been treated during the era of deinstitutionalization. This could be seen as an achievement if the readmission rate were not so astounding and the level of community care so fragmented.

The deinstitutionalization backlash occurred in the mid-1970s, when the effects of the flawed movement were pronounced (Kirschner & Pepper, 1981). Large numbers of mentally ill people appeared on city streets. There were huge ghettos of discharged patients in low-cost housing, proprietary homes, and deteriorating neighborhoods. Horrendous nursing home conditions existed, partially due to transfers of hospital-discharged mentally ill people. General hospital emergency rooms and psychiatric units were treating chronically ill persons, which produced "the revolving door" syndrome (Adams & Goldman, 1983). Politicians and clinicians alike began to refer to deinstitutionalization as disastrous.

The notion that chronic mental illness would vanish with the dissolution of institutions permitted policymakers to neglect the development of the necessary network of services. One disturbing effect of this has been the appearance of homeless mentally ill people. Shelters report that large numbers of their residents have prior state hospitalization (Ball, 1984). In 1984, there were an estimated 3 million homeless people in the United States. Anywhere from 25 to 50 percent of these people would have been residents of state mental hospitals in years past (Lamb, 1983).

Several documented generalizations can be made. The 1970s and 1980s saw the transformation of much of the homeless population from middle-aged alcoholics and skid row bums to former mental patients and never-treated mentally ill persons. The ranks of never-treated mentally ill people continue to swell as a result of harsh realities. There is a decrease in access to jobs, housing, education, and medical care for large numbers of people whose incomes are below the poverty level. The number of homeless people continues to grow, their average age is dropping, and their propensity for chronic physical and mental illness appears to be increasing (Kirschner & Pepper, 1981).

Out of frustration and fear, overwhelmed social systems designed to find solutions turn upon each other. Families of the mentally ill blame mental health and social service professionals, who point to restraints imposed by mental health and social service agencies. They, in turn, point to the paucity of federal funding and the intolerance of the public for local mental health programs. The public's intolerance for obviously psychotic "street people" leads to pressure on the criminal justice system to inappropriately arrest and jail these people.

Examining the Process of Innovation

To understand the deinstitutionalization process as an innovation, it is necessary first to separate the creative intention from its unintended, unplanned result. Four elements are involved in the birth of a program innovation. These include (1) the attack and rejection of traditional formulations, which produces discontinuity; (2) shifts in values, which result in new constellations of possibilities; (3) conflict between contrasting expectations; and (4) the recombination of elements in ways which are recognized as new and different. In addition, when the perception that there is a need for change is distributed throughout the community, the chances increase that innovation will result (Lasswell, 1959).

Deinstitutionalization easily fits these criteria for innovation. There was social pressure to redefine the shape and places of therapeutic intervention. Traditional treatment approaches were perceived as insufficiently responsive to the growing numbers of persons identified as having mental disorders, and to the accompanying growth of psychiatric hospital populations. The old beliefs of what constituted correct treatment were partially rejected. Hospitals were described as causing chronic mental illness in their patients, and it was said that they "drove people crazy" (Szasz, 1961). Psychotropic drugs introduced the illusion of a magical cure for mental illness. The legal system provided protection for the new innovation through defense of the right to care and residence in the least restrictive setting. Conservative fiscal reformers supported the new effort, believing it would result in cost trimming. There appeared to be a shared public ideology of shared responsibility for its most fragile members, who deserved an end to social isolation. There also seemed to be a consensus that mental hospitals were an affront to human dignity.

The underlying assumptions were that community care was the best care and could offer readily the range of interventions found inside the hospital, and that all patients and all communities were ready to assume this responsibility. With hindsight, it becomes easier to recognize what now appears to be a set of flawed assumptions which have helped to contribute to the present angry disappointment and cries of broken promises.

Proponents of deinstitutionalization did not agree on its definition. It has been alternately referred to as a value system, a theory, and a method or process of intervention.

It is known now that psychotropic drugs do not cure most chronic mental illness. They only ameliorate the symptoms, making life outside the hospital possible for longer periods of time when other social supports are available.

Although the public generally approved of the concept of treatment in the least restrictive residence, acceptance of mentally ill people and mental health programs did not keep pace with the need. Part of the difficulty was misinformation about the magical ameliorative effects of drugs, and the ability of all patients to comply with their own medication needs. Buoyed by the social protest movement and its philosophy of empowerment, civil rights activists affirmed patients' rights. The results of court action emptied hospitals into communities not prepared yet for the reality of patient need or for the range of local treatment programs needed to sustain them.

State government officials found that high-quality care still is expensive when rendered in the community. In addition, hospital operating costs rose dramatically so that it became impossible for the "money to follow the patient" from the hospital to the local community as was expected originally. The rise in the cost of care has caused the desertion of the fiscal conservatives who originally supported local mental health programs.

The enthusiasm and fervor that deinstitutionalization began with was based on the assumption of stable economic conditions, sufficient funding, housing, community acceptance, the belief that all patients could cooperate in their own treatment, and that disparate constituencies with incongruent values could remain united by congruent goals. As these assumptions sagged, the theory that the least restrictive environment was best began to topple.

The Future: Future Tense

Experience with deinstitutionalization in the past 2 decades raises a number of issues about innovation in social services. These fields do not lack for new or novel ideas. However, problems seem to occur when these bright ideas need translation into viable programs. Less creativity is used to put these good intentions into action. Perhaps the strength of the beliefs blots out the realities. The creation of a new social program requires the cooperation of a cast of thousands.

Social innovations cannot be copyrighted. Each of the groups supporting deinstitutionalization used the idea to support its own agenda. From one point of view, patient migration into the community was a creative way to cut costs. Without consideration for other concerns, cost cutting became destructive to clients and communities. The process of social innovation cannot easily be controlled in a democracy.

The history of mental health care reveals recurrent cycles during which institutions are found to be inhumane by muckrakers, there is impetus to change conditions, patients migrate into the community, their needs are largely unmet, and there is pressure to reinstitutionalize. However, people are not doomed necessarily to repeat the patterns of the past. Each historical cycle may be one part of a longer trajectory of novel recombinations. Although creativity involves "disposition to make and recognize valuable innovations" (Lasswell, 1959, p. 203), the social environments of each cycle contain different sets of facilitating and inhibiting factors that affect the validation of new solutions. The inhibiting factors surrounding the experience of deinstitutionalization already have been explored. Some time must be spent now on the facilitating elements.

The question raised by philosophers is, How should one classify a phenomenon that seems creative in one dimension and not in another? Lasswell (1959) suggested that "judgment can be focused by appraising a pattern according to its intrinsic elements" (p. 206). Those elements are the values and philosophy of the necessity to use the least restrictive environment possible for the patient. These values continue to be sound and accepted by the community and its legislature. The laws that forced open the door of institutions have been upheld repeatedly in the courts. It would seem that this enactment of society's good intentions finally has moved people beyond the "solution" of the past—to reinstitutionalize. People are left with what always follows a creative solution—the need to fill in the outlines. Although many attempts to do this have been flawed, the outlines remain.

It must be recognized that drugs now promise only amelioration, not the cure, of mental illness. The commonly accepted rate of chronicity appears to remain constant—approximately one-third of formerly mentally ill people have an enduring illness. As in any chronic illness, symptoms continue to emerge throughout life. For many people, supports must be provided throughout their lives.

The ardor with which all community care is condemned obscures many of the successes of that particular process. There are thousands more for whom community care *is* appropriate and who thrive in communities in which well-matched supports are available. Wholesale condemnation also obscures the work of some talented practitioners who, out of the need to deliver ongoing care to mentally ill people, create novel solutions daily.

Social workers must not confuse deinstitutionalization as a creative event with good or bad programs designed to meet a need. It is one thing to dream about a revolution and another to translate that dream into fiscally sound reality. Social workers must not confuse ambiguity, uncertainty, or even mistakes with total failure. Every creative encounter is a novel event. It is the environment tolerant of disorder that provides the basis for innovation.

References

Adams, N., & Goldman, H. (1983). Deinstitutionalization: The data demythologized. *Hospital and Community Psychiatry, 34*(2), 129–134.

Ball, J. (1984). A survey of the problems and needs of homeless consumers of acute psychiatric services. *Hospital and Community Psychiatry, 35*(9), 917–921.

Barron, F. (1963). The disposition toward originality. In C. W. Taylor & F. Barron (Eds.), *Scientific creativity: Its recognition and development* (pp. 139–152). New York: John Wiley & Sons.

Feldman, P., & Stadler, T. (1979). Phasing down state hospitals: Integrated versus non-integrated services. *Hospital and Community Psychiatry, 30*(5), 334–337.

Glick, I. (1979). Hospitals in the 1980's. *Hospital and Community Psychiatry, 30*(2), 125–129.

Greenhill, M. (1979). Psychiatric units in general hospitals. *Hospital and Community Psychiatry, 30*(3), 169–180.

Kirschner, M., & Pepper, B. (1981). The young adult chronic patient: An overview of a population. *Hospital and Community Psychiatry, 32*(7), 463–469.

Klerman, G. (1980). National trends in hospitalization. *Hospital and Community Psychiatry, 30*(2), 110–113.

Lamb, H. R. (1981). What did we really expect from deinstitutionalization? *Hospital and Community Psychiatry, 32*(2), 105–109.

Lamb, H. R. (1983). *Effective aftercare for the 1980s*. San Francisco: Jossey–Bass.

Lasswell, H. D. (1959). The social setting of creativity. In H. A. Anderson (Ed.), *Creativity and its cultivation* (pp. 203–221). East Lansing, MI: Michigan State University.

Lerman, P. (1980). *Deinstitutionalization: A cross problem analysis*. Washington, DC: U.S. Government Printing Office.

Macht, L., & Scherl, D. (1979). Deinstitutionalization: In the absence of consensus. *Hospital and Community Psychiatry, 30*(9), 599–605.

New York State Mental Health Committee. (1982). *Committee report to the New York State Commissioner of Mental Health*. Unpublished report.

Okin, R. (1985). Expand the community care system: Deinstitutionalization can work. *Hospital and Community Psychiatry, 36*(1), 742–745.

Shapiro, J. (1983). Patients refused admissions to psychiatric hospitals. *Hospital and Community Psychiatry, 34*(8), 733–735.

Szasz, T. (1984). *The myth of mental illness*. New York: Dell.

U.S. Department of Health and Human Services. (1980). *Toward a national plan for the chronically mentally ill: Report to the Secretary*. Washington, DC: U.S. Government Printing Office.

Implementing Innovations

Bromberg's discussion of deinstitutionalization suggests that there is seldom a single illumination but rather a series of needed illuminations with social ideas. The chapter brings to mind the story of Edison's experience of trying out 80 or so different filaments before he got the one he needed to make the first light bulb. It is so much easier to try out 80 different pieces of metal in a laboratory than to implement 80 different methods of deinstitutionalization. Verification of social ideas is exceedingly complex.

Bromberg's history of deinstitutionalization sharply illustrates Kingdon's (1984) point about social innovations—that brokers are more important than inventors. Social change involves the constant recombination of already familiar elements.

Bromberg's chapter suggests that program innovation cannot be designed as easily as an architect designs a building. Program innovation is much more emergent than planned. Thus, program innovators should plan for flexibility and adaptability, rather than set details in concrete.

To be open to innovation, organizations must be created to be capable of learning from mistakes and of acting on what is learned. As Pfeffer and Salancik (1977) asked, "How can structures be designed that incorporate a recognition of managerial fallibility and provide for the expression of alternative . . . ideas and that at the same time provide enough order to facilitate action?"

Pfeffer and Salancik (1977) suggested that innovation is not so much related to individual creativity (such as that possessed by the social entrepreneur) but that it is related to an organization's capacity to bridge the contradiction between learning what to do and the need to do. Their organizational suggestions relate to wider dissemination of information, procedures to facilitate the interaction of staff around problem solution, and the development of an incentive system that rewards managerial environmental scanning and problem finding (pp. 28–29).

Many social welfare ideas are similar to deinstitutionalization because of their lack of specification and development. This underdevelopment occurs

157

partially because the hardest job for a would-be innovator is to create legitimacy for a new idea.

The most common way to create legitimacy is to blur differences, leaving ideas vague so that potential opposition is blunted. In the short run this may be tactically correct. However, in the long run this can be disastrous— witness the history of deinstitutionalization. Well-planned strategies are needed to implement new ideas. A coalition of interests is needed, one that is powerful enough to allow concepts to develop. Developing such a coalition can be a creative act in itself.

For example, in studies of medical innovation certain influential doctors served as gatekeepers in persuading other doctors to adopt a new drug (Fine, 1981). There is a large body of empirical evidence in fields ranging from agriculture to aviation, which suggest that cultural adoption, a group process, always lags behind technical invention and innovation (Fine, 1981).

Organizational Resistance to Change

More needs to be learned about when and why professional gatekeepers, such as agency administrators, open and close their programmatic gates. As Taylor (1970) pointed out,

> A new social form is not introduced so easily. An innovative kind of school, a new way of dealing with poverty, a new procedure for resocializing delinquents . . . all are likely to disrupt complex and valued roles, identities, and skills. The disruption may have widespread and ramifying effects, so that whole [service systems] may be challenged and angered. (p. 70)

Inherently, change is unsettling to established relationships on a variety of levels, as are new ideas. This probably is the reason that most organizations tend to resist new ideas. Adams (1979) found that "the usual response is to scrub such ideas. There are many ways to do this. One is to overanalyze them, another is to laugh at them, still another is to ignore them" (p. 67).

According to Pettigrew (1985), change tends to be seen as either a single event or as a set of episodes, separate from the near- and long-term antecedents that gave events impetus, form, meaning, and substance.

Much of the literature on change and innovation implies a rational and linear process of change. Pettigrew suggested that these are deterministic stages or phases. "Each of these . . . is pregnant with its own worldview, model of human beings, and explanatory language. How are we to choose among growth and development, continuity and flow, life cycle and phase (thesis, antithesis, synthesis), contradiction, intrusion and crisis" (pp. 234–235).

He added,

> The practice question is thereby posed less in terms of how the change project or proposal, through whatever form of political agility or "authentic" process, can be implemented, and more in terms of how existing processes (inside and outside of an organization) can be speeded up, how the conditions that determine people's interpretations of situations can be altered, and how contexts can be mobilized to achieve practical effects, in order to move the organization, perhaps additively, in a different direction. (p. 244)

Weick (1979) made the point that a great deal of cognitive literature can be viewed as variations on the theme that organizational members simplify and vulgarize the data to which they are exposed. He stated that organizations "manage inconsistent information by collapsing or stretching time, by wishful thinking, by inferring the impossibility of implied action, or any one of numerous other techniques which have been documented repeatedly" (p. 68). He suggested that not much attention has been paid to the issue of how to reverse these tendencies of organizations (and their employees).

The Innovator As Organizational Actor

Young's chapter stressed the need for an innovator to possess social and political skills. The innovator must be an organizational actor. He or she has to know how to implement an idea for change in a complex, rather than simplified, organizational context.

Most of the social work literature views the problem of organizational change in narrow political terms—gaining control over resources is the crucial contest. As Gummer notes in the following chapter, the likelihood of any real changes taking place without the active support, or at least the neutrality of key organizational actors, is remote. However, the political perspective, with its emphasis on power and control, offers only a partial and short-term view of what an innovator must consider.

Adams (1979) described *contextual blocks* to innovation that develop from exposure to an implicit set of beliefs, and *environmental blocks* imposed by the immediate social and physical environment. Three examples of cultural blocks are the thoughts that "the more things change the more they remain the same," "it doesn't pay to risk," and "all problems can be solved by logic and experimentation." Three examples of environmental blocks are lack of cooperation and trust among colleagues, working for people who value only their own ideas, and a constant crisis atmosphere with no time for reflection (p. 53).

Adams (1979) made the point that organizations tend to routinize, decrease uncertainty, increase predictability, and centralize functions and controls. This tendency, he found, is at odds with innovation.

Groups and organizations reflect the conceptual blocks of their individual members: they have limited perceptions, are constrained by their cultures, respond emotionally to problems, are affected by their environments, and are limited in the intellectual strategies they employ. . . . Still groups can provide a rich store of information, perceptions, technical expertise, motivation and emotional and cultural resources to the creative individual. But it is essential that managers and participants in such groups be aware of and control those characteristics of the group or organization that can inhibit conceptualization. (Adams, 1979, p. 144)

This suggestion also applies to getting an innovation initiated and implemented. The innovator should begin with the assumption that the innovation will be difficult for others to understand, comply with, cooperate with, and follow through on. An innovator has to be a skilled implementer, able to get something accomplished—the new form is utilized, the program is started, the agency is restructured, and so forth. To implement, one has to be able to guide an innovation through the technological, institutional, political, staff, organizational, and environmental problems the innovation will confront and create.

Both social and technical skills are needed. An innovation needs a manager—someone who is specific about not only what is to be done, but also who is to do it, how it is to be done, what organizational changes are expected, and what the measurable objectives will be.[1] The manager must also be specific about the social processes involved in implementation: who has potential and actual power; the subphases and time required to get something done; how, when, and where to bargain; how to maintain a coalition if one is needed; how to handle initial failures; and so forth (Gergen, 1968).

The successful innovator knows the difference between a specific and a nonspecific innovation. Often, a potential innovation cannot be operationalized until that innovation is tried out. The innovator must learn from experience and encourage learning and self-design. Bromberg's history of deinstitutionalization illustrates the danger of not accepting this perspective.

Why Innovations Fail

In a sense, implementation involves a specification phase and an action, or "start-up," phase. The literature on implementation generally gives three reasons for failures in implementation: (1) poor planning, (2) insufficient power, and (3) strength of culturally ingrained standard operating procedures (Allison, 1971).

---

[1]The history of deinstitutionalization, as well as other social programs, suggests that often competence in implementation, let alone creativity, is in short supply.

In dealing with the last two reasons, logical thinking often must be joined with creative thinking. The ability to see the connections between the new and the old, to move toward the new, is the mark of the creative politician. Implementation skills are no less creative than those initially required for generating novel ideas.

Williams (1976) pointed out an innovator's need for logical (L-mode) and perceptual (R-mode) types of thinking. He found that "generally speaking, the big need . . . has not been for overpowering techniques but rather for reasonableness, sensitivity, and the ability to order and synthesize diverse pieces of information that often are fragmentary and conflicting" (p. 280). Successful innovators are bureaucratic virtuosos. They are great improvisers as they make connections between the new and the old.

In the next chapter, Gummer's points could be summarized by Pettigrew's (1985) findings:

> People who understand the political and cultural system of their organizations and the impact of changing economic and social trends on the emergence and dissolution of old issues, values and priorities and the rise of new ones, are at least beyond the starting gate in formulating, packaging and influencing the direction of organizational change (and innovation). (p. 243)

Harold H. Weissman
Editor/Senior Author

References

Adams, J. (1979). *Conceptual blockbusting.* New York: W. W. Norton.

Allison, G. (1971). *Essence of decision.* Boston: Little, Brown.

Fine, S. (1981). *The marketing of ideas and social issues.* New York: Praeger.

Gergen, K. (1968). Assessing the leverage points in the process of policy formation. In R. Bauer & K. Gergen (Eds.), *The study of policy formation* (pp. 181–203). New York: Free Press.

Kingdon, J. (1984). *Agendas, alternatives and public policy.* Boston: Little, Brown.

Pettigrew, A. M. (1985). Contextualist research: A natural way to link theory and practice. In E. Lawler, A. Mohrman, S. Mohrman, G. Ledford, & T. Cummings (Eds.), *Doing research that is useful for theory and practice* (pp. 221–248). San Francisco: Jossey–Bass.

Pfeffer, J., & Salarcik, G. (1977). Organizational design: The case for a coalition model of organizations. *Organizational Dynamics, Vol. 6*, pp. 15–29.

Taylor, J. (1970). Introducing social innovation. *Journal of Applied Behavioral Science, 6*, 69–77.

Weick, K. (1979). Cognitive processes in organizations. In B. Staw (Ed.), *Research in organizational behavior* (pp. 41–74). Greenwich, CT: JAI Press.

Williams, W. (1976). Implementation analysis and assessment. In W. Williams & R. Elmore (Eds.), *Social program implementation* (pp. 267–292). New York: Academic Press.

Overcoming Barriers to Innovation in Social Service Organizations

Burton Gummer

There is nothing more difficult to take in hand, more perilous to conduct, or more uncertain in its success, than to take the lead in the introduction of a new order of things.

—Niccolò Machiavelli

Innovation normally is associated with progressive times and political and social climates conducive to thinking about new ways of doing things. Indeed, the late 1960s and early 1970s were periods of considerable experimentation with new social services and ways of providing them. However, following this innovative period, social and political concerns shifted to issues of "uncontrollable" social spending, mismanagement of social agencies, and ways to curtail or reduce the growth of the "welfare state." Ironically, after 6 years of the most conservative national administration in modern history, interest in innovation now is on the rise again. This time, however, the interest is sparked by declining resources for social programs, rather than by the search for creative ways to spend the "social surplus" of the 1960s.

Although interest in innovation reappeared only recently in social services, the business community has been studying and experimenting with ways to promote innovations for the past several years. Prompted by the changing role of the U.S. economy in a global marketplace, and by the extraordinarily rapid pace of change in a number of business and manufacturing technologies, business analysts are producing a growing body of literature on the organizational and personal characteristics of the innovating firm and the innovating manager. These findings can be transferred successfully for use by social service organizations.

Ideological and Managerial Perspectives

Although social service organizations have much in common with other organizations, there are certain features unique to them. In general, there are two ways in which organizations develop. In the first, technological innovations, such as the silicon chip, foster the development of bureaucratic structures to coordinate technical work efficiently. In the second, social processes emerge, such as the appearance of large numbers of "runaway" adolescents and the accompanying changes in attitudes toward them, that define certain rules and programs, and the organizations that incorporate these programs and conform to these rules, as rational and legitimate.

As products of their communities, social agencies are tightly linked to community values, attitudes, and beliefs. Social agencies thus are highly ideological entities—besides doing things, they stand for things. Because most American communities are demographically diverse, they usually contain a number of different ideological positions on the problems that social agencies deal with. Consequently, many agencies are arenas where competing values and beliefs clash (Brager & Holloway, 1978; Sarri & Hasenfeld, 1978). When there is an agreement about service goals and procedures, it is usually an uneasy one—the result of one group's ability to gain dominance over others, at least for the present.

From this perspective, innovation takes on an important symbolic meaning. The goals and procedures of an agency are, among other things, the operational expression of the social and professional philosophies of dominant community and organizational groups (Miller & Phillip, 1983). Thus, proposals for changing goals or procedures through innovative practices can be seen as challenges to the established vision of the agency mission, and may be strongly resisted.

Many analysts of change and innovation in social agencies have highlighted this ideological dimension. In particular, there have been a number of studies on how employees might promote innovations that differ from, or contradict, established policies and procedures (Brager, 1967; Brager & Holloway, 1978; Miller & Phillip, 1983; Patti, 1974;Patti & Reznick, 1972). These studies assume a conflict of interest between top-level administrators and operating staff. This conflict often is taken to reflect an underlying conflict between ideological positions held by community elites and reflected in agency administrators, and those held by agency operating staff who see themselves as representing client interests (Martin, 1980).

These adversarial approaches to organizational innovation reflect, in part, the political and social climate of their times. The late 1960s and early 1970s were a time for challenging established institutions, and the "soft underbelly" of the precarious consensus that characterized many social agencies was a prime target. Innovation became a politicized concept, and the innovating social worker—as "change agent"—was an actor in a political drama aimed at liberating policies and programs from conservative or reactionary forces (Ad Hoc Committee on Advocacy, 1969; Miller & Phillip, 1983; Shattuck & Martin, 1969; Specht, 1969).

Ideology plays a more important role in social agencies than in most other nonprofit organizations, and a considerably greater role than in business organizations. However, it does not account for all of the variations in the characteristics of these organizations. In addition to being embodiments of community mores, social agencies also are formally structured organizations. As such, they are expected to be well managed, accountable to their sponsors, and successful in accomplishing their goals. Moreover, these two dimensions of social agencies—the ideological and the managerial—respond to different societal forces. Reich (1984) suggested that Americans

> tend to divide the dimensions of our national life into two broad realms. The first is the realm of government and politics. The second is the realm of business and economics. Our concerns about social justice are restricted to the first realm; our concerns about prosperity, to the second. (p. 4)

Depending on which realm, or "culture," is ascendant, different dimensions of the social agency will be highlighted. During the 1960s and early 1970s, when the government or civic culture predominated, the social agency was viewed largely in ideological terms. Since the mid-1970s, however, the business culture has moved to the forefront, and the social agency is seen increasingly in managerial terms.

From a managerial perspective, innovation is seen as an important technique for improving organizational performance by enhancing the ability to compete for resources. In business, product innovation is a major strategy for capturing new markets and securing existing ones. Accordingly, businesses invest considerable amounts of money in research and development. Analysts of governmental and non-profit organizations, however, point to the independence of these organizations from consumer markets, and to the test of profitability as a major difference between them and business organizations (Downs, 1967; Drucker, 1973). In social service organizations, there also is a lack of proprietary interest on the part of management. These three points often are given as the reasons why governmental and non-profit organizations are presumed to be less innovative than business organizations. However, the validity of that presumption is open to question. After reviewing the literature on incentives to innovate in public and private sector organizations, Roessner (1977) concluded that

> the answer to the question of whether there is anything intrinsic to public sector organizations that relegates them to lives less innovative than their private sector counterparts appears to be, theoretically, yes; empirically, maybe and maybe not. (p. 360)

Perhaps, then, like the hummingbird who, aerodynamically speaking, cannot fly, the social agency may be capable of innovation even though, theoretically speaking, it is not.

Theory aside, the pressures on social agencies to develop innovative responses to social problems exist, and come from a number of sources. Primary among these is competition for fewer public dollars. Although the bark of the Reagan administration may have been worse than its bite, there has been a significant reduction (estimated at around 10 percent) in federal outlays for social welfare programs (Bawden & Palmer, 1984). Moreover, the cuts have not been across the board, and the impact has been greatest on services for poor people. Like it or not, social agencies are having to compete with each other, as well as with other public service sectors for declining public funds.

A second factor promoting innovation is the growing interest in "privatization" of social and other public services. Many of the arguments in favor of transferring services from public to private auspices, especially proprietary auspices, originate with criticisms of the inefficiency and rigidity of governmental and nonprofit service bureaucracies (Starr, 1985). Whether or not these criticisms are valid is of minor importance, because they resonate with the prevailing conservative antigovernment and antiwelfare attitudes. As more and more businesspeople see human services as a market to be captured, governmental and nonprofit organizations will have to develop innovative programs to survive in what promises to be an increasingly competitive arena.

A third factor, environmental changes, traditionally has been the source of most organizational innovations. In addition to the political and economic dimensions, the social agency's environment consists of demographic and sociocultural elements. The American population continues to get older as life expectancy goes up, and more infirm as chronically ill and disabled people live longer. As the divorce rate continues to rise, the number of single-parent households also rises. These changes have produced problems such as "elder abuse," "aging out," "blended families," "latch-key children," and "urban nomads," all of which require innovative responses. Mores and values are changing apace with demographic changes. Since the 1960s, Americans have continued to rethink their traditional ideas about sex, family relations, addictive substances, the work ethic, discrimination, and almost every other important aspect of life. These forces exert continuous pressure on social agencies to rethink existing services that no longer may be needed, and to identify and develop services that are or soon will be needed.

Strategies for Organizational Innovation

Organizational innovation has been defined as the generation, development, and implementation of new processes, products, or services for the first time within an organization (Thompson, 1965). Unlike invention, which refers only to the generation of new ideas, organizational innovation entails the subsequent steps of translating ideas into organizationally usable forms and incorporating them into ongoing organizational practices. These phases of the innovation process require different skills and organizational structures to support them. The generation or "idea" phase, which often is taken mistakenly to stand for the whole innovation process, invokes visions of the lone genius and shouts of "Eureka!" The development phase, or the translation of ideas into usable products or processes, connotes the pragmatics and detail-mindedness of the engineer. Finally, the implementation stage, in which the developed idea becomes part of the routine behaviors of organizational members, conjures up a dual vision of the promoter who can sell an idea and the broker who negotiates and accommodates competing interests. These stages offer a framework for surveying some of the suggestions that have been made for improving an organization's innovating capabilities.

Generation

The creation of new ideas is an idiosyncratic and poorly understood process. Much depends on chance—the right person being in the right place at the right time. Allowing for this, there is some agreement that the generation of new ideas is more probable in organizations with complex tasks to perform and diverse staffs, than in those with simple tasks and homogeneous staffs. Wilson (1966), for instance, argued that

> in a complex task structure each member's task will to some extent be tailored by him to suit his own methods and style. . . . The greater the variety and complexity of rewards, the greater the incentive to conceive of ways in which

one's tasks can be altered to maximize the attainment of some particular mix of rewards that the member values. (pp. 200–201)

Much of the writing on personal characteristics desirable for an innovative thinker has its roots in the notion of the "marginal man." For example, Galbraith (1982) suggested that innovators generally have an irreverence for the status quo. "They often come from outcast groups or are newcomers to the company; they are less satisfied with the way things are and have less to lose if there's a change" (p. 21). Although innovative people may be marginal to the organization, they cannot be alienated from it, because the motivation to search for novel solutions to organizational problems usually is associated with an individual's perception of the organization as an avenue for professional growth.

Innovative thinkers also need detailed knowledge of the organization and its work. In particular, the innovator needs to know about those aspects of an organization that, in addition to being sources of problems, also present opportunities for developing novel responses. Drucker (1985) identified four such areas: (1) unexpected occurrences, (2) incongruities, (3) process needs, and (4) industry and market changes.

The typical managerial response to unexpected occurrences is "It shouldn't have happened here." From a management control perspective, this is understandable, because predictability and reliability are essential to efficient operations. If too rigidly adhered to, however, this attitude will suppress the recognition of new opportunities. For example, during the late 1950s family agency administrators were concerned about the decline in the average number of interviews per case. From the perspective of the long-term treatment approaches then prevalent, this constituted a problem. However, for practitioners and researchers experimenting with brief treatment methods, this provided additional motivation to test the relative merits of brief versus long-term treatment.

Incongruities refer to discrepancies between expectations and outcomes. During the 1960s, for example, Mobilization for Youth experimented with having teenagers provide services to younger children. The teenagers providing the services benefited more than the kids receiving them. Although ostensibly a service failure, this discrepancy contributed to the thinking of people interested in self-help groups and served as important data for what eventually became known as the "helper-therapy" principle.

Process needs are problems that grow out of an organization's operating procedures. In the social services, for example, the plight of foster children "in limbo" was a significant factor in the development of computerized information systems for tracking the "careers" of foster children.

The social service equivalent of *industry and market changes* involves the emergence of new social problems and/or alternative ways of dealing with existing problems. Drucker's (1985) observations on how industries respond to these changes has many instructive points for social administrators:

> When market or industry structures change, traditional industry leaders again and again neglect the fastest growing market segments. New opportunities rarely fit the way the industry has always approached the market, defined it, or organized to serve it. Innovators therefore have a good chance of being left alone for a long time. (p. 70)

What many social workers see as encroachments on their professional domains by the newer "human service" occupations or people totally outside the social service, also can be viewed as the ability of nontraditional service providers to take over existing service sectors that social workers are unwilling to remain in (public assistance), or to capture emerging areas that social workers are reluctant to enter (long-term personal care) (Austin, 1984; Mandell, 1983).

Stages of Innovation

Generation

In addition to having a staff capable of generating new ideas, the innovating organization must tailor administrative practices to innovation. Creativity usually is associated with an atmosphere free from external pressure. According to Thompson (1965), "a person is not likely to be creative if too much hangs on a successful outcome of his search activities, for he will have a strong tendency to accept the first satisfactory solution whether or not it seems novel or the best possible" (p. 12).

Frequently, creative people will be motivated and rewarded by the work itself and the opportunity to pursue their ideas autonomously. If necessary, additional motivation can be obtained by promotion and recognition for innovating performance. Since many innovative people are likely to be professional peers, recognition will be an important reward. This includes the opportunity to present innovative ideas at professional meetings and in publications. To provide these opportunities, the organization will have to alter its notions of secrecy and ownership of ideas developed within it.

Development

The development of new ideas into operational forms usually is a trial-and-error process with many false starts and setbacks. To support this, an organization must provide resources in the form of uncommitted money, time, skills, and good will. As Quinn (1985) noted,

Introducing a new product or process to the world is like raising a healthy child—it needs a mother (champion) who loves it, a father (authority figure with resources) to support it, and pediatricians (specialists) to get it through difficult times. (p. 79)

Managing innovations also requires a different attitude toward resources than does routine management. In routine management, the manager views resources as something to be *controlled*, while to the innovator, resources, including other peoples' resources, are something to be *used*. Therefore, the manager of an innovation project should adopt an entrepreneurial approach to resources, acquiring even their temporary use to promote the innovation project.

Implementation

The implementation of even routine policy or programmatic changes is highly problematic in organizations like social agencies, where operating personnel have considerable discretion and can shield themselves from administrative oversight (Smith, 1965). The difficulty is compounded when the innovation to be implemented has been introduced and developed by people other than those responsible for carrying it out. In his research on policy innovations in nearly 100 social service, hospital, and government organizations, Nutt (1986) identified four implementation strategies: (1) implementation by intervention, (2) participation, (3) edict, and (4) persuasion. Each reflects a different style of leadership and can be applied successfully in particular situations. None provides a panacea for the problems of implementation.

Squaring the Circle: Implications for Practice

Getting an organization to develop and adopt new goals or ways of doing its work is a difficult—some would say impossible—task. Most organizations—and all social agencies—are the scenes of continuous discussions (and intermittently bitter debates) about what the organization has accomplished, what it is accomplishing, and what it should strive to accomplish in the future. Disagreements over the nature of an organization's past, present, and future mean that at any given time organizational leaders will be told by some factions that

> survival requires prompt changes of policy and by other factions to keep the course of the organization steady as it goes. . . . [S]ome will propose daring forays into untried fields, others will demand equally drastic shifts backward toward older practices, and some will counsel only incremental departures. . . . Each will insist that the existence of the organization will be placed in jeopardy by the policies urged by the others. (Kaufman, 1985, p. 48)

If left unchecked, these competing perspectives can produce organizational "stalemate" in which the only thing that all members can agree to do is nothing (Hirschhorn, 1978). Moreover, it may be—as some analysts argue—that there really is nothing that can be done to correct a stalemated situation. Organizational survival, they argue, ultimately depends on luck, since organizations are buffeted by random environmental forces and attempts to rationally deal with this amount to little more than magical rituals (Gimpl & Dakin, 1984; Kaufman, 1985). Others, however, are more hopeful about the prospects for purposeful action to correct undesirable situations. Their research on organizational innovation suggests a number of precepts that managers and staff well might heed.

The first of these is top management's commitment to innovation. In their research on innovation successes and failures, Delbecq and Mills (1985) found that organizational leaders played a key role in very innovative organizations. They created special funds to support innovative work, and established special committees to review and evaluate innovative proposals. In this way, the innovation proposal immediately became part of an organization's overall strategic planning process, rather than the pet project of one person or unit:

> The review body does not pay for the self-serving projects of "prima donnas." By assigning one of its members to work with the advocate and his or her project group . . . the committee guarantees that the study is an *organization* project—as opposed to Engineer Smith's or Dr. Jones' project. (Delbecq & Mills, p. 28)

Besides making specific resources available for innovative work, top managers play an equally important, although less tangible, role in creating an atmosphere or culture supportive of innovative work (Quinn, 1985). Innovative leaders project a vision of the organization's future development and point out general areas in which innovative work should be done. The innovative manager's task is to create a developmental framework within which different employees can identify how their own efforts and creative ideas can facilitate the organization's movement.

Delbecq and Mills (1985) also found that, paradoxically, organizations with little innovation simultaneously were guilty of narrow parochialism and illusions of grandeur. Frequently, advocates of innovations, in consultation with one or two colleagues, determine the "demand" for the new idea by speculating among themselves and adding only selective data that support their notions. There then is a rush to "implement directly, immediately, and on a large scale" with the commitment of a great amount of resources "to assure success" (p. 32). On the other hand, in innovative organizations, proposals are scrutinized by specially created feasibility study groups that substitute "search behavior" for creative speculation. Keys to the search for information are "closeness to the average potential user" and knowledge about previous design successes and failures obtained from a broad sample of creative thinkers both within and outside the organization (pp. 30–31). The review is followed by a formal decision. Because consensus is rare, some formal voting mechanism is used to identify the review committee's judgment:

No single reviewer, as a minority critic, can veto any project. . . . Advocates . . . expect to incorporate modifications and do not demand that the "purity" of the original proposal be maintained. Mutual adjustment rather than hard bargaining among study group members is the norm. . . . The advocate does not carry the entire burden of possible failure on his or her shoulders. . . . The project was, after all, a shared organizational judgment. (p. 32)

The decision to go ahead with the project is followed with a small, controlled pilot study conducted by people who have already adopted the innovative idea. The enthusiasm of early adopters (who often are advocates) allows them to be

patient with glitches and to contribute to as well as support the necessary product modifications and organizational adaptation needed for new innovations. . . . [P]ilot studies help maintain the attitude that the initial implementation is clearly experimental and the results will require further modifications before direct, large-scale implementation can occur. (p. 33)

Social service organizations are simultaneously rational instruments for accomplishing goals and political arenas for resolving or accommodating conflicts of interests. These two dimensions form the context within which innovators cast themselves in adversarial roles against top administrators. This often is a rational response to the political realities of organizations in which multiple constituencies vie for control of key agency processes and policies. Although this makes political sense, it no longer makes managerial sense, as researchers identify the structures and practices associated with successful organizational innovations. One conclusion to be drawn from the research on organizational innovation is that it is a total organizational effort. All segments of the organization have to be involved—management, operating staff, clients, and technical specialists and consultants. The disagreements in the literature center on when and how different organizational constituents should be involved, not whether. The likelihood of any real changes taking place without the active support, or at least the neutrality, of key organizational actors, is remote.

All organizations face the challenge of change—the challenge of adapting their practices in the face of a rapidly changing environment. The obstacles confronting social agencies are many and difficult. In many ways they reflect the turbulence and confusion which characterize contemporary American life. Unfortunately, they also mirror the disagreements within the social welfare community. What is at stake is not the actual survival of social agencies—innovative or not, they will limp along. However, if social workers are to resume an influential role in shaping decisions and practices regarding the welfare of Americans, they must develop the will, the expertise, and the creativity needed for these times.

References

Ad Hoc Committee on Advocacy. (1969). The social worker as advocate: Champion of social victims. *Social Work, 14*, 16–22.

Austin, D. M. (1984). Observations on the search for an institutional base for social work. *Social Work, 29*, 485–487.

Bawden, D., & Palmer, J. (1984). Social policy: Challenging the welfare state. In J. Palmer & I. V. Sawhill (Eds.), *The Reagan record* (pp. 177–215). Washington, DC: The Urban Institute Press.

Brager, G. (1967). Institutional change: Perimeters of the possible. *Social Work, 12*, 59–69.

Brager, G., & Holloway, S. (1978). *Changing human service organizations: Politics and practice*. New York: Free Press.

Delbecq, A. L., & Mills, P. K. (1985). Managerial practices that enhance innovation. *Organizational Dynamics, 14*(1), 24–34.

Downs, A. (1967). *Inside bureaucracy*. Boston: Little, Brown.

Drucker, P. (1973). On managing the public service institution. *The Public Interest, No. 33*, 43–60.

Drucker, P. (1985). Entrepreneurial strategies. *California Management Review,* *27,* 9–25.

Galbraith, J. R. (1982). Designing the innovating organization. *Organizational Dynamics, 10*(3), 5–25.

Gimpl, M. L., & Dakin, S. R. (1984). Management and magic. *California Management Review, 27*(1), 125–136.

Hirschhorn, L. (1978). The stalemated agency: A theoretical perspective and a practical proposal. *Administration in Social Work, 2*(4), 425–438.

Kaufman, H. (1985). *Time, chance, and organizations: Natural selection in a perilous environment.* Chatham, NJ: Chatham House.

Mandell, B. R. (1983). Blurring definitions of social services: Human services versus social work. *Catalyst, 4*(3), 5–21.

Martin, P. Y. (1980). Multiple constituencies, dominant societal values, and the human service administrator: Implications for service delivery. *Administration in Social Work, 4*(2), 15–27.

Miller, H., & Phillip, C. (1983). The alternative service agency. In A. Rosenblatt & D. Waldfogel (Eds.), *Handbook of clinical social work* (pp. 779–791). San Francisco: Jossey-Bass.

Nutt, P. C. (1986). Tactics of implementation. *Academy of Management Journal, 29*(2), 230–261.

Patti, R. J. (1974). Organizational resistance and change: The view from below. *Social Service Review, 48*(3), 367–383.

Patti, R. J., & Resnick, H. (1972). Changing the agency from within. *Social Work, 17*(4), 48–57.

Quinn, J. B. (1985). Managing innovation: Controlled chaos. *Harvard Business Review, 63*(3), 73–84.

Reich, R. B. (1984). *The next American frontier.* New York: Penguin Books.

Roessner, J. D. (1977). Incentives to innovate in public and private organizations. *Administration & Society, 9*(3), 341—365.

Sarri, R. C., & Hasenfeld, Y. (1978). The management of human services— A challenging opportunity. In R. C. Sarri & Y. Hasenfeld (Eds.), *The management of human services* (pp. 1–18). New York: Columbia University Press.

Shattuck, G. M., & Martin, J. M. (1969). New professional work roles and their integration into a social agency structure. *Social Work, 14,* 13–20.

Smith, D. E. (1965). Front-line organization of the state mental hospital. *Administrative Science Quarterly, 10,* 381–399.

Specht, H. (1969). Disruptive tactics. *Social Work, 14,* 5–15.

Starr, P. (1985). The meaning of privatization. *Project on the Federal Social Role* (Working Paper No. 6). Washington, DC: National Conference on Social Welfare.

Thompson, V. A. (1965). Bureaucracy and innovation. *Administrative Science Quarterly, 10*(1), 1–20.

Wilson, J. Q. (1966). Innovation in organization: Notes toward a theory. In J. D. Thompson & V. H. Vroom (Eds.), *Organizational design and research* (Vol. I, pp. 193–218). Pittsburgh, PA: University of Pittsburgh Press.

Institutionalizing Innovations

Just as an innovator may not be the inventor or the originator of an innovation, so the person who gets the organization committed to trying out the innovation may not be the person who successfully implements or institutionalizes it. As Gummer noted, different skills are needed for different phases of innovation.

The final phase, institutionalization, is as crucial as the earlier phases. Once a new program is tested successfully it should be made part of the service array of a social work agency. There is nothing more wasteful than a useful and vital program that dies once the innovator leaves the agency.

The following memorandum illustrates this waste, both personal and organizational:

> I was supervising an MSW [master of social work] student who was designing a teen pregnancy program as part of her school assignment. She was mildly invested in the program's survival. Her driving force was to complete the course requirement. As her field work supervisor, though, I was as concerned about program survival as about her education. Some of the program design guidelines that I offered to this student included:
>
> 1) Work within the existing structure. One of my priorities was "a good fit."
>
> 2) Get approval from all superiors before beginning work. Without approval the design process would have been a waste of time and energy.
>
> 3) Ask for suggestions from anyone who could sabotage any aspect of the program. Spend the time to contact and meet with all collateral personnel.
>
> 4) Get information from existing teen pregnancy programs on their operation and structure. This would guide the design to address noted gaps and necessities.
>
> 5) Oversee the entire range of function (including clerical, administrative, and social work) during the initiation period, in order to be immediately aware of any problems which might arise.
>
> 6) Document all work for administrative purposes. If the program design was well documented it might have a greater chance of survival.

174

7) Have the energy and initiative to follow through and solve problems as they arise.

8) Above all, get the program started. A program which has begun has a greater chance of continuing.

I think these were pretty good guidelines, yet during the [following] academic year . . . all of the programs which I helped design, initiate, or implement stopped running in any recognizable form. This has led me to the sobering insight that although a strong theoretical background can offer the designer a deeper "resource well" to draw from, program survival depends upon more than a solid design.

Since my return to [the agency], I have been asked to design a program for mastectomy patients. My social work impulse urges me to design a program and include enough disciplines in the hope that someone might be motivated to continue the struggle for survival. My educated intuition informs me that under the best of circumstances the program will not survive six months after I leave in September. A metaphorical stillbirth, leading to a paper on postpartum depression in program design.[1]

Designing a program is not the same thing as institutionalizing it. The writer of the memo understandably focused on problems of implementation, overlooking the problems of institutionalization. The teenage pregnancy program never became an innovation. Institutionalizing a program requires that its funding be stabilized so as not to be viewed as a drain on organizational resources and that its procedures be integrated into the existing organizational routines. Also, any changes the new program has created in the existing organizational power and status systems must have been accommodated. In the following chapter, Finnegan amplifies these issues.

Finnegan also suggests that competence in administration, like clinical competence, rests on the ability to possess a repertoire of schemas or patterns of action and response that can be reworked and recombined as events unfold. His chapter draws attention to the connection between money and innovation, and implies that a creative administrator must have well-defined and subtle cognitive maps of various financial machinations.

Harold H. Weissman
Editor/Senior Author

---

[1] W. Kugelman, personal communication, July 1987, of a case vignette used in teaching administration.

Personal Social Services: Impact of Innovative Financing on Innovative Social Services

Daniel J. Finnegan

The funding source of a program can be as important to the program's success as any other variable. Because of this, there is a critical need for creativity and innovation in financing social services. Over the past 30 years, expenditures for major social welfare programs have risen tremendously. Financing mechanisms have been used both to encourage and to control the expansion of personal social services. Social workers must understand how these mechanisms work and how they can dramatically affect their practices.

Financing Mechanisms

Historically, four methods have been used to finance personal social services. These services are as follows: (1) project grants-in-aid, (2) block grants, (3) fee-for-service schemes, and (4) prospective payment systems (PPSs).

Project Grants-in-Aid

Specificity is a key feature of a *project grant*. A fixed amount of money is awarded for specific expenditures made during a specific period. Expenditures for personnel, equipment, travel, contractual services, and so forth are limited to the amount authorized by the provisions of the grant. In addition, project grants typically are authorized for specific activities, such as training, research, or services. However, these grants seldom directly relate the amount of the award to measures of productivity. Generally, a service provider must demonstrate only that the monies awarded are spent in accordance with the approved budget plan.

The amount of funding does not depend on the provision of a specific quantity of services.

Block Grants

Block grant funds can be used to support ongoing operations as well as new approaches to service delivery. The recipient of the block grant is given considerable flexibility to respond to local needs and conditions.

Two features of block grants are noteworthy. First, the recipient of a block grant usually is a unit of state government, not the community agency providing services. Consequently, the agency must apply to the appropriate unit of state government for funding, not to the federal government. Second, the state government receiving the block grant generally determines how the funds provided are spent. Unlike project grants, decisions about how much can be used for personnel or travel expenses or for equipment purchases are made by the state government. Within broad limits, state officials also decide how much of the block grant funds should be used to support services for one target population or another. For example, in allocating an Alcohol, Drug Abuse, and Mental Health Block grant, state officials decide on the amount used to support drug abuse detoxification programs or day treatment programs for chronically mentally ill people.

Fee-for-Service Schemes

Reimbursement for allowable costs is a third financing mechanism used by federal and state government, and also by private insurers. Under this approach, a service provider is reimbursed for all (or some predetermined percentage) of the costs incurred in providing services to an eligible client. The amount of reimbursement depends upon the amount of costs incurred. The more costs incurred, the greater the level of reimbursement. Medicaid and Title IVB (foster care for children) are examples of programs financed by this mechanism.

The reimbursement approach to funding is not used widely today. The open-ended nature of the contract leaves the financial commitment of the funding agency indeterminate. Opportunities to provide services to more clients, or to provide more services per client, leave the funder too little control over the total amount to be reimbursed. However, the reimbursement approach has had a lasting impact. It introduced the notion of paying a service provider for a specific service transaction for a specific client. Reimbursement was the precursor of the fee-for-service systems, which are emerging as the current dominant financing mechanisms.

A *fee-for-service* approach provides a fixed payment for the provision of an identifiable service to an eligible client. The fee is determined before the service is provided. Providers project both the amount and cost of their services. These estimates provide a basis for negotiating payment rates. Once an appropriate rate is established, payment is made as services are rendered.

PPSs

PPSs currently are being used to pay for physical health care services. Experts are debating their suitability for reimbursement of mental health care and treatment (Goldman, Pincus, Taube, & Regier, 1984; McGuire & Scheffler, 1986), and their applicability to other forms of social services probably also will be investigated.

The prospective payment method is an extension of the fee-for-service approach. Instead of basing payment on individual units of service, however, payment is based on episodes of care given or on number of eligible clients served. For example, Medicare's reliance on diagnostic related groups is a PPS based on episodes of care. Providers are paid a fixed mount, based on the clients' diagnosis. The specific amount of services used by the client does not affect the amount of payment.

Lessons from the Past

Each of the financing mechanisms has had a significant impact on social services agencies. Changes have occurred in financial management practice, in service organization and delivery, and in the populations targeted for services.

A fictional account follows to illustrate the extent and nature of these changes. This example considers the operations of a fictitious nonprofit community mental health agency in 1960, 1975, and 1985. Although imaginary, the experiences of this agency are representative of the experiences of many community agencies during the past 30 years.

Rapid Expansion

The Marion County Mental Health Clinic was incorporated in 1959 as a nonprofit community agency in a medium-sized Midwestern city (population 175,000). Initially, the clinic operated on a small budget of $25,000 per year. The clinic provided outpatient counseling services to adults experiencing mild to moderate mental health problems. Individuals with more serious mental health problems were treated in the nearby state mental institution.

The clinic relied on private philanthropy and donations for most of its funding. An endowment of $75,000 could be expected to generate an additional investment income of $3,000 to $5,000 annually. A small, but significant, amount of other revenue came from patient fees.

At the clinic, financial record keeping consisted of a cash receipts and disbursements journal, a checking account, and a clients' billing journal. The amounts of all cash received were entered in the cash receipts and disbursements journal upon receipt. A short note identifying the source of the money accompanied each journal entry. Similarly, all cash expenditures were entered in the journal, along with a short note identifying the reason for the expenditure. All cash receipts would be regularly deposited into the agency's checking account. All disbursements would be made in the form of checks drawn on that account. Finally, a journal recording the amounts billed and received from each client was maintained.

The clinic faced few demands for accountability. Each month the clinic director, a psychiatrist, included a brief summary of the clinic finances in his oral report to the board of directors. The board's treasurer provided a more formal summary of the bank balances based on his review of the clinic's financial records. Signatures of two clinic board members, the president and the treasurer, were required on all checks. The treasurer monitored the clinic investments that were secured with the $75,000 endowment. Any changes in the way the funds were invested needed the full approval of the board of directors.

Over the next 15 years the clinic greatly expanded its operations. In January 1968, the National Institute of Mental Health (NIMH) awarded the clinic a $600,000 capital construction grant. As a condition of the grant award, the clinic agreed to expand its services to include the following five "essential" services: (1) inpatient services; (2) emergency services; (3) outpatient services; (4) partial hospitalization services (such as day treatment); and (5) consultation and education services.

A second project grant from NIMH was received by the clinic in 1970 to help support the costs of staffing these essential services. Additional project grants continued for the next several years. The monies provided by the grants were based on matching monies the clinic generated from other sources.

Between 1970 and 1975 the clinic participated in several other NIMH project grant programs. By 1975, the clinic was designated as a comprehensive community mental health center and required to provide 12 services. In addition to the five essential services, the agency offered services for children and elderly, screening services, follow-up care for people released from state and county mental hospitals, transitional residential services, alcoholism and alcohol abuse services, and drug abuse services. The state department of mental health, Marion County Board, and the United Way also funded the expansion of services.

Meeting New Accounting Needs

New expansion required several changes in the financial management practices of the agency. First, the sheer volume of monies being handled necessitated a more systematic accounting of receipts and expenditures. Typically, the center received funds authorized by as many as five different grants. At the same time, applications for continued funding and for new services were under review. Also, the center constantly was planning new grant submissions. An integrated financial accounting system had become essential to adequately plan and acquire the necessary resources to carry out the expansion of services.

In 1965, the mental health center implemented a fund accounting system, which enabled the staff to trace receipts and expenditures for each funding source. The accounting system also permitted the tracking of total receipts and expenditures for management planning and control.

Each funding agency had different service priorities, forcing a second change in the financial management practices of the mental health center. An accounting system able to distinguish among the various service activities of the center was needed. In 1970, the fund accounting system was changed so that the different types of services to which a particular receipt or disbursement was related could be identified.

In 1974, the center shifted to an accrual-based accounting system. Rather than measure center performance on the basis of cash transfers (disbursements and receipts), the center measured performance by matching the revenues earned with the associated expanses incurred. When a service was provided, the Center recognized the associated revenue generated as earned.

Importantly, the shift to an accrual basis meant that the value of in-kind benefits were included in the center accounts. The value of these benefits could often be used as matching funds, permitting the centers to demonstrate that it generated support from other sources when applying for a state or federal grant.

For example, the accrual accounting system placed a monetary value on the hundreds of hours of donated time by the volunteers manning the mental health crisis line. The value of this donated time was used as matching support when state funding was sought for the salary of the coordinator of the crisis services.

The funding arrangements of the center became increasingly complex. Each of the funding organizations preferred a unique array of services. At the same time, the center's administrators and the board of directors had their own priorities. The center's director had to be able to reconcile these multiple sets of priorities.

During this period of rapid expansion, meeting the concerns of the funding agencies was complex, but not particularly difficult. A more or less tacit agreement developed between the center and the various funding organizations. The state department of mental health put the bulk of its funding into services for the chronically mentally ill and alcoholic people. The county board funded outpatient services, crisis emergency services, children's services, and consultation and education services. NIMH provided monies for expansion.

Competition Becomes Fierce

The availability of funds for the mental health center changed considerably between 1975 and 1985. Securing funding from traditional sources became much more difficult. New sources, particularly private insurance and employee assistance programs (EAPs), became more attractive.

NIMH funding for program expansion evaporated. The numerous NIMH project grant programs were merged with several others into the Alcohol, Drug Abuse and Mental Health block grant. As a recipient of the block grant, the state department of mental health distributed the monies to community agencies. The community mental health center had to compete with the rapidly rising number of other community mental health, alcoholism, and drug treatment agencies located throughout the state. At the same time, the state's institutional programs were placing significant demands on its state's limited resources. Consequently, the competition for scarce state resources became fierce.

Several other Marion County community agencies also actively sought state and local funds for their mental health services. Philanthropic sources could not be relied on for general support as readily as in the past.

181

United Way had begun to tie its funding to priority services. Several private foundations began to redefine their mission to produce a strategic impact on specific social problems.

Although competition for funds from traditional sources was intensifying, two new sources emerged: (1) private insurance and (2) employee assistance programs. A growing public acceptance of the existence and need for treating mental health problems emerged. Unions pushed for extension of insurance benefits to include new mental health coverage. Although the general escalation of health care costs limited the amount of coverage that could be secured, some minimal provisions were obtained.

EAPs also began to be used to fund a variety of social services, particularly treatment services for alcohol and drug abuse. Employees often could seek counseling services on their own. More frequently, however, employees whose job performance appeared to be suffering because of personal problems were required by their employer to seek assistance.

Responding to Competition

The increasing competition for funds did not produce significant changes in the financial record keeping practices of the community mental health center. However, some important changes in financial management practices did occur. First, the center became much more aware of how the costs of its services compared with those of other agencies. In previous negotiations with the state mental health department, the current year's expenses, plus reasonable increases for inflation and service expansion, had provided the basis for future funding. However, because many community agencies throughout the state now were providing similar services, the state department of mental health started comparing the costs of the center's services with those of other service providers.

Second, the center began to depend on each of the service programs to be self-supporting. The expenses of a program (including a share of indirect costs) were not expected to exceed revenues. If revenues did not cover expenses, program directors were expected to reduce expenses.

Third, the center became much more aggressive in seeking payment from clients, private insurers, and EAPs. Sliding fee schedules were used to ease the financial burden for poorer clients. Clients were billed for missed appointments for which they had not given advance notice of cancellation. Clients missing more than five scheduled appointments without advance warning were dropped and replaced.

Along with changes in financial management practices, some changes in the organization and delivery of its services were instituted. Most important, significant differentiation between professional tasks occurred. Each client was assigned to a case manager, whose primary task was the design and implementation of a case treatment plan. The case manager seldom became involved in the actual provision of service. Rather, other professionals in the center were relied upon for specific types of services. Consequently, the practitioners in the center became more specialized. Short-term treatment modalities were used more frequently. Activities that did not relate directly to specific client needs involved in treatment decreased.

Visions of the Future

The fictional story of the mental health center provides a review of recent trends and clarifies the important impact that financing mechanisms have had on the development of personal social services. Future changes in financing mechanisms can be expected to produce similar impacts.

A greater reliance on the purchase of service agreements can be expected to increase the number of different services that are funded. However, the kinds of activities performed within a service category will become much more standardized. As a result, professional autonomy is apt to decrease.

A greater use of capitation methods also is likely to occur in the next 20 or 30 years. Under *capitation*, agencies would be paid a specified amount per client, regardless of the type or amount of services the client is provided. Capitation methods are apt to emerge because of an inherent weakness in the purchase of service mechanism. Contracting on a fee-for-service basis permits funding agencies to control the content of individual service transactions with a client. It does not give these agencies adequate control over the total use of services by clients. In particular, there is no incentive for the service provider to ration services among clients. On the contrary, the provider has an incentive to oversupply the willing client with services.

The capitation method has some distinct advantages over fee-for-service mechanisms. First, the capitation method does give the funding agency greater control over total payments on behalf of a client. Second, there is an incentive for the service provider to substitute less costly services for higher cost services. Third, there is an incentive for the service provider to deliver only the most appropriate services to the client.

A capitation method of financing provides a funding agency with predictability. The service provider is offered an incentive to provide services at minimum cost. The attractiveness of these two features is apt to outweigh any concerns about the responsiveness of the service system to the individual client.

The social work profession must be prepared for the increasing use of capitation methods of financing. Steps must be taken to empower clients who are in need of services. The competence and independence of the case management role must be strengthened if case managers are to act effectively on behalf of clients and their individual needs.

What is seen as good financing may be bad for effectiveness and adequacy of client services. Likewise, good service may be seen as wasteful and unaccountable from a financial point of view.

A great deal of administrative and financial talent is needed to handle these real strains in a creative manner. Without this talent, there will be continuing shifts in concern from client need to client reimbursability; frantic efforts to move the burden of funding from one level of government to another; sharp rises in costs and concomitant attempts to cut funds and reduce services; and, ultimately, a fiscal environment that consistently thwarts the capacity of creative practitioners to develop service innovations.

References

Goldman, H., Pincus, H., Taube, C., & Regier, D. (1984). Prospective payment for psychiatric hospitalization: Issues and questions. *Hospital and Community Psychiatry, 351*(5), 460–464.

McGuire, T., & Scheffler, R. (1986). Research issues in reimbursement of mental health services: Conference overview. *The Journal of Human Resources, 21*(3), 289–292.

An Innovative Work Climate

Although some innovations do not require funding, other good ideas go nowhere without it. Thus, it becomes increasingly difficult to innovate without a thorough knowledge of financing. Herzlinger (1977) suggested that many executives of nonprofit organizations have not realized the vital importance of financial sophistication, that

> rarely does one hear that executives in non-profit organizations are good with numbers. More frequently the accolades are [that they are] creative, innovative, or caring. Indeed some managers of non-profits view their lack of quantitative skills as a rather endearing imperfection—like having freckles. (p. 84)

In addition to this need for financial sophistication, innovators also must realize the need for a work environment that supports innovation. Innovation occurs in an environment that either can support innovation or constrain it. Innovators must be aware of the effect their work environments have on innovation. Research shows that agencies that support innovation employ managers who allow subordinates to learn from their mistakes by not dwelling on them, who stretch policy to accommodate new ideas, who are good listeners and able to respond to staff in useful ways, and who are tolerant of "half-baked" ideas, realizing that this is a stage most ideas have to go through (Campbell, 1978).

Van Gundy (1984) suggested that the quality of interpersonal relationships in work groups also affects the quantity of creative responses considerably. He suggested that, among other qualitative concerns, interpersonal trust, acceptance of deviant behaviors, open confrontation of conflicts, and respect for others' feelings are vital to creativity.

To be successful, an innovator must create a context in which ideas can survive and prosper. At the minimum, an innovator has to have a supportive group within an organization (Pettigrew, 1985). Once this group exists, it must find a way to create organizational legitimacy for change.

Innovations, whether they are programs, procedures, or new problem definitions, must be accepted by others. Nothing can be more stifling than to have one's innovative ideas rejected, ignored, or taken as evidence of one's disloyalty or personality deficits. Nystrom and Starbuck (1984) suggested that organizations may develop a kind of innovative inertia, that

> they encase their learning in programs and standard operating procedures that members execute routinely. These programs and procedures generate inertia, and the inertia increases when organizations socialize new members and reward conformity to prescribed roles. As their successes accumulate, organizations emphasize efficiency, grow complacent, and learn too little. To survive, organizations must also unlearn. (p. 53)

Crises often force organizations to confront their usual ways of operation. Often when top managers are fired, the result is a change in perspective as their replacements bring in fresh approaches. Those interested in promoting innovation have a number of options to avoid such drastic changes and crises. First, dissent can be encouraged. Information and interpretations of information can bring to light differing assumptions and expose potential dangers. Legitimizing dissent encourages unlearning. Second, change is always occurring in organizations. If these changes are interpreted as learning opportunities, there are real opportunities to unlearn and promote innovation. A strike is an opportunity to unlearn standard operating procedures and learn how to cut operating costs. A central facility breakdown is an opportunity to unlearn a system of control and learn another, such as decentralization (Nystrom & Starbuck, 1984).

March and Olsen (1979) suggested that the design of organizations can legitimize change and promote innovation by ensuring both playfulness and reason as aspects of organizational functioning. Echoing the poet Emerson's belief that "a foolish consistency is the hobgoblin of little minds," they found that

> this is partly a matter of making the individuals within an organization more playful by encouraging the attitudes and skills of inconsistency. It is also a matter of making organizational structure and organizational procedure more playful. Organizations can be playful even when the participants in them are not. The managerial devices for maintaining consistency can be varied. We encourage organizational play by permitting (and insisting on) some temporary relief from control, coordination, and communication. (p. 81)[1]

---

[1]March and Olsen (1979) saw change in organizations with ambiguous goals and unclear technologies as crucially affected by situational events—for example, who is involved, what other problems exist at the time, what preferred solutions "are looking for problems," and what actual choices about what must be made at particular times.

Value of Skepticism

Yet, inconsistency, in and of itself, is not an organizational virtue. An organization also must value skepticism. As March and Olsen (1979) pointed out, what is needed is a "theory that does not assume that experience (automatically) produces wisdom and improves behavior" (p. 134). Experience can be the best as well as the worst teacher.

Usually, there is no shortage of skepticism, which often works against innovation. Because of earlier organizational experiences with innovations that did not work, it can be difficult to get a "hearing," to get encouragement to keep working on an idea, or to get preliminary funding for exploratory pretests or trials. As ideas are developed and implemented, prior experiences also may make management leery of providing the needed sanction, resources, and support when unanticipated problems emerge. There also may be problems when an innovation conflicts with other projects or with competing ideas, when it causes power struggles, or any of a host of other difficulties which can emerge when a system has to accommodate an innovation.

Unlearning is much more difficult than learning from experience for individuals. This is even more true for organizations. To create a more innovative and skeptical organizational environment, a sense of timing and playfulness are important. For example, to air the unmentionable, an organizational analog to the role of court jester may be needed.

Organizations face many pressures to innovate: new social problems emerge in public consciousness, funding patterns change, competition from other groups or sectors develops, and so forth. However, there are equally strong pressures to maintain the status quo. "Factors such as reinforcement, overload and socialization undoubtedly focus members' attention on a relatively small number of relations present in the relational algorithm, and these biases in turn seal off many possibilities of new interpretations of organizational events" (Weick, 1979, p. 63).

One successful organization followed March and Olsen's (1979) prescription for combining reason and playfulness in combatting dampers on innovation. Nystrom and Starbuck (1984) found that

> Company G actually appointed a vice-president for revolutions, who stepped in approximately every four years and shook up operations by transferring managers and reorganizing responsibilities. When asked how he decided what changes to make, he answered that it made little difference so long as the changes were large enough to introduce new perceptions. Statistics show that productivity rose for about two years after each shakeup, then declined for the next two years, until another shakeup initiated another productivity increase. (p. 61)

There is considerable disagreement in the literature on how best to structure and design organizations to promote innovation. Much of the current critique focuses on the theoretical and practical inadequacies of highly rational and linear theories of innovation and planned change.

Given this uncertainty, it is unwise to expect that when one thinks of an innovation, the organization will accept it with open arms. A better approach is to have a long-range perspective toward creating a seriously playful organizational environment conducive to innovating. Weick (1977) suggested that "we should invent some organizational equivalents of an off-off-Broadway experimental theater . . ." (p. 43). Weick recommended that organizations sponsor experimental designs by encouraging "galumphing."

> Galumphing is the "patterned voluntary elaboration or complication of process, where the pattern is not under the dominant control of goals." Stephen Miller argues that play or galumphing preserves adaptability because it provides a way to develop novel designs. . . . What play basically does is "unhook behavior from the demands of real goals." The person gains experience in combining pieces of behavior that he would never have thought of combining given the practical problems that confront him. . . . People discover capabilities [in themselves] they had overlooked before. (p. 43–44)

Examples of galumphing are not difficult to imagine if the goal of temporary relaxation of existing patterns of communication, coordination, and control is kept in mind. Switching jobs for 1 week a year, creating a special "skunkworks" department for new projects where policies and procedures are relaxed, or holding an annual "assumption day" where all the unspoken assumptions about clients, staff, and administration are scrutinized, followed by a "reversal day," when some of these actions are reversed, are all examples of such environments.

Harold H. Weissman
Editor/Senior Author

References

Campbell, D. (1978). The psychology of creativity. [Audiotape.] Available from the Center for Creative Leadership, Greensboro, NC.

Herzlinger, R. (1977, January/February). Why data systems in nonprofit organizations fail. *Harvard Business Review, 55*, 81–86.

March, J., & Olsen, J. (1979). *Ambiguity and choice in organizations*. Bergen, Norway: Universitetsforlaget.

Nystrom, P., & Starbuck, W. (1984). To avoid organizational crises, unlearn. *Organizational Dynamics, 12*(4), 53–65.

Pettigrew, A. (1985). Contextualist research: A natural way to link theory and practice. In E. Lawler, A. Mohrman, S. Mohrman, G. Ledford, & T. Cummings (Eds.), *Doing research that is useful for theory and practice* (pp. 222–274). San Francisco: Jossey-Bass.

Van Gundy, A. (1984). How to establish a creative climate in the work group. *Management Review, 73*(8), 24–28; 37–38.

Weick, K. (1977, Summer). Organizational design: Organizations as self-designing systems. *Organizational Dynamics*, 43–44.

Weick, K. (1979). Cognitive processes in organizations. In B. Staw (Ed.), *Research in organizational behavior* (pp. 41–74). Greenwich, CT: JAI Press.

Summation of Part Three

The danger in writing about innovation is that one's ideas can sound something like a scouting credo: be open; be flexible; be prepared, honest, playful, and loyal. In general, these are good guidelines. However, they offer little specific help in determining how much preparation or flexibility is needed, or to whom one should be loyal. Also, lists of guidelines often may give little importance to the role of the environment. The subtle patterning of behavior and beliefs by the environment (or agency) is ignored.

Part Three has focused on both the individual innovator and on the context with which the innovator must deal. Young has articulated the need for social entrepreneurs and described their skills. Turner pointed out that practice wisdom cannot become an innovation until it is proceduralized so others can try it out. Bromberg discussed the constellation of social and political factors that an innovator must consider in promoting innovation. She also suggested that practitioners not be demoralized by partial failures, such as deinstitutionalization. Rather, it should be understood that social innovation is a disorderly process in a democracy, where the environment often can be controlled only partially. Innovation, therefore, proceeds through trial and error.

As Cole (1988) pointed out,

> the best ideas rarely come in shiny boxes. They come off the wall. . . . Off the wall means, simply coming from someplace unexpected. Being open to the unexpected is what play is all about.
>
> In this sense, democracy is a very playful form of government. Making mistakes is built into the system, along with the means for correcting them.
>
> Play is the name we give to this freedom to go out on a limb with the full knowledge that we might fall flat on our faces. (p. C16)

On a less playful note Finnegan dispelled the notion that innovation can be divorced from its funding and regulatory environment. Gummer provided a sophisticated view of organizational dynamics. He explained what innovators need to know about their agencies, such as incongruities, process needs, and market changes; and what skills they need to possess in each phase of innovation—the inventor's skills for generation, the engineer's skills for development, and those of the broker or promoter for implementation.

The chapters and commentary in Part Three tell the would-be innovator, whether a top executive or the lowliest worker, to pay attention to their environments, to think about the organizational factors that affect either tasks or people: management controls, reward systems, pattern of communication and feedback, interpersonal relationships, and so forth. As Pettigrew (1985) pointed out, one either must work toward creating a supportive work climate, or suffer diminishments in creative possibilities.

By combining work and play, organizations can support individual creativity and organizational innovation. Dandridge (1988) described the supportive dynamics of such seriously playful activities as workplace rituals, ceremonies, or celebrations.

(1) Participants may experience and build competence useful in the common practice of work; useful behavior can be "practiced" in the ceremony. This can include skills in temporary leadership, social skills, and so on.

(2) Individuals can transcend their work role and experience a sense of cooperativeness or community. The unity of the organization can be seen, or the place of a department within that organization better understood. . . .

(3) Certain kinds of ceremonies may direct attention to values, roles, or goals of the organization . . . rituals indicate [their] importance [to] the organization. . . .

(4) An inspirational ceremony may lead the participants to experience new vitality or renewed energy.

(5) When a ceremony or ritual provides a haven from a problem, it facilitates coping.

(6) New lines of communication may be created, or different lines not usually permitted within a hierarchy may be used, leading to better integration of work units or new information in vertical communication.

(7) Lessons are taught and status is changed, often in the context of fun. . . . (p. 258)

A practical approach to examining the organizational effects on innovation would be to do an innovation audit. Try asking the following questions: What supports are there for the generation of ideas? Is there information or time with which to innovate? Are there structures or rewards for innovation? To what extent does the agency allow the development of ideas? Are new innovations ever tested? Are organizational crises viewed as natural experiments? What is the administration interested in learning?

What is the agency's history in idea development? How was the latest innovation in the agency implemented? Is there any history of failed implementation? Are there professional or personal interests that support or hinder implementation of innovations? Who has the talent and power to manage the implementation of an innovation? Has the agency ever had any interest in verifying its operating assumptions? Does it have any capacity to rigorously evaluate its programs or procedures? Are work and play integrated in ways that promote innovation?

These questions are not exhaustive. Making an audit of an agency's capacity to generate, design, develop, verify, and adopt ideas would take a great deal of time and effort. Yet the personal and organizational payoffs could be considerable. An organization's posture toward innovation might be changed. At the worst, innovators might find it better to focus their creative efforts on updating their resumes, than on butting a stone wall of resistance.

Harold H. Weissman
Editor/Senior Author

References

Cole, K. C. (1988, November 30). Play by definition, suspends the rules. *New York Times*, p. C16.

Dandridge, T. (1988). Work ceremonies: Why integrate work and play. In M. Jones, M. Moore, & R. Snyder (Eds.), *Inside organizations: Understanding the human dimension* (pp. 251–259). Beverly Hills, CA: Sage.

Pettigrew, A. (1985). Contextualist research: A natural way to link theory and practice. In E. Lawler, A. Mohrman, S. Mohrman, G. Ledford, & T. Cummings (Eds.), *Doing research that is useful for theory and practice* (pp. 222–274). San Francisco: Jossey–Bass.

PART FOUR

Social Movements: Nourishment for Creative Practitioners

Social Movements and Creativity

The only person who likes change is a wet baby.

—Roy Z-M Blitzer

All stage or phase theories, including those related to creativity, must demarcate the shift from one phase to the next. With creativity, what indicates that saturation has been reached and the next phase should begin?

Unfortunately, there are no clear indicators. More is known about what is not an indicator than what is one. The object of saturation is not simply to gather information, but also to see problems from a variety of perspectives (Edwards, 1987).

Seeing different configurations, perceiving analogies which formerly were overlooked, and broadening the gestalt require individual effort and perseverance. Yet there is a social dimension to saturation. The environment in which one works and the experiences one has affect one's ideas and views of reality. The use of R-mode, analogic, synthesizing thought processes alone will not provide a new perspective.

In the social work profession, social movements have offered new perspective on problems, priorities, and social needs. The movements change social workers' views of reality by highlighting what often is buried deeply in their consciousness of the environment. At times, programs developed by social movements are taken over by social work agencies. At other times, agencies develop the programs for which social movements have agitated.

The close relationship between social work and social movements has been acknowledged for a long time. Leading social workers such as Jane Addams also were the leaders of social movements for women's rights, protection of child labor, public health, and electoral reform. Porter Lee's (1937) famous *Social Work: Cause and Function* enshrined the dual emphasis of social work in the profession's literature.

At times, the differences between a profession of cause and one of function have brought divisiveness and dispute. However, most social workers now accept that these distinctions can complement, rather than exclude, each other. As Miller and Philipp (1983) pointed out,

195

When certain social conditions give rise to new client groups, the existing network of social agencies (for reasons of funding, legitimacy and social sanction) cannot possibly be a source of help for some of these groups. In these instances, the alternative service agency (shelters, hot lines, self-help groups, etc.) may arise outside of the conventional network and act as gadfly to the profession.

In the context of clinical practice, the alternative service agency becomes a stimulus for change and innovation. These changes occur not only in regard to the organization of service delivery but also in regard to the theory and technique of intervention. In the long run, the alternative service agency becomes an important factor in the way the profession of social work grows and amends its practice. This is not to say that in the short run the alternative service agency is not a source of considerable stress for the enterprise of social work and social welfare. (p. 779)

The first chapter in Part Four highlights the problems that settlement houses have had in maintaining their innovative focus. When cause becomes function, the scope of innovation is limited by a host of parameters which Stuart clearly delineates.

For the past 30 years, settlement houses increasingly have entered into symbiotic relationships with government. Where once settlements were self-supporting, they now are dependent on government for the majority of these funds. The rules and regulations on receiving these funds and the reactive state of mind created by this dependence ultimately have led to less innovation.

Social settlements were not in the forefront of dealing with the problem of homelessness in the 1980s. Were they lacking in creativity, or had they become inappropriate locales for dealing with homelessness? According to Miller and Philipp (1983), they were inappropriate locales. However, this might change in the future as society accepts the legitimacy of concern for the problem.

The profession loses a great deal when social workers do not grapple with the concerns of new and emerging client groups and social problems, such as homeless people and homelessness. These losses include the opportunities that different experiences provide in challenging traditional explanations of problems and making possible new and potentially creative explanations; limitations on organizational adaptiveness because the challenge is not taken up; costs to the profession because other and, perhaps less able, groups fill the void; and the chance to adapt traditional knowledge to new groups and problems, which often can be applied very usefully.

For the creative practitioner, these losses can have serious ramifications. Agency contexts can congeal rather than open; the experiences from which new connections can be drawn are narrowed and limited; support from colleagues for innovation is less likely to occur; and necessity for change, the oft-noted mother of invention, is lessened. Saturation cannot occur.

Harold H. Weissman
Editor/Senior Author

References

Edwards, B. (1987). *Drawing on the artist within: A guide to innovation, imagination, and creativity* (Fireside ed.). New York: Simon & Schuster.

Lee, P. (1937). *Social work: cause and function.* New York: Columbia University Press.

Miller, H. & Philipp, C. (1983). The alternative service agency. In A. Rosenblatt & D. Waldfogel (Eds.), *Handbook of clinical social work* (pp. 779–791). San Francisco: Jossey–Bass.

Settlement Houses: Changing Sources of Innovation in Social Work

Paul H. Stuart

Finding ways to foster innovation is a serious concern for the social work profession. Fears often are expressed about stale and ineffective social work methods and the danger of the profession becoming irrelevant to the solution of social problems. Yet a narrowing of scope, a sense of retrenchment, and an increasing conservatism seemed to characterize the social work profession in the 1980s. The buoyancy that characterized the profession in the 1960s and 1970s seems to be long gone. Are there new ideas? Where are they coming from? What are the conditions which lead to the development of innovations?

History of Settlement Houses

Some answers can be derived from looking at the history of settlement houses, one of the oldest forms of social agency. The earliest settlement houses were inspired by new Protestant interpretations of Christian social obligations. Settlement houses share a common heritage with the institutional church and the Social Gospel, two other late nineteenth century innovations in religious life. In 1884, Samuel Barnett established Toynbee Hall, the first settlement house, in an English–Irish slum district in London's East End. Toynbee Hall was to be a place where Oxford students could move into the slums and participate in the daily life of the poorer classes. In this sense, it had much in common with other nineteenth-century reform movements aimed at the poor, such as the Salvation Army; the Charity Organization Society; and, in particular, Thomas Chalmers' efforts to "rechurch" Glasgow in the 1820s. Chalmers attempted a parochial management of the poor, proclaiming a "principle of locality" as a guiding principle in help for the poor (Kellogg, 1934).

Barnett's experiment created quite a stir, in part because of his access to the British upper class. Many visited Toynbee Hall, among them the Americans Stanton Coit, Jane Addams, and Robert A. Woods, all of whom later founded settlements in the United States based on the model of Toynbee Hall.

The American settlements, though based on an English model, soon came to differ from their English predecessor. Clubs and small group activities were much more developed in the American settlements from the start; women dominated the American settlements, and men were more prominent in the English houses; and, perhaps as a result, there was more attention to the problems of young children and youths and to concerns about health in the settlements in the United States. Although most American settlements started modestly, by 1900 many had large investments in buildings and equipment. Paid staff members appeared relatively early in the American settlements, many of which shed their religious affiliations. American settlements responded more quickly to changes in their neighborhoods than did Toynbee Hall. The East End neighborhood surrounding the settlement became Jewish in the 1890s, but this change had only a gradual effect on the program of the settlement. American settlements, in contrast, were much more sensitive to changes in the ethnic composition of their neighborhoods (Reinders, 1982).

American settlements emphasized reciprocity. Addams (1892) said that in the settlement, the friendly visitor "should also be the friendly visited" (p. 237). Like the English settlements, the American settlement houses conducted research on neighborhood problems and got to know their neighbors as people rather than "cases." Spontaneity and responding to the most immediate need were thought to be vital, as was a flexible spirit. Addams warned settlements to "hold programs lightly" (Berry, 1965, p. 107) and be prepared to turn their programs over to more permanent organizations. Throughout the early settlement literature, there is a theme of resistance to institutionalization, an experimental spirit, and a view of the settlement as a means to an end—a tool or temporary expedient.

Only four settlements were established in the United States before 1890, but the movement grew rapidly during this decade, especially after the Panic of 1893, which led to the most severe economic depression of the nineteenth century. By 1895, more than 50 settlements had been established (Schlesinger, 1933). Five years later there were more than 100 (Bremner, 1956), including several in rural areas in the South (Ingram, 1937). In 1896, 19 of 27 settlements responding to a survey conducted by the Social Settlement Committee of the National Conference of Charities and Corrections had no in-house religious services. The program generally involved clubs and in-house activities and the sponsorship of municipal reform activities (Reynolds, 1896; Social Settlement Committee, 1896).

During the early 20th century, settlement leaders warned against the tendency toward institutionalization. White (1911) noted that there were 500 settlements in the United States, although the term was loosely used, "implying a somewhat vague conception of the essential idea" (p. 48). Settlements were confused with missions, with charity organizations, and with educational efforts. Although settlements might be involved in all of these areas, the essential value of the settlement movement lay in its flexibility and its closeness to its neighbors. Settlements were in a unique position to know peoples' needs, to initiate reforms and preventive work, and to use their facilities to test the value of new ideas:

> A concrete case of individual need comes to the attention of a settlement resident, and in the attempt to meet the need, it is seen to be only a symptom of a larger social need. Then follows an effort to meet the larger need, and the settlement is the natural place for the effort to be tried out. It is in this way that settlements have become experiment stations in social work. (White, 1911, p. 62)

Changing neighborhoods presented a special problem. White (1910) called for the establishment of settlements in new neighborhoods to follow neighbors as they left old districts. Quoting Robert S. Woods, McDowell (1910) responded that the settlement was "an attitude of mind," not a building or even a program, and that settlement workers had to assume that this attitude was contagious (p. 246). Neighbors who left the immediate vicinity of the settlement could create their own clubs and associations, indeed their own neighborhoods, without a settlement (McDowell, 1910).

Because of physical plant investments, few settlements moved with their neighbors. Although there were instances of failure to adapt to new conditions, many settlements made efforts to adjust to changing neighborhoods and to ease the process of neighborhood transition. The focus on the local community, so important in the early settlements, continued (Patterson, 1981). After World War I, many settlements shifted their interests to providing neighbors with experiences in the dramatic and visual arts. Settlement work increasingly was viewed as a neighborhood service, and settlement houses were seen as group work agencies such as the contemporary YMCA, YWCA, Boys' Clubs, and city recreation departments (Williamson, 1929). Recreation and art fit well into the settlements' flexible program; recreation was liberating, wrote Mary K. Simkhovich (1930), Director of New York's Greenwich House, because it involved the development of self-expression and self-understanding.

With some exceptions, settlements concentrated mainly on the provision of a group work service during the 1930s. The "central objective for settlement programs" was "personality development through group relations," wrote Helen Hart (1931, p. 292), headworker of Pittsburgh's Kingsley House. Although some settlements helped organize the unemployed during the Great Depression, most houses, particularly those receiving funds from the community chest, confined themselves to providing recreation services (Trolander, 1975).

In the 1940s, the major emphasis was on the professionalization of settlement house employment, the development of group work, and the expansion of in-house programs. The expanding black population of cities in the 1950s, and the settlements' difficulties in relating to these newcomers, resulted in a reexamination of the settlement role and a return to social action, research, and local organizing (Pernell, 1970). During the 1960s, the availability of federal funding for antipoverty projects dramatically affected the settlement program, as many settlements introduced programs, such as Head Start, which federal agencies would support (Switzer, 1973).

Settlements and Social Work Innovation

Settlement houses were significant sources of social work innovation, particularly in the years before World War I. In part, this resulted from the strategic position of settlement houses. The settlements were found in big-city neighborhoods, which included many clients, both potential and actual, of other social agencies. In part, the innovations resulted from the deliberate lack of structure and agenda which characterized the early settlements. The settlements were dominated by volunteers before 1920, and this volunteer spirit was critical in the flexibility which settlements espoused. In addition, the close association between settlement houses and other early social agencies made it possible for the settlements to exert an influence on the entire field of social work. The settlements provided a way for volunteers to affect all of social work.

In the United States, the tension between organized charity and the settlement movement, much celebrated by historians, did not exist to the extent that it did in England. In America a much more cooperative atmosphere prevailed, particularly in the early years (Reinders, 1982). In 1986, McDowell (1896) surveyed 16 settlements on relations with organized charities; 15 reported extensive cooperation. Settlement residents served as friendly visitors, and settlements served as information and referral centers, directing clients to public and private charities (Lathrop, 1894).

Several years before World War I, when the Red Cross introduced casework services "above the poverty line" in its home service program, settlements were experimenting with "the application of the C.O.S. [Charity Organization Society] method to families above the poverty line" (Simkhovitch, 1909). Casework, Simkhovitch argued, provided a means for settlements to engage in preventive interventions with neighbors; the settlements could show caseworkers how to engage in a helping relationship without the subordination implicit in the relationship between a COS visitor and a dependent charity client. Elsewhere, Simkhovitch (1932? [probably 1922]) pointed out that settlement residents had "normal human relationships" with neighbors; they could show how to help clients to help themselves (p. 3). A normal relationship with the client was seen as a prerequisite to preventive intervention, and an emphasis on prevention was a hallmark of modern charity. At a time when charity experts were decrying the failure of many district agents to "really *know*" their neighborhoods, this was a welcome contribution (McLean, 1909).

The settlement was viewed by its residents as the "general practitioner" in social work. "Out of an unselective and close association with all kinds of people," Hall (1971) wrote, "our programs and our opportunities to affect social change must spring" (p. 61). Settlements pioneered the information and referral function, and used that function to identify gaps in available services. In the process, a variety of new agencies and organizations were initiated, preferably in the public sector if the settlement residents could make the case convincingly enough. Unlike COS workers, settlement residents advocated public services as a means of institutionalizing the specific services that people needed. Settlement leaders always favored institutionalizing needed services, rather than the settlements.

The settlement program itself was ideally shaped by neighborhood needs. Hull House provided a day nursery, for example, not because the residents wanted to, but because the neighbors' need for child care during working hours would not otherwise be met (Addams, 1897). As Lathrop

(1894) wrote,

> Every activity of [Hull] House has sprung out of some neighborhood need; and it has thus been perhaps a necessity, at any rate a natural development, that it should undertake many things, as it realized the untoward conditions about it, rather than that it should do a few things with the thoroughness which a laboratory implies. (p. 314)

The primary effort was not to build programs, however, but to convince others to meet the need which the settlement discovered. The settlement "interpret[s] foreign colonies to the rest of the city in the light of a professional obligation," Addams (1908, p. 155) wrote. Typically, the interpretation was broad, and included the identification of needed services and programs that could be carried out by others.

The settlements' emphasis on the neighborhood was not unique; COS also emphasized the importance of locality. Both movements drew inspiration from Chalmers and other British poor law reformers who emphasized the "principle of locality." However, the settlements contributed the idea of approaching the neighborhood without preconceptions or a previously determined agenda. Unlike a mission, White (1911) wrote, "The settlement . . . does not approach its neighborhood with preconceived notions as to what must be accomplished for the neighborhood's regeneration" (p. 55).

Such an approach was well suited to learning the neighborhood on its own terms. Whether in the hands of a settlement resident, a neighborhood worker, or a sensitive caseworker, the technique of approaching the neighborhood without preconceptions was a powerful tool for generations of social workers (Fantl, 1964). The widespread use of volunteers, combined with an ideology which viewed them as the equals of paid staff members, was an essential contributor to the openness and flexibility of the early settlement movement.

Not only was the service agenda to be developed on the spot, in response to local conditions, but ideally the neighborhood would be in charge of making the decisions. Simkhovitch (1932? [probably 1922]) wrote that community development must be "*by* the community as well as *for* it" (p. 4). As settlements moved into group work and recreation, they brought this principle of empowerment with them and applied it in work with groups. Group work supervisors had to learn how to work with group leaders without making decisions for them, advised Swift (1935).

The contribution of the settlements to empirical research and the development of new services is well known. The settlement movement's contributions to social work include the stress on the importance of approaching new situations without preconceptions, an open attitude toward filling gaps in services, and an orientation toward doing whatever is necessary to improve a situation.

Speaking to the National Conference of Social Work in 1930, Addams (1930) illustrated the profession's function as a gap filler: "Social workers were the pioneers in certain movements afterwards taken over by medicine and law" (p. 51). She recited a striking list of accomplishments, including the campaign against tuberculosis, the development of occupational health, venereal disease prevention, governmental maternal and child health programs, the juvenile court, legal aid societies, and, in the field of education, vocational guidance. She continued:

> I do not claim any special perspicacity on the part of the social worker. I should say that if he has at times seen the need, before the profession involved saw it, it may be due to the fact that . . . it may be possible for the social worker, living in the midst of divers groups whose history, language and customs show the tremendous variability of human nature, to find clues to a new life pattern. . . . (p. 54)

Innovation Today: The Need for Free Spaces

Evans and Boyte (1986) argued that *free spaces*, or voluntary associations located "between private lives and large-scale institutions where ordinary citizens can act with dignity, independence, and vision," are essential for democratic renewal and change in American society (p. 17). They described such "free spaces" as black self-help groups during slavery, the Knights of Labor, the settlement movement, and the civil rights movement of the 1950s and 1960s. The social work profession, like American society, may need its "free spaces" to respond to changing conditions. Such free spaces should provide an opportunity to experiment, while being close to the profession's central concerns of the clients and their problems.

Settlement houses are constrained, to some extent, in performing an innovative role today because of their dependence on grants-in-aid and purchase of service contracts. Governmental funding restricts innovation because contracts and grants provide little space for the unusual or untried (Kramer & Grossman, 1987). In addition, the role of the volunteer has long been subordinated to that of the paid professional staff member, in settlement houses as in other social agencies (Davis, 1967; Lubove, 1965).

Unfortunately, professional education also can limit innovation to the extent that mastery of a skill may result in an unwillingness to abandon that skill. Schools of social work must educate students to be innovative practitioners. Too frequently, students are trained only to use specific techniques. Brilliant's (1986) complaint that schools of social work fail to educate students to assume leadership positions may be a reflection of an increasingly narrow and technical emphasis in social work education.

The response of the profession to the problem of homelessness provides a test case for these concerns. Homelessness, among the most visible social problems today, has attracted considerable public and professional notice. However, with a few notable exceptions, neither schools of social work nor settlement houses have been in the forefront of efforts to provide programmatic and innovative solutions to this problem. Settlements have lacked the freedom to demonstrate fresh approaches with this population, and schools have been relatively isolated from the problem. Only recently have substantial government funds become available. The most innovative responses have come from organizations on the fringes of organized social work—from the urban missions, from the Catholic Worker movement, and from the Salvation Army. These organizations differ from settlements in that they are defined more by their mission than by any one method of helping; the vast majority of their funds do not come from governmental sources, permitting them greater flexibility; they often use volunteers committed to dealing with a single concern; they tend to not see their program as bounded by their physical facilities; and they retain considerably more flexibility as to the time and means of access to services.

An exception is provided by two recent attempts by schools of social work to become involved in the provision of innovative services to homeless people. In the first attempt, the School of Social Service at St. Louis University and the Salvation Army Emergency Lodge of St. Louis developed a program designed to place homeless people in permanent housing (Hutchison, Seawright, & Stretch, 1986). In the second attempt, faculty and students at the School of Social Work at Western Michigan University studied community reaction to a new social service—an experimental residence for formerly homeless people in Kalamazoo, Michigan (Pawlak, Skurski, Creamer, Grendy, & Bishop, 1985). The St. Louis project was funded by federal grant monies awarded to the school and the agency, while the Kalamazoo study was supported by the School of Social Work. Both efforts represent collaboration between the school and a segment of the practice community.

To promote innovation relevant to the profession's needs, schools of social work need to be open to influence from the field, and settlements need to be free to innovate through reducing their dependency on purchase of service contracts. Creating partnerships between settlement houses and the schools would accomplish both objectives. In addition to the aforementioned two examples, a number of models have been proposed, including placing practitioners-in-residence in schools of social work and providing faculty members with academic leaves in social agencies, including settlement houses. Although the allocation of new resources would be required, the job of creating free spaces ultimately is one of creating a state of mind—as was the case in the early settlement movement. The consequences of creating this new state of mind should be positive for the profession, the schools, and the settlements.

References

Addams, J. (1892, October). Hull House, Chicago: An effort toward social democracy. *The Forum, 14,* 226–241.

Addams, J. (1897). Social settlements. *Proceedings of the National Conference of Charities and Corrections* (Vol. 24; pp. 338–346). Boston: Geo. H. Ellis.

Addams, J. (1908, May). The Chicago settlements and social unrest. *Charities and the Commons, 20,* 155–166.

Addams, J. (1930). Social workers and the other professions. *Proceedings of the National Conference of Social Work* (Vol. 57; pp. 50–54). Chicago: University of Chicago Press.

Berry, M. E. (1965, January). Mr. Gans is challenged [Points and viewpoints]. *Social Work, 10,* 104–107.

Bremner, R. H. (1956). *From the depths: The discovery of poverty in the United States.* New York: New York University Press.

Brilliant, E. L. (1986, September/October). Social work leadership: A missing ingredient? *Social Work, 31,* 325–331.

Davis, A. F. (1967). *Spearheads for reform: The social settlements and the Progressive Era, 1890–1914.* New York: Oxford University Press.

Evans, S. M., & Boyte, H. C. (1986). *Free spaces: The sources of democratic change in America.* New York: Harper & Row.

Fantl, B. (1964, June). Initial insights into Hunters Point. *Smith College Studies in Social Work, 34,* 178–185.

Hall, H. (1971). *Unfinished business: In neighborhood and nation.* New York: Macmillan.

Hart, H. (1931). The changing function of the settlement under changing conditions. *Proceedings of the National Conference of Social Work* (Vol. 58, pp. 289–295). Chicago: University of Chicago Press.

Hutchison, W. J., Seawright, P., & Stretch, J. J. (1986, November/December). Multidimensional networking: A response to the needs of homeless families. *Social Work, 31,* 427–430.

Ingram, F. M. (1937, May). The settlement movement in the South. *World Outlook, 27,* 12–14, 38.

Kellogg, P. U. (1934). Social settlements. In E.R.A. Seligman (Ed.), *Encyclopedia of the Social Sciences* (Vol. 14; pp. 157–162). New York: Macmillan.

Kramer, R. M., & Grossman, B. (1987, March). Contracting for social services: Process management and resource dependencies. *Social Service Review, 61,* 32–55.

Lathrop, J. C. (1894). Hull House as a sociological laboratory. *Proceedings of the National Conference of Charities and Corrections* (Vol. 21; pp. 313–319). Boston: Geo. H. Ellis.

Lubove, R. (1965). *The professional altruist: The emergence of social work as a career, 1880–1930.* Cambridge, MA: Harvard University Press.

Addams, J. (1908, May). The Chicago settlements and social unrest, *Charities and the Commons, 20,* 155–166.

McDowell, M. E. (1896). The settlement and organized charity. *Proceedings of the National Conference of Charities and Corrections* (Vol. 23, 123–127). Boston: Geo. H. Ellis.

McDowell, M. E. (1910). Discussion of Gaylord White's paper. *Proceedings of the National Conference of Charities and Corrections* (Vol. 37, p. 246). Ft. Wayne, IN: Archer Printing Co.

McLean, F. H. (1909). Social problems of the smaller cities. *Proceedings of the National Conference of Charities and Corrections* (Vol. 36; pp. 107–118). Ft. Wayne, IN: Ft. Wayne Printing Co.

Patterson, J. T. (1981). *America's struggle against poverty, 1900–1980.* Cambridge: Harvard University Press.

Pawlak, E. J., Skurski, M., Creamer, D., Gundy, J., & Bishop, A. (1985, June). A view of the mall. *Social Service Review, 59,* 305–317.

Pernell, R. B. (1970, July). The privilege of these terrific years. *Public Welfare, 28,* 251–255.

Reinders, R. C. (1982, March). Toynbee Hall and the American settlement movement. *Social Service Review, 56,* 39–54.

Reynolds, J. B. (1896). The settlement and municipal reform. *Proceedings of the National Conference of Charities and Corrections* (Vol. 23; pp. 138–142). Boston: Geo. H. Ellis.

Schlesinger, A. (1933). *The rise of the city, 1878–1898.* New York: Macmillan.

Simkhovitch, M. K. (1909). The case work plane. *Proceedings of the National Conference of Charities and Corrections* (Vol. 36; pp. 138–148). Ft. Wayne, IN: Ft. Wayne Printing Co.

Simkhovich, M. K. (1930). The place of recreation in the settlement program. *Proceedings of the National Conference of Social Work* (Vol. 57; pp. 372–377). Chicago: University of Chicago Press.

Simkhovitch, (1932? [probably 1922]). Case work as the settlement sees it. Box 6, Folder 40, National Federation of Settlement Papers, Social Welfare History Archives, University of Minnesota.

Report of the Social Settlement Committee. (1896). *Proceedings of the National Conference of Charities and Corrections* (Vol. 23; pp. 166–175). Boston: Geo. H. Ellis.

Swift, A. L. (1935, October 24). Training aspects of group work. Paper presented at the Group Work Section, New York State Conference of Social Work, Buffalo, Box 10, Folder 25, National Federation of Settlement Papers, Social Welfare History Archives, University of Minnesota.

Switzer, E. (1973, December). Chicago settlements, 1972: An overview. *Social Service Review, 47,* 581–592.

Trolander, J. A. (1975). *Settlement houses and the Great Depression.* Detroit: Wayne State University Press.

White, G. S. (1910). The settlement problem of a changing neighborhood. *Proceedings of the National Conference of Charities and Corrections* (Vol. 37, pp. 240–246). Ft. Wayne, IN: Archer Printing Co.

White, G. S. (1911, January). The social settlement after twenty-five years. *Harvard Theological Review, 4,* 47–70.

Williamson, M. (1929). *The social worker in group work.* In American Association of Social Workers, Job Analysis Series, No. 2. New York: Harper & Brothers.

A Warehouse of Experience

In addition to Stuart's findings, another factor that may account for the recent less innovative character of settlements is that staff members no longer live in the settlement houses. Is a 9 a.m. to 5 p.m., 5-day work week experience the same as being in a place for 24 hours, 7 days a week?

The live-in experience is certainly a far richer one. The feelings and perspectives gained must be different, both qualitatively and quantitatively. The motivation to deal with a problem is different when one is living constantly with it.

The cues one picks up on a daily basis, the nuances of each day, and the meanings people attach to their problems are necessary bits of information that have to be sifted through and stored for real saturation to occur. A warehouse full of ideas and concepts, feelings, and experiences is needed for the mind to begin the next phase of the creative process—incubation. A half-empty warehouse limits the chances for the final creative phase—illumination.

One of the guidelines for the saturation phase is to look at the shadows of a problem, at what might be left out (Edwards, 1987). How does one see shadows in social problems? What one sees in the shadows depends on the exact nature—the reality—of the lighted shapes. Paradoxically, therefore, the ability to extrapolate into unknown areas depends on the ability to see known areas accurately, without gaps or distortion.

For saturation to occur and to sharply illuminate the shadows, information has to be compared and contrasted, and seen in both proportion and perspective. One way of experiencing contrasts or anomalies is exposure to those who see problems differently. If an agency will not or cannot experiment with radically different approaches, then creatively inclined workers need to seek out those that will take such approaches.

Kerson in her chapter on self-help groups illustrates different methods of helping, and different explanations of the causes of social and personal problems. The potential for fruitful discussions with professional social workers is readily apparent.

Yet, there can be problems for social workers working with self-help groups. Some groups take an overtly antiprofessional stance. Others are based on values antithetical to those of the profession. Here, creative practitioners or agencies should not respond angrily or defensively, but simply admit differences and offer the possibility of mutual learning.

In one sense, one's experiences form a well, which serves as a source for creative efforts. It may be that the highly creative person is able to experience more and then register experiences with greater intensity, creating a wider, deeper well from which to draw.

Sensitivity to stimuli is probably a precondition for creativity. Immersing oneself in self-help groups will not guarantee creative ideas. It is necessary for any experience to be judged according to some criteria (Wilson, 1986).

Wilson suggested that, to gain creative responses to experiences, individuals first need an overall frame of reference,

> a largeness, a generosity toward impressions which enables the creator to accept irreconcilable modes, resolving them if possible, but encompassing them if necessary . . . for the tension between widely various ideas must be maintained without compromise, without arbitrarily narrowing one's vision in the interests of psychic ease. (p. 49)

Second, experiences with self-help groups must be digested, explored, put in order, and compared with one's professional knowledge—one's cognitive maps. Sensitivity to the unusual, the unexpected, the out-of-the-ordinary in self-help groups may then provide the spark for a first insight into creative adaptation of these experiences.

Harold H. Weissman
Editor/Senior Author

References

Edwards, B. (1987). *Drawing on the artist within: A guide to innovation, invention, imagination, and creativity* (Fireside ed.). New York: Simon & Schuster.

Wilson, R. N. (1986). *Experiencing creativity*. New Brunswick, NJ: Transaction Books.

Lending Vision: Ways in Which Self-help and Voluntary Efforts Promote Practice Creativity

Toba Schwaber Kerson

Self-help and voluntary efforts usually arise because society is not meeting a need. They often are formed outside of the mainstream, and outside of what currently is acceptable practice. This "outsider" status generally comes about because the problem that the group addresses is considered unworthy in some way, because society does not want to spend what it would take to alleviate the problem, or because society does not know how to treat or rectify the situation. The first kind of group may be formed to address gay rights; the second, to gain welfare rights; and the third, to help middle-aged children of frail, demented elderly parents to deal with problems they face.

Many groups fit all three categories. For example, alcoholism has been a problem in American society for many years. Social drinking is acceptable, but drunkenness is not. Although there now are many public programs for the treatment of alcoholism and other substance abuse, they are relatively new, and were created only after the courts recognized that alcoholism was a disease. Because it is estimated that there are between 6 million and 10 million alcoholics in the United States, it can be argued that the number of public programs is insufficient.

The most successful treatment for alcoholism after detoxification is Alcoholics Anonymous (AA), an international self-help organization with an estimated 1.25 million members in 42,000 groups (Donovan, 1984). Al-Anon is a self-help group separate but parallel to AA which is described as a fellowship for relatives and friends of alcoholics. Throughout the world there are 20,000 Al-Anon groups, including 2,500 groups for teenagers only called Alateen. These self-help groups have become so well established—through success, longevity, membership, and geography—that they are highly valued treatment approaches (Kerson, 1985).

Social Work and Self-help/Voluntary Efforts

Self-help and voluntary groups have much to teach professional social workers, just as social workers have much to offer such efforts. According to many professionals, the relationship is one-sided. Although they may admit grudgingly that the power of peer support can bring beneficial change for those in a self-help situation, professionals often think that they can effect more change. Conversely, many proponents of self-help groups demean professional help as making people feel sick and dependent. The best solution is a give-and-take between professionals and self-help proponents.

The dictionary (Murray, 1971) defines a *professional* as

> following a vocation in which a professed knowledge of some department of learning or science is used in its application to the affairs of others or in the practice of an art founded upon it. This is applied specifically to the three learned professions of divinity, law, and medicine; also to the military profession. A professional is engaged in one of the learned or skilled professions or in a calling considered socially superior to a trade or handicraft. (pp. 1427–1428)

Two aspects of this definition are helpful in examining the relationship of professional help and self-help. One is the concept of superiority. If there is a superior, there must be an inferior (Kerson, 1978). The second is the notion of the application to the affairs of others, which implies a service to someone else. Social workers always have had particular difficulty with a definition of the professional role which includes an assumption of superiority, because it does not fit well with the social work value system, particularly the importance placed on the client self-determination (McDermott, 1982).

Volunteers in Social Work History

Self-help groups and volunteers promote practice creativity by finding ways to cajole, demand, and sometimes force professionals and society to view the world the way they do. This type of approach played a large role in social work history, when volunteers saw the pain of others and insisted that society attend to this pain.

Carola Woerishoffer found ways to make society aware of the plight of the women laundry workers (Lewis, 1986). Jane Addams originally was a volunteer who found ways to make society aware of the problems of poor laborers in Chicago, the need for municipal reform, and for peace (Hoover, 1986). Robert Treat Paine volunteered to help develop safe, affordable housing for the working people of Boston (Harmond, 1986). These early social workers were defining needs that then were outside the existing services which society was willing to support (Miller & Philipp, 1983). Now, most social workers work within agencies, meeting needs that society recognizes.

How do social workers honor their training, their ability to intervene effectively, their knowledge of social problems, and the dispassion that they must develop as self-protection, while being receptive to creative practice techniques learned from self-help groups and volunteers?

Learning from Self-help Groups

Self-help groups have been defined as

voluntary, small group structures for mutual aid and the accomplishment of a special purpose. They are usually formed by peers who have come together for mutual assistance in satisfying a common need, overcoming a common handicap or life-disrupting problem, and bringing about desired social and/ or personal change. The initiators and members of such groups perceive that their needs are not, or cannot be, met by or through existing social institutions. Self-help groups emphasize face-to-face social interactions and the assumption of personal responsibility by members. They often provide material assistance, as well as emotional support: they are frequently cause-oriented, and promulgat[ing] an ideology or values through which members may attain an enhanced sense of personal identity. (Katz & Bender, 1976, p. 9)

As Anderson and Anderson (1981/82) pointed out, "Society always tends to fall back on segregation as a way of dealing with awkward members" (p. 15).

Increasingly . . . the initiative has come to lie entirely with the counselors, who either reject expert help contemptuously or accept it only on the same basis as legal help from solicitors. In the field of general health in particular there has been a burgeoning of self-help groups . . . for sufferers of almost every conceivable symptom. Their philosophy often attests that fellow-sufferers understand best what is needed, and can usually meet the need directly or indirectly if properly organized. . . . Outsiders signify dependence, weakness and incompetence, and thereby undermine an important political message—the right to power. (Westman, 1979, p. 5)

People who join self-help groups exclude others who do not share their problem. The self-help group process is not always positive. A woman

Serious Play

who joined a support group after a mastectomy said that she had to quit the group because she was developing "tunnel vision." The group was supporting her in defining herself solely in terms of her cancer. Another client said that he could not join the multiple sclerosis group to which he was referred because everyone in the group was significantly debilitated, and he was not. At that point in his illness, the group would have been a detriment.

Generally, however, self-help groups have the ability to turn what might be viewed as a negative into a positive. The group identification becomes a positive, rallying force, and people often feel passionately about their cause (Anderson & Anderson, 1981/82).

Self-help groups empower their members. Volunteer organizations almost always empower their volunteers, and sometimes also empower the groups for which volunteers are working (VanderAvort & VanHarberden, 1985). This empowerment, which somehow is greater than the usual effect of direct practice, casework, or psychotherapy is a critical goal for social workers. The form a group takes, whether it is closed or open, meant to change members' views of themselves or society's view of the members, is less important than its ability to empower its members. From this empowerment comes the group's creativity, support, passion, and sense of mission that is so striking to professionals. A social worker working with a self-help or volunteer group can set the stage, provide the place, give a short speech about the rules of the situation, and offer help if it is requested, but then must hope that creative and helpful work will transpire (Steinman & Traunstein, 1984).

Creative Solutions for Professionals

Social workers have much to learn from self-help groups. Some of the creative contributions of self-help groups that social workers could make creative use of in their practices include problem definition by clients, self-direction in choice of a particular group, helping oneself by helping others, sponsorship, using old techniques in new ways, finding new vehicles for expression, group trust, moving from reality to fantasy, and willingness to advertise. Experience with volunteer groups can teach the importance of emotional involvement, and how to recruit and maintain a useful group.

At a glance, experiences with self-help groups and volunteers would seem to be quite different. After all, self-help groups help only their members, and volunteers help others. Still, the issues both types of groups face, such as maintaining momentum, finding the right group, level of involvement and satisfaction, and working creatively to solve problems, are not all that different. Each type of group can lend a vision to social work professionals. Examples generally are culled from the experiences of individuals in small groups. Techniques may be generalized from each context.

Problem Definition and Choice of Group

A depressed 53-year-old man whose son died of acquired immune deficiency syndrome at age 30 went to two different professionals who insisted that he had to accept his anger about his son's homosexuality before he could mourn his death. The man told a third professional from whom he had sought help that he was not crazy, just sad. The rest of the family had finished mourning and he had not. Therefore, the family members had gotten angry with him and decided that he was mentally ill. The social worker told him about several self-help groups and suggested that he visit each of them. When the man did choose a group, one primarily for parents who had lost young children to cancer, the social worker was sure it was the wrong one. However, she knew that the man could not afford to have anyone else tell him he was wrong. The man went to the group that affirmed his feelings (Videka-Sherman & Lieberman, 1985). The group helped the man to mourn and move on with his life. He helped himself by finding a group that defined his problem as he saw it (Klass, 1984/85).

A physician referred a woman who had had an iliostomy to an Ostomy Club, but she refused to go. Instead she formed her own support group to meet what she believed were much different needs. Later, when the group became a national organization and widened its focus, she left the group.

These two examples demonstrate the importance of choice to the client. By choosing their own self-help groups, these people defined their need in ways which others had not understood. In the first example, the man found the solace he needed by joining a group that recognized his sadness. In the second situation, the woman had to begin her own group to meet her own needs. As the focus of the group shifted, the group no longer met her needs, and she moved away from it.

Another self-help group member described the differences between weight loss groups. People must pay to attend Weight Watchers meetings, where they talk almost constantly about food and can obtain the nutritional information which the Weight Watchers organization feels that they lack. On the other hand, Overeaters Anonymous (OA) is free, and group members do not talk about food. Like AA, OA works through inspiration and the teaching of responsibility. A second person had tried both of these groups, but instead joined a small group of overweight people who met several times a week at work for diet information and emotional support. Such oversimplified differences point up the importance of choice of self-help group. To be helpful, a social worker should present the full range of possibilities.

Helping Oneself by Helping Others

An 87-year-old widowed grandmother was housekeeper, carpooler, and the emotional and social pivot for her working children and grandchildren. The cancer that she had developed required a laryngectomy. As a result of her illness, the fact that the chemotherapy made her sick, and the struggle to learn to talk again, she became depressed.

Only to help other people, the woman joined the 12-week 65 Plus group at the cancer center. She quickly became the group champion on how to deal with doctors, and how to get good medical care. The phrase she used with the radiologist who was orchestrating her care, "Boy, I'm going to let you be in charge," became the slogan of the group. By the end of the group, the woman was feeling strong enough to resume much of her housekeeping. She never articulated her feelings or motivations (Norman, 1983). However, while helping others, she had helped herself.

Sponsorship

By now the grandmother of self-help groups and certainly mother of all of the kinds of "Anonymous" groups, AA uses the concept of sponsorship. When alcoholics join AA, they are assigned a sponsor. Sponsors do not tell their charges what to do, but they do share their own experiences. Often, these experiences are powerful in helping new members understand that they are not alone in their experiences and that these events are survivable and quite common. Thus, new members begin to feel a sense of support and membership, rather than isolation.

A volunteer counselor in a YWCA camp used the same sponsorship concept in recounting how she taught an 8-year-old girl to feel good about herself when she was not chosen by either team captain for a game of kickball. The child felt hurt until the counselor shared her own feelings in a similar experience.

Social workers also can help clients through discussions of empathy or self-disclosure. Being able to empathize and share the feeling of having, in some way, "been there" is a powerful therapeutic tool. This is not to say that social workers should pretend to have had experiences that they have not had. However, at some time everyone has experienced loss of control and been left out or left behind. These examples demonstrate the creative value of the kind of commitment one feels in sponsorship, and the use of those feelings to help someone feel more connected and in control.

Finding New Vehicles for Expression

Some Vietnam war veterans have used self-help groups to address problems that were not addressed by the Veterans Administration. Through his Army assignment in a psychiatric hospital, a man met many Vietnam veterans whose needs were not being met. Out of the frustration he felt in being unable to meet such needs, he formed an organization called Citizen Soldier, which helped Vietnam veterans upgrade their discharges and be examined for symptoms of Agent Orange exposure. Another Vietnam veteran channeled his anger about the war and the treatment of soldiers by forming a theater troupe, which wrote and performed plays about their experiences. The first group concentrated on social action; the second, on the expression of their feelings.

Moving from Reality to Fantasy

A woman joined a support group for the newly separated. Most of the women in the group were angry and overwhelmed by too little money and emotional support and too much responsibility for children, work, and home. The women liked each other, were helpful about day-to-day problem solutions, and found appropriate professional advice and consultation, but one of them mentioned that she got more anxious when she came to the group because she realized there was so much to do. She suggested that they take 15 minutes of each meeting and pretend that they were young, single, and responsible for no one but themselves. That plan worked so well that the group also decided to have an occasional session called "fantasies for the future" in which they focused on a time when they would have enough time, money, and a positive view of themselves and their lives. They decided to use these fantasies like daydreams to help with stress reduction or insomnia. These artificial, fantasy exercises worked beautifully (Toombs & Toombs, 1985).

Willingness to Advertise

In a recent metropolitan daily newspaper issue, 16 self-help and volunteer groups were listed, including everything from cancer and divorce support groups to groups for writers and business communicators. Perhaps agencies should advertise what needs they fill, what pains they soothe—in specific terms. In that way, they could see advertising as a way to clarify the community's definition of agencies. Why are more social workers not interviewed on talk shows or for newspaper columns about the problems that the social workers address in their agencies?

Self-help groups are not worried about self-aggrandizement or appearing entrepreneurial, because they have a clear message they want carried to those people they believe they can help. Several professionals who also are involved in self-help groups have said that they are comfortable advertising for their voluntary associations, but could not possibly advertise in the same way for their agency because it would sound as if they were doing it only to make money.

Borrowing a Vision for Creative Practice

Self-help and voluntary endeavors can lend vision to social work in many ways (Schwartz & Zalba, 1971). Basically, self-help groups comfort and/or mobilize their members. Members often identify passionately with the group's goals. The sense of mission fuels pride in belonging. A group often decreases members' anxiety by demonstrating problem commonality. Because someone in a group probably has experienced what another member is going through at the moment, the group can avoid problems endemic to working with certain groups. For example, it is harder for drug abusers or those with eating disorders to "con" others who have the same problems, or for adolescents or those people with chronic illnesses to feel isolated when they know others share their feelings and fears.

Self-help groups also can help social workers to broaden the range of what they consider helpful. What a person in need considers help may be quite different than what social work theories and values lead practitioners to conclude.

Often self-help groups point up the inability of social workers to accept limited goals and different values. Clients may set priorities with which social workers disagree. Serious professional consideration of these differences can be a fruitful source of innovation.

To get the maximum benefit from experiences with self-help groups, professionals need to pay attention to the unexpected, to what seems to clash with professional practice wisdom, and question that wisdom. Tension between such ideas is one source for creative thinking.

References

Anderson, D., & Anderson, I. (1981/82). The development of the voluntary movement in mental health. In J. Norbeck (Ed.), *The mental health yearbook, 1981/82* (Reprint; p. 15). Wokingham, England: Van Nostrand Reinhold.

Donovan, M. E. (1984). A sociological analysis of commitment generation in Alcoholics Anonymous. *British Journal of Addiction, 79*(14), 411–418.

Harmond, R. (1986). Robert Treat Paine. In W. Trattner (Ed.), *Biographical dictionary of social welfare in America* (pp. 583–585). New York: Greenwood.

Hoover, D. W. (1986). Jane Addams. In W. Trattner (Ed.), *Biographical dictionary of social welfare in America* (pp. 13–15). New York: Greenwood.

Katz, A. H., & Bender, E. I. (1976). *The strength in us: Self-help groups in the modern world.* New York: New Viewpoints.

Kerson, T. (1985). *Understanding chronic illness.* New York: Free Press.

Kerson, T. S. (1978). The social work relationship: A form of gift exchange. *Social Work, 23,* 326–327.

Klass, D. (1984/85). Bereaved parents and the Compassionate Friends: Affiliation and healing. *Omega: Journal of Death and Dying, 15*(14), 353–373.

Lewis, M. R. (1986). Emma Carola Woerishoffer. In W. Trattner, (Ed.), *Biographical dictionary of social welfare in America* (pp. 787–789). New York: Greenwood.

McDermott, F. E. (1982). Against a persuasive definition of self-determination. In H. Rubenstein & M. H. Bloch (Eds.), *Things that matter: Influences in the helping relationship* (pp. 77–88). New York: Macmillan.

Miller, H., & Philipp, C. (1983). The alternative service agency. In A. Rosenblatt & D. Waldfogel (Eds.), *Handbook of clinical social work* (pp. 779–791). San Francisco: Jossey–Bass.

Murray, J.A.H. (Ed.). (1971). *Oxford English dictionary* (compact ed.). Glasgow, Scotland: Oxford University Press.

Norman, W. H. (1983). Self blame in self-help: Differences in two weight-loss groups. *Journal of Applied Social Sciences, 8*(1), 137–153.

Schwartz, W., & Zalba, S. (Eds.). (1971). *The practice of group work.* New York: Columbia University Press.

Steinman, R., & Traunstein, D. M. (1984). Self-help organization in Edinburgh and two north-eastern American regions: Some initial comparisons. *International Journal of Comparative Sociology, 25*(3–4), 255–262.

Toombs, G. I., & Toombs, M. E. (1985). Dream appreciation: A personal growth group. *Group, 9*(2), 3–15.

VanderAvort, A., & VanHarberden, P. (1985). Helping self help groups: A developing theory. *Psychotherapy, 22*(2), 269–272.

Videka-Sherman, L., & Lieberman, M. (1985). Effects of self help and psychotherapy intervention on child loss: The limits of recovery. *American Journal of Orthopsychiatry, 55*(1), 70–82.

Westman, J. C. (1979). *Child advocacy.* New York: Free Press.

Experiencing Experience

The creative professional must be able to withhold judgment—to entertain the possibility that anomalies highlighted by inconsistencies between, for example, the reality of how self-help groups help and social work theories of help, may be the beginnings of new discoveries. Fascination with the unexpected—the anomaly—can trigger the creative process. The bridge between competence and creativity is constructed by intertwining different perspectives—different knowledge, ideas, values, feelings, and attitudes about the world. The issue is not whether a perspective is right or wrong, but rather the ability to entertain differing perspectives, such as that of the social worker and that of the self-help group.

Sensitivity to experience is a precondition of creativity. It is important for those interested in making the most of their creative potential to consider what they are most sensitive to in their experiences. This sensitivity could be a clue to where creative talents lie. What registers with greatest intensity—places, things, events, people, smells, feelings, or sounds? What does not register? The mind cannot manipulate or retrieve what has not been stored in it.

However, sensitivity alone does not guarantee creativity. As Wilson (1986) pointed out, "An extremely sensitive person may never learn how to use . . . [structures] or have the energy necessary for disciplined expressive action" (p. 38).

A person's attitude toward use of time also affects his or her ability to put experiences to creative uses. Those people who believe that "time is money" are unlikely to be able to let go of a problem, and to let it incubate.

Although some people can work creatively under pressure, for others the desire to solve a problem immediately can be detrimental if it rules out relaxation, condemns playfulness, and increases anxiety. Feeling rushed and controlled by time can limit one's patience and one's sensitivity to experience. A freedom from pressure is needed for playing with ideas and allowing them to incubate.

No one has been able to estimate the specific duration needed for any of the phases of creativity. The existence or duration of each phase can differ with the problem and with the individual. Referring to his discoveries about the movement of planets in the seventeenth century, Kepler (as cited in Edwards, 1987) noted that "eighteen months ago, the first dawn rose for me; three months ago, the bright day; and a few days ago, the full sun of a most wonderful vision; now nothing can keep me back. I let myself go in divine exaltation" (p. 223).

Most critics of the stage theory of creativity see it as mechanistic, and argue that creative work is a series of illuminations, combining several processes at the same time. They dispute the theory that one "Aha!" provides the insight. Rather, they see insight as preceded by a series of smaller, though not less significant "Aha!"s.

If this is the case, then the issue becomes how to get these recurrent small illuminations. In the chapter that follows, Maluccio suggests how client feedback can be a source of new and continuing insights for social workers.

Client feedback can add to the well of knowledge that is drawn upon in making creative connections. It also can supply a continuing source of new data and impressions that can help to recharge social workers' creative batteries.

Again, without a strong desire to solve a problem, one is likely to give up. Whether there are a series of small illuminations or one large illumination, periods of frustration, stalemate, and lack of progress are bound to occur. Maluccio's chapter shows how client feedback served him as a source of both ideas and inspiration.

Harold H. Weissman
Editor/Senior Author

References

Edwards, B. (1987). *Drawing on the artist within: A guide to innovation, invention, imagination, and creativity* (Fireside ed.). New York: Simon & Schuster.

Wilson, R. (1986). *Experiencing creativity.* New Brunswick, NJ: Transaction Books.

Client Feedback and Creativity in Social Work

Anthony N. Maluccio

Client feedback can be a source of creativity in social work—a vehicle for stimulating the creative impulse and helping to realize the creative potential that, according to some theorists, exists in every human being to some degree (Bruner, 1970). This chapter illustrates this theme through a discussion of a study on client feedback.

In a study on client feedback, clients' views on the process and outcome of clinical social work practice were explored, then compared with the views of their social workers (Maluccio, 1979).[1] The study focused on client and social worker expectations and their impact on helping activities, clients' and social workers' perceptions of the factors that influence the helping process and its outcome, and their satisfaction with the helping process and its outcome. The interviews included open-ended questions asked of all respondents and specific questions probing clients' or social workers' views, impressions, feelings, and perceptions. The same questions were asked of both clients and practitioners.

Following are selected findings from the study:

- There were major differences between the expectations of clients and those of social workers. For instance, clients expected help in solving concrete or discrete problems in their lives. Social workers, on the other hand, expected changes in personality structures or resolution of

---

This chapter is adapted in part from Maluccio, A. N. (1979). *Learning from clients*. New York: Free Press.

[1]The study was conducted at an urban, sectarian family service agency staffed by social workers with master of social work degrees (MSWs). It included a randomly selected sample of 33 clients from diverse socioeconomic backgrounds who had sought help primarily with marital or parent–child problems. See Maluccio (1979) for further study details.

underlying problems. In most cases, the discrepancies were dealt with successfully through the client–social worker contracting process.

• Clients preferred to have active social workers who would provide concrete services and suggestions or advice, whereas social workers stressed the value of talking and listening. Some of the social workers' methods, such as the emphasis on talking, were puzzling to clients. As one woman said, "I can't say she [the social worker] did a lot of counseling other than listening; I don't understand what listening had to do with counseling."

• In most cases, clients and social workers concurred that the agreed-upon goals had been achieved and that clients had benefited from the service. However, there were striking differences in their levels of satisfaction: in essence, most clients were satisfied with the outcome, whereas most social workers were dissatisfied or ambivalent. Furthermore, social workers usually were not aware of the positive impact that they had on clients. During the course of treatment, they rarely solicited feedback from clients about the outcome of their intervention.

• In general, clients presented themselves as autonomous human beings who are able to enhance their functioning through help received from the social worker, as well as their own internal strengths and social networks. On the other hand, social workers tended to view their clients as reactive, with continuing problems, underlying weaknesses, and limited potentialities. After treatment, social workers continued to express doubts about their clients' ability to cope with current life challenges or future crises.

• Finally, clients and social workers also differed in their perceptions of the major influences on the helping process and its outcome. Social workers attributed more importance to the client–social worker relationship. Clients emphasized the positive role of life experiences or events, and of social supports or other resources in their social environment. For example, one client said that she felt "so good" after a recent promotion that "I wanted to go on and live my life, even though my husband and I had decided to get a divorce." In contrast, her social worker reported that the "promotion was a mixed blessing. . . . It demonstrated that people thought highly of her, but it also put more pressure on her to perform."

The clients' more positive perceptions of life experiences and resources in their social networks were impressive. Among other aspects, clients highlighted "their satisfaction in participating in meaningful life activities;

the importance of rewarding work and appropriate job changes; the pleasure of giving of themselves to others through volunteer service; and, in short, the satisfaction of doing" (Maluccio, 1979, p. 188). Clients believed that they were better able to function and grow as they experienced their impact on the environment, and thus enhanced their competence and self-image (White, 1963).

Implications of the Study

As these findings suggest, and as other researchers also have shown (Mayer & Timms, 1970; Rees, 1979; Sainsbury, Nixon, & Phillips, 1982), clients and social workers have different perspectives on the helping process. This is not surprising; after all, clients and social workers bring to their encounter different roles, expectations, and frames of reference. However, the experience of listening to clients through a study such as this can awaken, or reawaken, various practice concerns. It can make more alive the phenomenon of interpersonal helping in general, and clinical social work in particular. Finally, it can lead social workers to question certain basic assumptions and redefine various basic concepts.

Closely examining client feedback can help social workers to respect people's strengths, resources, and the rich range of ways through which they cope with life challenges and environmental stresses. Social workers must realize "the value of viewing and treating clients as active and striving human beings rather than as creatures laden with pathology and bound by psychic and/or environmental determinism" (Maluccio, 1979, p. 201).

As Goldstein (1984) pointed out, when practitioners enter into a client's situation, they "become involved not with abstractions such as a diagnosis, a clinical category, or a statistic, but with the very real, perplexing, and often enigmatic problems of living" (p. xi). Although social workers should be guided by their preferred theories or practice modalities, they should not be constrained by over-preoccupation with them. They are, at best, incomplete representations of human realities and experiences.

Practitioners must learn to go beyond the emphasis on the client–social worker relationship as the major vehicle of help. In many cases the relationship is an important instrument; but often it is only one of the many variables leading to change in the client's functioning or situation. For example, the receptionist in the agency where the study was conducted played a significant therapeutic role. Client after client talked abut how helpful it was to talk with this woman while waiting for their appointment. Social workers were aware of the receptionist's contribution but did not fully appreciate it. In several cases, for instance, the clients reported that they were ambivalent or resistive about continuing in treatment, but did so because of the receptionist's encouragement (Maluccio, 1979).

Finally, social workers must learn to appreciate the triggering function of their intervention. In many cases in the study, it was evident that the social worker's actions (such as helping a client to work through feelings about a spouse or encouraging another person to change jobs) enabled the clients to mobilize resources in themselves or their environment. In effect, the social worker's input triggered a process of self-examination, growth, and change in the client:

> As some clients talked, there was the suggestion of an almost regenerative quality to their functioning; as they had the experience of coping more effectively and gaining some mastery over their environment, they went on to rekindle dormant capabilities and develop new coping patterns. (Maluccio, 1979, p. 189)

Using Client Feedback in Social Work

In his discussion of education for creativity in the sciences, Weisner (1967) observed that

> there must be encouragement and stimulation of imagination and unconventional interpretations of experience in general; this is particularly true in problem-solving activities. It is important, especially in childhood and early youth, that novel ideas and unconventional patterns of action should be more widely tolerated, not criticized too soon and too often. (p. 96)

In light of various deterrents to creativity in social work, such as "bureaucratization and rigidity of structure" (Rapoport, 1968, p. 17), Weisner's exhortation may be said to apply not only to children and youths, but also to social work practitioners, students, and educators. Social workers constantly must resist pressures to maintain the status quo or provide simplistic answers for complex problems.

As the study showed, client feedback can help practitioners to remain alert in this regard. Whatever methods are used to obtain it, client feedback is another valuable means of examining one's theories, monitoring one's practice and services, and improving one's skills. By being tuned into clients' perspectives, social workers are able to determine better which methods are effective, which approaches may need to be modified, and which assumptions on human behavior and clinical practice should be questioned. Social work educators also can learn what knowledge and methods must be taught to their students to prepare competent practitioners.

By listening to clients and by thinking about their particular perspectives, social workers are more likely to become engaged in the creative process in a way that leads to innovation—that is, to "contributions that have novelty and value" (Weisner, 1967, p. 93). In short, client feedback ultimately can enhance social work practice and service delivery, contribute to theory building, and enrich the education of future practitioners.

Enhancing Practice and Service Delivery

The systematic gathering of clients' views and impressions can serve as a means of monitoring social work practice and as an essential component of program evaluation and planning. The study of client feedback, for example, generated a number of practice implications in areas such as the role of client and social worker expectations in the initial phase of the helping process, the dynamic nature of client–social worker contracting, the need for systematic collaboration between formal and informal helpers, and the significance of social networks and support systems in the client's environment (Maluccio, 1979).

At the agency level, the "clients' views can help to maintain accountability, identify service gaps or deficiencies, influence policy formulation and decision-making, and initiate changes . . ." (Maluccio, 1979, p. 203). Researchers have demonstrated the value of client feedback in evaluating programs and implementing changes in service delivery in such settings as community mental health (Landsberg, 1977); family service (Dailey & Ives, 1978); and child welfare (Bush, Gordon, & LeBailly, 1977). Researchers also have shown that clients can play direct roles in service delivery, such as consumer advocates (Weisner, 1967), as resources in staff development programs, and as aides to other parents of children in foster care (Maluccio, Fein, & Olmstead, 1986).

Contributing to Theory Building and Research

Participation in the study inspired the creation of the new social work perspective of competence-centered social work practice (Maluccio, 1981, 1983, 1986). Competence-centered social work practice is a perspective that holds that the promotion of competence in human beings

227

is the overall goal of social work. This practice embodies a set of attitudes, principles, skills, and strategies designed to promote effective functioning in clients by

- focusing on their unique coping and adaptive patterns
- mobilizing their actual or potential strengths
- using their life experiences in a planned fashion
- emphasizing the role of natural helping networks
- using environmental resources as major instruments of help

The evolvement of this perspective can be traced directly to what the author heard and learned from clients in the client feedback study. The findings influenced him to delineate client strengths and potentials, life experiences, and environmental resources as the cornerstone of this emerging conception of social work practice. The fresh perspectives of clients can help social workers to raise new questions, formulate new hypotheses, or identify new concepts. Involving clients can help ensure that theory building in social work is grounded in human experience. In addition, clients can contribute to theory building by playing new roles in research. Current as well as former clients, for instance, might be involved as consultants in the formulation of research projects. They also might be employed to obtain the views of consumers of an agency's services, or as resource persons in data analysis and interpretation.

Involving clients in research roles is not common. In the client feedback study, for example, although the social workers were asked to examine the research design and methods, a few representative clients also could have helped to refine or clarify some of the research questions.

Enriching Social Work Education

Educators also can model the use of client feedback, not only by incorporating the results of related research in their teaching, but also by bringing clients into the classroom. This can be accomplished through the use of audiovisual aids and by inviting clients into the classroom to share their views in person. "Clients can serve as collaborators in formal and informal educational programs: through their special insights, they can help students and practitioners to appreciate the richness of the interpersonal helping process" (Maluccio, 1979, p. 206).

Above all, emphasis on client feedback can help to nurture the creative potential in teachers as well as students. It can reinforce the "basic habit of maintaining a skeptical, actively critical point of view toward all knowledge and opinion" (Weisner, 1967, p. 96). It can support "the longing or search for a new object or state of experience" that is the essence of the creative process (Arieti, 1976, p. 6). Finally, it can be an antidote for the pull toward rigid and doctrinaire thinking that sometimes emerges in our teaching and learning.

Learning from Clients

Social workers and educators can learn from clients through a mutually rewarding process in which both social workers and clients help each other to change and grow. Clients experienced satisfaction by participating in the feedback study. Many expressed surprise and pleasure that someone would be interested in their views. Other clients indicated that the research interviews helped them to review their experience with the agency and to appreciate or consolidate their gains. Their sense of competence and self-esteem evidently were enhanced through involvement in the study.

In contrast, social workers in the study tended to express doubts about their effectiveness—and, therefore, about their competence. Obtaining client feedback could have the additional benefit of making practitioners feel more competent, as they become more aware of the positive impact that they often have on their clients' functioning and situations. Their ego drive toward mastery would be promoted, and their capacity for creativity and innovation could then be more effectively mobilized (Rapoport, 1968, p. 13).

References

Arieti, S. (1976). *Creativity: The magic synthesis*. New York: Basic Books.

Bruner, J. S. (1970). *On knowing: Essays for the left hand*. New York: Atheneum.

Bush, M., Gordon, A. C., & LeBailly, R. (1977, September). Evaluating child welfare services: A contribution from their clients. *Social Service Review, 51*, 491–501.

Dailey, W. J., & Ives, K. (1978, April). Exploring client reactions to agency service. *Social Casework, 59*, 233–245.

Goldstein, H. (Ed.). (1984). *Creative change*. London: Tavistock Publications.

Landsberg, G. (Ed.) (1977). Consumer feedback research in a community mental health center. In W. Neigher, R. J. Hammer, & G. Landsberg (Eds.), *Emerging developments in mental health program evaluation* (pp. 367–375). New York: Argold Press.

Maluccio, A. N. (1979). *Learning from clients: Interpersonal helping as viewed by clients and social workers*. New York: Free Press.

Maluccio, A. N. (Ed.). (1981). *Promoting competence: A new/old approach to social work practice*. New York: Free Press.

Maluccio, A. N. (1983). Planned use of life experiences. In A. Rosenblatt & D. Waldfogel (Eds.), *Handbook of clinical social work* (pp. 134–154). San Francisco: Jossey–Bass.

Maluccio, A. N. (1986, September 13). Promoting social competence: Doing what we can do best. Paper presented at the NASW Clinical Social Work Conference, San Francisco, CA.

Maluccio, A. N., Fein, E., & Olmstead, K. A. (1986). *Permanency planning for children: Concepts and methods.* London and New York: Tavistock Publications.

Mayer, J. E., & Timms, N. (1970). *The client speaks: Working class impressions of casework.* Boston: Routledge and Kegan Paul.

Rapoport, L. (1968, June). Creativity in social work. *Social Services Review, 38,* 139–161.

Rees, S. (1979). *Social work face to face.* New York: Columbia University Press.

Sainsbury, E., Nixon, S., & Phillips, D. (1982). *Social work in focus.* Boston: Routledge and Kegan Paul.

Weisner, J. B. (1967). Education for creativity in the sciences. In J. Kagan (Ed.), *Creativity and learning* (pp. 92–102). Boston: Beacon Press.

White, R. W. (1963). *Ego and reality in psychoanalytic theory.* New York: International Universities Press.

Incubation

Because it is impossible to predict how long it will take to solve a problem, anxiety about whether one ever will solve it is to be expected. No one can say when one is saturated. Is feeling bloated with information the same as saturation? Is yet another round of client feedback needed? When should the next phase begin?

The time between saturation, or preparation, and illumination has been termed *incubation* (Edwards, 1987). Incubation can be a short or long period, from weeks to months or years. It is not known exactly how ideas are incubated.

There is general agreement that when an idea is incubated the creative process shifts from a conscious effort at problem solving to a more unconscious one. As Edwards (1987) explained, "At some point in the process, often when fatigue or frustration sets in, the problem is 'set aside' or 'given over.' The problem shifts to a different realm, so to speak, to develop or grow under conditions that are different than usual thinking" (p. 223).

Countless reports exist of people waking suddenly with the solutions to problems, of people playing golf or painting and getting insights into work problems, and of similar illuminations when people were not trying consciously to solve these problems. As Edwards (1987) found, it appears that people can think without consciously trying to:

> The brain, focused on the problem and saturated with information linked to language but arranged in the form of visually patterned images, reaches a point at which the complexity and density of information is greater than can be handled in usual ways.

> This point, I believe, is somehow "recognized," and makes itself known at a conscious (L-mode) level. Beset with anxiety, the person casts about for some way out of the dilemma. "What shall I do? Give up? What—walk away from all that work? Something has to be done about this!" Finally, weary and perhaps even despairing, the conscious mode says, in effect, "All right. You

find the answer." This deliberate "giving over" of the problem, I believe, puts it out of conscious control, thus enabling (or perhaps allowing is a better word) R-mode, which is capable of dealing with enormous complexity, to "think aside." In its spatial manipulation of complicated structures, R-mode "looks at" the densely packed information simultaneously and globally, searching for "fit," seeking meaning, until the parts fall into place and the key to the structural unity of the data—the organizing principle—is "seen" at last. (pp. 224–225)

Perkins (1981) gave a more mundane view of incubation. Instead of viewing incubation as extended unconscious thinking, he emphasized setting a problem aside and returning with a fresh eye for strengths and weaknesses. Time off provides physical refreshment, fruitful forgetting, losing a commitment to an ineffective approach and noticing previously overlooked clues (p. 57). In a sense, one recovers one's good judgment through incubation.

Guidelines for incubation are needed. It is likely that one does not "give over" a problem just once. In fact, there may be many "giving overs," or even a return to the earlier phases of creativity.

According to Edwards (1987), Norman Mailer has said that when he has a problem with plot or character in writing, he actually programs his unconscious, as is done in self-hypnosis, to come up with an answer when he returns to his writing (p. 225). Whether this mental programming actually is possible, or even required for everyone, is open to question.

A more plausible heuristic relates to understanding the process a person goes through in letting go of a problem temporarily but still remaining mentally connected to it. There is an element of playfulness involved—a temporary suspension of rules with the full knowledge that one will return to those rules.

During incubation a person's mind may begin to play with the material absorbed during saturation. During this mental play, ideas and objects are rearranged and recombined, new boundaries are set, and a new solution that had not been perceived before is created.

As Blatner and Blatner (1988) explained, "Nature has a wonderful way of motivating its organisms through pleasure. In order to ensure the accomplishment of essential tasks, eating is enhanced by taste, and procreation is motivated by sexual tension and enjoyment" (p. 35). If thinking is an essential task, then play also may enhance thinking because play is pleasurable.

It is important to distinguish between play and playfulness. Blatner and Blatner (1988) described this difference with an example: Play is riding a bike; playfulness is riding "no hands." The playfulness that occurs in the incubation phase depends on the innovator first knowing how to play.

Self-help groups provide a good example of the incubation process in action. Group members can create new rules, revise old ones, and act in ways that others might consider foolish—in effect, they are being playful with existing ideas. Innovations are tried and discarded, people get involved and drop out, groups are formed and disbanded, and new groups emerge.

This flux creates a good deal of experimentation and trial and error learning. In some ways, this process can be viewed as social incubation, where new arrangements and relationships are being tried out in socially unplanned ways.

Huizinga (1955) pointed out that "to dare, to take risks, to bear uncertainty, to endure tension . . . are the essence of the play spirit" (p. 51). The self-help group gives its members the chance to play with conventional roles and rules. It is the play spirit that allows one the freedom to incubate—to think differently, to relax the rules of logic.

If one is to overcome the inevitable anxiety of the saturation phase, patience, courage, and confidence also are required. Studies of creative people show that they possess these traits. Whether they possessed them to a lesser degree earlier, and their success at creative endeavors then reinforced these traits, is unclear. Yet, it is clear that emotions and motivation play a part in creativity.

Motivation drives the personality to bring order out of disorder, and provides the well from which resourcefulness and the desire to restore equilibrium are drawn. Self-esteem, the capacity for autonomous action, and tolerance for ambiguity are required for the motivation to create (Bromberg, 1987).

Writers with a broad perspective on creativity describe an interactive process of person, situation, and motivation. In the next chapter, Fabricant shows the importance of the environment in supporting creative endeavors. It usually is not enough that an individual be persistent, courageous, and determined. The communal feeling developed in the alternative sheltering services he describes played a crucial role in sustaining staff commitment, dedication, and creativity. Fabricant also points out the role social necessity, or social crises, play in spurring creative approaches. Perhaps social work, more than any other profession, operates in a milieu that cries out for innovation.

Harold H. Weissman
Editor/Senior Author

References

Blatner, A., & Blatner, A. (1988). *The art of play.* New York: Human Services Press.

Bromberg, E. (1987). *Creativity and social work.* Unpublished manuscript.

Edwards, B. (1987). *Drawing on the artist within.* New York: Simon & Schuster.

Huizinga, J. (1955). *Homo ludens.* Boston: Beacon Press.

Perkins, D. N. (1981). *The mind's best work.* Cambridge, MA: Harvard University Press.

Commitment, Perseverance, and Social Innovation: The Sheltering Movement

Michael Fabricant

Throughout the history of social work in the United States, social movements have played a pivotal role in focusing the attention and creative energy of the profession. These forces have reshaped basic assumptions and practices of social work on at least three occasions during the past century. During the 1890s (Settlement House), 1930s (Rank and File), and 1960s (Poor People's), social movements emerged in response to the dynamic interplay between environmental forces and the deteriorating condition of poor people. Although these movements were distinct, they did share a similar commitment to altering specific socioeconomic conditions. Additionally, they shared some of the basic characteristics of a "norm (or reform) oriented movement" as discussed by Smelser (1963):

> An attempt to restore, protect, modify or create norms in the name of a generalized belief. Participants may be trying either to affect the norms directly [for example, efforts of a feminist group to establish a private education system for women] or induce some constituted authority to do so [for example, pressures from the same group on a governmental agency to support or create a public co-educational system]. Any kind of norm—economic, educational, political, religious . . . may be the subject of such movements. (p. 302)

Each of the three movements emerged in response to social or economic turbulence. These shifts in the social order, such as the rising tide of homelessness, economic depression, and so forth, pinpointed the inability of traditional institutional arrangements to meet the expanding and/or changing nature of social need. Innovation became necessary.

235

Innovation is necessary again today, to help the ever-growing number of homeless people in the United States.

Homelessness is not a new phenomenon. Clearly, however, the magnitude of this social problem has grown substantially during the 1980s.

The confluence of five factors, including (1) federal disengagement from low and moderate income housing creation, (2) a systematic gentrification policy of low income housing destruction, (3) the reduction of entitlement grants, (4) the tightened eligibility criteria of many entitlement programs, and (5) the policy of deinstitutionalization without accompanying support services, have combined to affect a substantial rise in the number and shift in type of citizens who are becoming homeless.

This rapid shift in the structure and magnitude of homelessness has had substantial consequences for social service agencies. In general, agencies are unprepared to meet the needs of homeless people because of lack of flexibility, expertise, and resources.

Most social service agencies are organized to meet the needs of their clients through carefully delineated services. For instance, services usually are provided on-site between 9 a.m. and 5 p.m. Additionally, services are given to treat a single problem, such as substance abuse, disease, or delinquency. Finally, most problems are addressed and resolved after a number of client visits. However, the provision of services to homeless individuals and families requires greater flexibility. Clients may be unwilling or unable to visit an agency for services because of a range of experiences associated with living on the streets. Additionally, categoric definitions of assistance often will not meet the needs of the homeless citizens, who combine physical and emotional problems with material needs. The circumstances or threat of living on the streets creates an urgent need for immediate help. The "red tape" inherent to large public welfare agencies often makes this kind of help impossible.

Many social workers are not familiar with, nor have they been trained to understand, the range of emergency entitlements that may provide some form of relief to the homeless. Additionally, social workers and their agencies often have not developed the most basic skills necessary to locate a meal and short-term shelter at a reasonable price for a homeless person. Finally, many agency-based models of practice encourage an objectivity, a rationality, and a distancing from the client that is inappropriate for a group that is desperately isolated and in substantial need of intimate forms of human connection that offer hope.

Innovative Agency Alternatives

The initial push for change in this situation came from concerned citizens, many of whom subsequently have become regional and national leaders in the movement to shelter and house homeless people. This emergent leadership shared certain basic characteristics. To begin with, they acted because of a sense of mission. In effect, they could no longer accept what Mitch Snyder described in a December, 1986 Washington, DC, speech as "the horror of human bodies littered all over the street like so much garbage." Their individual responses to the problem often were framed by their own professional or personal skills. Consequently, lawyers attempted to resolve these issues through the courts. Alternatively, those trained in counseling or social work frequently attempted to create shelter space that was an alternative to the squalid conditions of most public shelters.

Five innovative alternative agency administrators were interviewed, and their comments are provided to provide insight into creative, effective ways of dealing with homeless people. They are (1) Rita Zimmer, executive director of Women In Need, New York, New York; (2) Tilly Schuster, of the Henry Street Settlement and president of the board of trustees of Women In Need; (3) Peggy Schorr, former clinical director of Community Access, New York, New York; (4) Colleen McDonald, director of Olivieri Center, New York, New York; and (5) Joan Driscoll, director of the Elizabethan Coalition to House the Homeless, Elizabeth, New Jersey. Zimmer (personal communication, April 15, 1986) noted

> I started out on the street with a big glass bottle to collect money for homeless women and children. The money was used to acquire shelter beds. After a while a church stepped in and offered permanent space for a shelter. It was a thrilling moment but as you can see our beginnings were modest.

Welcoming Homeless People

There are a number of problems plaguing social workers' attempts to help homeless people. Governmental budgets provide only woefully inadequate quantities of housing, shelter beds, food and other services, severely undermining practitioners' and agencies' efforts to meet the needs of homeless people.

Just as critically, the often rigid structure and delivery of social services has deflected the poor away from vital services. Rigid intake criteria; excessive documentation demands; categoric definitions of service; cold, impersonal, and on occasion, hostile responses to expressions of need too often characterize the homeless person's experience with highly bureaucratic forms of social services, such as welfare and large municipal shelters. These standard responses to critical need ultimately deny or delay the delivery of service and thus further sap the hope, self-esteem, and strength of homeless people.

In response to these problems, innovative providers began to develop and offer services that provide an alternative to bureaucratic prescriptions. In contrast to the constricted choices and lack of hospitality of the bureaucracy, alternative agencies are organized to develop new programs that welcome and strengthen homeless people. An environment of hospitality is a characteristic feature of the innovative shelters, apartment programs, and advocacy organizations working with homeless people. Schuster (personal communication, September 13, 1986) described the importance of providing such an environment:

> Part of what has kept our program fresh and creative is being able to keep perspective on what is important. For instance, we are overloaded with paperwork and state regulations. But when a woman walks in the front door we stop everything and make our best effort to mobilize resources to meet her need. You just have to be able to truly meet and encounter people as they enter the program. Otherwise you've lost half the battle before you've begun.

Schorr (personal communication, November 19, 1986) put it this way:

> When someone walks in the door, they can't be treated with disrespect. When they walk in you almost have to visualize their being somewhere, living somewhere and having quality in their lives. You have to immediately struggle to see it so they can see it and also begin to connect to you. That's the key. Because if they see that you're looking at them as a stinking lump of flesh then that's the way they'll feel and respond.

Narrowing the Distance

Homeless people are isolated and therefore need human encounters and relationships. The technical, rational models of social service delivery emphasize social objectivity, expert distancing, and hierarchy in client–social worker relationships. However, alternative social agencies serving homeless people have found that it is particularly critical to narrow the distance between the social worker and the client. Only in this way can the alienation, distrust, and isolation that are characteristic of life on the streets be penetrated. As Schön (1982) suggested, it is critical to seek out connections to the client's thoughts and feelings. Just as important, a sense of the homeless person's fundamental equality and worth must be incorporated into the practice relationship. Each of these features of a more reflective practice are necessary ingredients for enabling homeless people to regain a sense of control over their own lives. McDonald (personal communication, September 8, 1986) explained that

> homeless people have a real sense of hierarchy—they've been defined by everybody and everyone reinforces that they're at the bottom. That distance between them and everybody else has isolated them. I firmly believe that strengths don't emerge and change can't occur when people are isolated. It's therefore so important that the distance and sense of hierarchy with homeless people be bridged.

Schorr (personal communication, November 19, 1986) agreed:

> My experience working with homeless people is that narrowing the distance between them and me offers so much opportunity for creative clinical work. When you're feeling, as homeless people do, that you're at the bottom then you're also feeling low levels of [self-]esteem. I think this reduces the probability that they will contribute in any serious way to a relationship with a social worker. It's my job to bridge the gap to contribute to an increase in esteem. Only in this way will they be willing to risk in the relationships and will their talents begin to surface. These are prerequisites for identifying and building upon the homeless persons' many areas of strength.

To narrow the distance between the social worker and homeless person, the social worker must invest enough time in the relationship. The availability of this time depends greatly on the size of the social worker's caseload, or the breadth of his or her responsibility. Therefore, relatively low staff/client ratios are emphasized, and where possible, enforced by alternative agency administrators:

> We are very insistent upon low client/staff ratios and really attempt to control the size of a caseload. We try to limit the caseload to one worker for every fifteen clients. We find that when we exceed these ratios it becomes very difficult for the worker to build on client strengths or even dialogue with homeless people. The lower ratios allow more time for solutions to emerge from the process and the process here is very important because many homeless people wind up on the street as a result of systemic and personal processes. It is therefore very important that alternative constructive processes be allowed to develop. The alternative is that the worker is reduced to some form of crisis management which in the long run accomplishes very little. (Zimmer, personal communication, April 15, 1986)

Sharing the Power

There are a variety of approaches that have been developed by alternative social service agencies to narrow distance, build on client strengths and empower homeless people. However, the unifying theme of these approaches is that each of these agencies has surrendered some part of the "turf" to homeless people. This democratic restructuring may be as organizationally modest as offering greater equality in practice relationships, or as substantial as the development of new governing bodies that involve homeless people. Only by creating the opportunity for homeless people to shape their present environment can they develop the necessary self-esteem and learn the skills needed to regain control of their lives outside these sheltered settings. This sharing of power is an expression of respect that gives value to the homeless people's experiences and opinions. Just as important, this approach offers homeless people choices, and thus some measure of control over their lives. The dynamic relationship between the democratization of structure and the empowerment of homeless people is described in the following statements:

> People function better if they are an involved and vital part of their environment. For instance . . . we trained many clients on how to live in an apartment. This training was initially done by staff. Over time, however, more and more of this training was done by clients. You could almost see the jump in their sense of esteem. In effect we took some of their strengths, gave them an opportunity to put them to work, and not only did they do a marvelous job; they built on these strengths. (Schorr, personal communication, November 19, 1986)

> We have a self-governance structure. The women have an opportunity to change everything from the content of the meals to the services. They truly have a voice in every facet of agency life. At times we as staff may have to identify when we are pressed against our limits and really can't make changes immediately. . . . But at least we go through the process and together attempt to find an answer to the problem. It is through processes like this that many women learn that what they have to say is important and that they can make a difference. (Zimmer, personal communication, April 15, 1986)
>
> What we're trying to offer the homeless are choices. It's important that the choices available be explicitly identified. Too often the women I work with feel that everyone else or someone else is controlling their lives. By offering choices some of the control is placed back in the hands of these women. The area of choice may be as modestly defined as accepting or denying certain realities associated with being homeless and understanding the conse-

quences of denial or acceptance. The important thing is that only by seeing choices and therefore control can we contribute to a process of empowerment. (McDonald, personal communication, September 8, 1986)

The alternative structure and content of these services has created a demand for a distinctive work force and recruitment process. The kind of process that has been created to identify able candidates is outlined by Schuster (personal communication, September 13, 1986):

It is particularly difficult to recruit people for the kind of practice being developed in this agency. To begin with, during recruitment we ask a lot of personal questions. The candidate's answers to these questions and personal qualities that may surface during the interview are balanced against formal educational criteria. For instance, we want to know about their values, temperament and flexibility. We also want to know how open they are to this population and how willing they are to acknowledge what they don't know. Finally and perhaps most importantly, we need to see if they have an appreciation for the difficulties experienced by homeless people.

From Agency to Community

As homeless persons begin to feel they are an essential part of the life of the agency, and as social workers are recruited not only to sustain this involvement but to find new and creative ways to build upon it, the agency gradually is transformed into a community. Four elements critical to the first stage of this transition already have been identified: (1) hospitality, (2) narrowing of distance, (3) a sense of control, and (4) the ability to make choices within the agency environment. However, the transition from living within an agency of mutual respect and concern to a community involves an array of factors that ultimately congeal about a depth of interpersonal bonding that is both more varied and risky. Both the staff and the homeless persons in these agency/communities must feel secure enough to take risks, to create new ways to transform their daily experience and push against their present limitations. As McDonald (personal communication, September 8, 1986) said,

Staff needs to be supported in their development of ideas. They have to be willing to take the risk of expressing crazy creative ideas and not feel that their ideas will be stolen or that they will have their legs shot out from underneath them. They must be able to present ideas and leave with dignity and a continued sense of possibilities.

Clients shouldn't be forced to do things they don't want to do. This place binds staff with residents, residents to residents and staff to staff. These new relationships allow each of us collectively to see possibilities in each other than individually we would never have seen.

In social work agencies, there has been a trend toward the development of highly specialized or focused services. In general, a single agency will respond only to a particular client need. The agency's interest may be in the client's legal problems, drug dependence, lack of a job, or absence of shelter. Present funding patterns and the training of many professional staff members tend to reinforce this highly specialized, and often fragmented, response to human need.

A richer and far better multidimensional response of alternative agencies for the homeless is outlined by Driscoll (personal communication, September 25, 1986):

> Homeless people have more than sheltering needs. They have critical health problems, are often illiterate and frequently families do not have the necessary child care to do an effective housing search. Consequently we created a literacy training program with volunteers, a health program in conjunction with [a] hospital, and are in the midst of attempting to develop a child care center. These new programs and others which will follow were not created out of thin air. They represent an attempt by this agency to meet needs as they are articulated by homeless people.

Learning from Past Mistakes

There are a range of problems that have and will continue to plague empowerment service agencies. As has already been noted the content of these services depends on low staff/client ratios. However, given fiscal realities and the swelling homeless population, agencies may have little control over these ratios in the future. Consequently, social workers may be forced into forms of crisis management. Increasingly, agencies will be forced to provide empowerment services and also to meet the daily demands of government and of those homeless citizens who remain in crisis.

The initial vision, energy, and sense of mission of agency leadership and staff may erode over time. The combination of new demands and less time can drain their momentum and sense of direction. This point is important particularly because it was just this array of factors that undermined similar community-based programs in the 1960s and 1970s.

Additionally, growth may pose a threat to these programs. These agencies may no longer have the capacity to function as an alternative to bureaucratic agencies if they require similar centralizing organizational structures to manage their new tasks. Again, this was the fate of similar programs 2 decades ago.

Clearly, if the integrity of empowerment service programs is to be retained, then these agencies and their leadership must learn a number of vital lessons from their predecessors. Solving the problems of homeless persons depends on it.

A balance must be struck between the growth of the agency and the need to maintain the communal facets of its leadership. The absence of such a balance will result in many losses, the most critical of which may be the creative or innovative impulse. As Schuster and Zimmer (personal communication, April 14, 1986) pointed out, respectively:

> After the passion and zeal subsides because, in part, you're called upon to do so much, the day to day reality begins to set in. You begin to deal with your own limits and the limits of the program. It's at that point that you have to create a balance between being able to say you can't meet the universe of needs of all people . . . thus avoiding burnout [and] at the same time continuing to struggle to find new and better ways to provide service.

> As we continue to grow it is very tricky to achieve a balance between a structure that holds things together but also offers an opportunity to be flexible and spontaneous. We haven't found any answers to this question. As we continue to grow, we continue to experiment and know that if the agency is to remain on the cutting edge of meeting the needs of homeless people then agencies must remain aware of this tension and continue to struggle with it.

References

Smelser, N. (1963). *The theory of collective behavior.* Glencoe, IL: Free Press.

Schön, D. (1982). *The reflective practitioner.* New York: Basic Books.

Summation of Part Four

Alternative agencies and self-help groups offer many lessons in innovation and creativity. The creation of voluntary groups is a quintessential American trait—termed the "civic religion" of American democracy by De Tocqueville in the early nineteenth century. No one can deny the creative energies these groups have loosed over the years, or the wealth of information on social creativity they provide.

Self-help groups are instruments fashioned "to exploit powerful principles of personal change and reform" (Powell, 1975, p. 756). In a sense, they provide social workers with a form of client feedback, often revealing different sources of motivation for change than those that may be expected. Sensitivity to the unexpected is one of the characteristics of creative people. Powell offered an example:

> In Alcoholics Anonymous patients admit that they are powerless over alcohol and that their lives have become unmanageable. They believe that a power greater than themselves can restore them to sobriety. This view generally conflicts with the clinical view that powerlessness must be overcome and that the only person who can overcome it is the client himself or herself. Certainly, most clinical treatment does not begin with having the client admit powerlessness. Yet as Gregory Bateson suggests about this organization:
>
> > Implicit in the combination of these steps is the extraordinary—and I believe correct—idea: the experience of defeat not only serves to convince the alcoholic that change is necessary; it is the first step in that change. To be defeated by the bottle and know it, is the first "spiritual experience." The myth of self-power is thereby broken by the demonstration of a greater power. . . . Philosophically viewed, the first step is not a surrender; it is simply a change in epistemology, a change in how to know about a personality in the world. (p. 764)

The idea that creative innovators are gifted people is limited. The great innovators all had experiences from which they derived new ideas or connections. Their ability to make use of these experiences often is what distinguishes them from their less innovative colleagues.

For example, the terms *system* and *system boundary* refer to the interconnection of a set of individuals, groups, and organizations related to a particular problem or concern. Although it often is possible to map out these interconnections, the map essentially is static. Thus, the admonition to think systemically may be of limited use in getting new ideas for solving problems. Alternative organizations and self-help groups expand the interconnections—they expand the playing field, the players, the rules, and the goals. In essence, they create a "new ball game," a new system.

Social movements can provide a fresh perspective on troublesome problems. However, although creative, some of the new systems can be destructive and should be resisted vigorously. The horror of mass murder at Jonestown, Guyana, began as the People's Temple, a more or less traditional, religiously sponsored grassroots community organization.

Nevertheless, novel connections between previously disconnected elements are central to invention. Creativity partly is related to having intuitive and imaginative powers. Yet intuition and imagination alone do not produce creativity—they work with and through experience. A steady diet of the same type of experience and the same kind of explanatory explanations of experience ultimately can be enervating to a person's creative powers.

To ensure a variety of experiences in social work, a more open profession is needed—one that accepts uncertainty, tolerates questioning, and checks its assumptions among others—a profession that structures itself to maintain a creative balance between continuity and change.

Crucial supports for innovation are less likely to occur in a profession that models itself solely after professional forms and structures that give overriding emphasis to credentials and territorial concerns. These pursuits result in a closed profession and closed professional minds.

A professional culture that is open to multiple sources of information must be nurtured. An open profession could have standards, credentials, values, and preferred ways of operation. Yet an open profession would not try to monopolize service to people in need—an undesirable, impossible goal.

The hallmark of an open profession is its stance toward the world. What Stuart reminds us was said of settlements in earlier times could well be said of an open profession: "It is an attitude of the mind, not a building or even a program" (p. 319); "it doesn't approach a neighborhood with preconceived notions" (p. 324); and "it is an orientation toward doing whatever is necessary to improve a situation" (p. 325).

Fabricant's and Kerson's chapters remind the reader how important the roles of passion and emotion are in "doing whatever is necessary." The social work profession would be wise to mold passion, rather than squelch it. Alternative groups, agencies, and programs provide a functional outlet for these feelings.

The chapters in Part Four describing the profession's involvement with self-help groups, social movements, and the consumer movement also offer a structure for institutionalized self-criticism. Landau (1973) has called for the institutionalization of criticism—a process that

> require[s] strong alternatives, rival programs, adversary plans . . . [and] permit[s] policy makers, planners, and program analysts [by having bases of comparison] to protect against undue specialization, the trained incapacity to think, premature closure of a field, ideology disguised as fact, and Gresham's law of decision making. (p. 542)

Landau's ideas suggest that creativity and innovation will be undercut without a structure of self-criticism in a profession. The social work profession is fortunate to have had a long relationship with a variety of social movements and self-help groups, as well as an interest in client feedback. As an addition to systematic program evaluation, these movements and groups provide a means of comparison, a way to spot errors, as well as ideas and directions for innovation. For those who aspire to make the transition from being competent to being both competent and creative, positioning themselves in an organizational and professional milieu open to criticism is important. Such milieus support creativity and innovation through their willingness to pay attention to discrepancies, anomalies, and contradictions in their work. If the capacity to improvise is indeed one of the key links between individual competence and creativity, then much of what transpires in self-help groups can be viewed as social improvisation. From a societal point of view, this type of improvisation is important. It may demarcate the link between the competent and the creative society—a society that encourages individual creativity.

Harold H. Weissman
Editor/Senior Author

References

Landau, M. (1973, November/December). On the concept of a self-correcting organization. *Public Administration Review, 33*, 533–542.
Powell, T. (1975). The use of self-help groups as supportive reference communities. *American Journal of Orthopsychiatry, 45*, 756–764.

PART FIVE
A Creative Approach to an Innovative Career

Playing While Working: Creative Planning for an Innovative Career

Harold H. Weissman

The play's the thing, Wherein I'll catch the conscience of the King.

—William Shakespeare, Hamlet

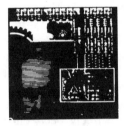

There is still much to be learned about creativity and innovation. However, there is a base of knowledge from which practical guides on achieving a creative, innovative career can be drawn.

There are at least 100 different definitions of creativity. Some definitions focus on the unique process of creative thought, others on the novel product created. Here, *creativity* refers to the capacity to produce unique ideas or products. *Creative capacity* is the result of the mix of traits and talents that activate a process of thought or action. In this process, synthesis, intuition, and imagination combine with logic, reason, and analysis to produce novel solutions or actions. There also are many different definitions of the process of innovation. However, there is agreement that new inventions or discoveries become innovations only if and when they are accepted by others. Innovations can be developed through trial and error and linear, logical thinking. As such, they are innovations, but not a product of creative thinking. Innovations also can be produced through a creative process that combines logical, convergent reasoning with more divergent perceptual reasoning processes.

In reality, it is unlikely that anyone will be innovative without also being somewhat creative. Where does the problem solving that intelligent people are capable of end, and creative problem solving begin? The line between the two processes is murky.[1]

Usually, one attacks a problem with ordinary, sequential logic. If logic does not provide a solution, then the problem may not have a single cause, or may not be defined adequately. More divergent thought processes may be required.

According to Hermann (as cited in Gordon & Zemke, 1986), "The trick to unlocking creative potential . . . is not to try and shove everyone further toward intuitive modes of thought, but to teach people how to tap into their less-preferred modes, whichever those might be. Balance (with logic) not just intuition is the key" (p. 39). Seeing creativity as related solely to idea generation has led to the emphasis on intuition. Yet many innovative processes, such as the design and development of ideas, require both logical and analogical thought processes.

It is unlikely that anyone is completely logical or completely intuitive. When someone is referred to as creative, what is meant is that they have a greater capacity to move freely between divergent and convergent modes of thought.

Can people be taught to move freely between the two modes? The argument among the experts revolves not about whether creativity can be taught, but whether people trained in thinking techniques will be more creative on the job. In business terms, can a dollar and cents figure be put on the results? Is it financially worth the effort?

In addition, the notion of the centrality of thought processes for understanding creativity has been disputed:

> The essence of invention isn't process but purpose. Purpose is what organizes the diverse means of the mind to creative ends. First and most simply, on many occasions people try to be inventive as such. Scientists seek new phenomena and theories, artists strive to develop fresh styles. It's odd that this has been so overlooked as an important explanation for creative accomplishment. (Perkins, 1981, p. 106)

---

[1]Fruitfully challenging and crossing frames of reference are not such difficult or exceptional matters as one might suppose. Events of this sort can occur in many quite straightforward ways. Processes like noticing, which do most of their work within major frames of reference, constantly cross smaller frames of reference inside them. Processes like reasoning and understanding, whose main business, it might be said, is maintaining coherent and consistent frames of reference, can both detect anomalies and coordinate different frames. Extraordinary invention really does borrow the means of mundane thought (to notice, to remember, to associate, and to choose) (Perkins, 1981, pp. 98–99).

There is no definitive answer to these questions and disagreements. However, based on laboratory testing with control groups, there is sound evidence that those people trained in creative thinking and problem solving are superior in analytical thinking, in divergent thinking, and in ability to suspend judgment and generate options. Gordon and Zemke (1986) concluded that

nobody is promising that a little training will turn Dagwood Bumstead into Albert Einstein. . . . We know that creativity isn't like IQ. . . . It isn't even correlated very highly with IQ. [Yet] Dagwood Bumstead is naturally creative to some degree. Training in certain techniques can make him more so. . . .

Training can do three things. . . . You can help people discover their own creativity—how creative they really can be. You can help them remove the blocks they've put in their own way. And you can teach them creative-thinking skills; because creative thinking can be a learned skill instead of a talent. (p. 41)

Which of the creative training techniques or methodologies work best? Gordon and Zemke (1986) described the following techniques: lateral thinking, question lists, brainwriting and brainstorming, visualization, morphological analysis, synectics, or forced fit/forced relationships.[2] Research indicates that a key distinction is whether the problem calls for a resourceful solution (something is broken and needs fixing) or an original solution, in which a whole new approach is needed (pp. 32–33).

People skilled in visualization seem to do better with the problems needing original solutions. Those trained in brainwriting seem to do better with resourceful solutions. The balance in succeeding with either type of problem is achieved with brainstorming (Gordon & Zemke, 1986). At this point, however, each of the methodologies have dedicated proponents who can present anecdotal evidence of the method's success (Gordon & Zemke, 1986, p. 41).

The ability to be creative and come up with novel ideas or actions also is related to factors other than cognitive skill or talent. Personality, values, beliefs, motivation, and situational and historical factors also play roles. *Satori*, the Japanese word for creativity, implies a broad perspective— insight and enlightenment are the results of practice and patience.

Studies of people defined by others as creative show that these people are highly productive. Their biggest accomplishments, it seems, come after years of trying, rather than from a divine spark as viewed by Dante.

---

[2]See Gelfand (1988) for examples and exercises related to using a variety of these training techniques.

The ability to persevere, to be challenged by complexity, and to take risks are important traits.

Yet the organizational context affects those within it. Studies of creative people show them to be confident and persevering. Broad (as cited in Edwards, 1987) said, "The Eureka myth overlooks the long period of gestation for breakthroughs. Even in the vagueness and confusion, before the light comes, people know something is there, but they're not quite sure what it is yet" (p. 222). An oppressive environment lowers the odds on the gestation of creativity and innovation.

Organizational or situational factors such as a minimum of red tape, acceptance of failure, open communication, and sufficient resources, among others, were related to highly creative productivity. Obstacles to creativity were noted as too much control, tight deadlines, lack of boundary crossing, and lack of rewards (Gordon & Zemke, 1986, p. 41).

It has been theorized that there are different kinds of intelligence. Experts are debating whether there also may be different kinds of creativity. A different mix of traits and abilities may be required in different spheres of activity. For example, one theory describes seven different kinds of intelligence or "know-how," including the body control displayed by athletes and dancers, musical talent, interpersonal skills such as being able to read another's feelings, as well as more academic abilities such as mathematical and logical reasoning (Goleman, 1988, p. C11).

If so, then it is possible to consider that the usual list of traits and attributes—tolerance for ambiguity, ability to suspend judgment, access to intuition, and so forth—is limited. Certainly, great innovators, deeply involved in a social process of getting ideas tried out and accepted, as well as persevering in the face of resistance, must be perceptive about other people's feelings and concerns. The focus of creativity training may have to be expanded. The present limited focus may to an extent explain the current inability to predict carryover of creativity training into on-the-job situations.

Importance of Creativity

Is social work an art? As Rapoport (1968) said, art is a perceptual, rather than a conceptual, medium. Art is a representation of the artist's feelings.

> The artistic process involves [more or less] controlled purposeful activity which is guided by various aesthetic laws and principles. The end result of this process is the artistic product. In social work we can speak only of a

process and not a product, though we can state that the process should lead to some satisfying result. (pp. 141–142)

The effectiveness of services cannot be judged primarily on the basis of aesthetic principles, nor are social work processes primarily perceptual.

Is there a place for artistry—the use of imaginative and intuitive modes of expression and thought—in social work? Absolutely. Nevertheless, one still can find in the literature arguments over social work as either science or art (Davis, 1988; Nagel, 1988; Thayer, 1988). What usually is missed in these discussions is that there is a good deal of artistry (creative leaps) in science and a good deal of science (systematic rigor) in art.

All professions are involved in a constant process of shifting substantive ideas and practices, derived through artistry, into a more routinized craftsmanship. That is one of the functions of a profession. However, a narrow *empiricism* —the belief that if something cannot be verified immediately, it cannot be used—is in error. All ideas need development. Often, this development comes only through trial and error.

Social workers abdicate their responsibilities if they deal only with something that can be proven easily or definitely. Social work is concerned with problems that are complex, and probably not permanently solvable in a democratic society—crime, addiction, neglect. Rittel and Webber (1977) called these problems "wicked" because they do not have a finite beginning or end, or one definable cause or solution (p. 135).

Partial resolution of wicked problems sometimes can be achieved by perceiving the problems in a different way, from a fresh approach that transcends dead-end, stalemated positions and finds different challenges or opportunities. Artistry is needed in dealing with wicked problems.

In all professions, there are zones of practice in which there are no clear solutions, based on established knowledge and principles. Therefore, all professionals must be able to improvise, to come up with innovative or creative solutions. All discussions of the art of medicine, the art of psychiatry, the art of social work hinge on this fact:

> Engineering technologies, powerful and elegant when judged from a narrowly technical perspective, turn out to have unintended and unpredicted side effects that degrade the environment, generate risk, or create excessive demands on scarce resources. . . . [A social worker] may discover that his client is unwilling to listen to his attempts to describe the situation's uniqueness and uncertainty, insisting on an expert answer that specifies one right way. He will be caught, then, in a thicket of conflicting requirements: a wish to keep his job, a feeling of professional pride in his ability to give

usable advice, and a keen sense of his obligation to keep his claims to certainty within the bounds of his actual understanding. (Schön, 1987, p. 6)

Social workers operating at any level—client, organization, or policy—are troubled by indeterminate zones of practice when there is uncertainty, uniqueness, and value conflict. For example, many situations practitioners deal with embody value conflicts; for example, the rights of the parents versus the rights of the child. Technical problem solving depends on the prior construction of a well-formed problem (Schön, 1987). When there is uncertainty about just what the problem is, the mechanics of diagnosis fall short. Artistry or creativity is required.

Talented social workers must be talented improvisers. Resources almost always are scarce. Knowledge of many problems is limited. Policies and programs, no matter how well conceived, cannot completely fit the complexities and exigencies of life. Great improvisers make novel, creative connections.

More important than the argument about whether social work is a science or an art, is the question of whether there are artistic principles that can guide social workers as they improvise (England, 1986). There certainly are techniques of creative thinking that can be taught, but these do not comprise a practice theory of improvisation.

A plausible hypothesis is that different combinations of intuition and logic are needed to improvise at different stages of the knowledge development process. Intuition probably predominates in the generation of novel ideas and logic in their verification (Figure 1).

Bell (1984) suggested that improvisation at work is aided when attention is paid to quality.

While the urge to create characterizes all of us, some individuals in the workplace are accorded special status for their skills, imagination and accomplishments. . . . These individuals enhance the intrinsic rewards of the work experience of others (by their improvisations), serve as symbol makers for the occupational group, and increase the feeling of community by means of their presence and participation (as well as stimulate others to emulate or outdo them). (Jones, Moore, & Snyder, 1988, p. 243)

In the above sense of an aesthetic appreciation of the quality of work, there are similarities between social work and art. Improvisers have an aesthetic sense of quality. This sense affects both them and others, organizationally and professionally.

Another related issue about innovation needs to be scrutinized before summing up the case for promoting creativity in individuals and in the

Figure 1. Knowledge Development and Cognition

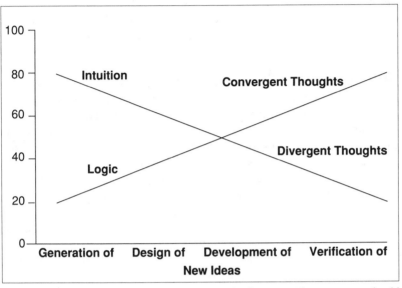

The graph and percentages in Figure 1 are meant to be illustrative. The percentages should not be taken literally. Similarly, it is likely that dichotomies such as quantitative versus qualitative research and science versus art do not represent logic versus intuition, but rather differential use of the two at different times.

profession. This is the myth of the inevitability of the emergence of ideas. Some theorists believe that the locus of creativity is in a group, rather than in an individual. Others share Plekhanov's (as cited in Gruber, 1983) view that "like a locomotive, history has its inevitable course; the individual's role is to get on board" (p. 4). Ideas are socially conditioned and determined, and as such their emergence is inevitable.

In this view, individual creativity and artistry are less important than social or organizational forces. Thus, the focus of efforts should be on creating a milieu that promotes creativity. Yet, downgrading the importance of individuals and focusing on the social environment leaves open the question of why certain inventions did not appear when conditions seemed conducive. The Aztecs had a highly developed civilization, including commerce between distant cities, but never invented the wheel. The Chinese invented gunpowder, had armies and engaged in warfare, but never invented the gun (Gruber, 1983).

255

Neither a crude social determinism nor a biological determinism is useful. The creativity of the individual social worker is extremely important in making advances in the field. Likewise, the milieu in which social workers practice will have a great impact on the way creative capacities are utilized.

Enhancing Individual Creativity

Rapoport noted the crucial distinction between artistry and creativity. She defined *creativity* as intuitive thought or action that is innovative and that forges something new, such as a new therapeutic approach or a novel way of delivering services. By *artistry*, Rapoport meant the ingenious and imaginative use of what is known. She believed that social workers are called upon constantly to apply their knowledge and skill artistically and that this artful application is what distinguishes a profession.

It is necessary to maintain the distinction between artistry and creativity. Creativity is a precious resource about which much more knowledge is needed. It is more likely that this learning will occur if the words creativity and artistry are not used synonymously, even though there is undoubtedly a high degree of overlap in skills or capacity.

Is the artistic imagination that makes novel connections between what is known different than the creative imagination that forges something new? Or is the distinction merely one of focus—of trying to do something new, as opposed to trying to do the usual in a better way? Or is the only distinction a semantic one?

Is the difference between creativity and artistry more one of motivation? Rapoport (1968) suggested that the creative impulse results from a strong desire to bring order out of chaos—to understand, to complete, and to order. The artistic motivation may be a totally different one.

Although in this study a sharp distinction between the artistic and the creative has not been drawn, finding the answers to these questions is important. The answers are more likely to be found if when, where, and why the term creative applies is examined. At present, the term is used much too loosely.

Creativity and competence in this text are viewed as a continuum. The focus here has been on the transition area where one trails into the other. Not much has been said about the creative far end of the continuum.

Many experts contend that there are levels of creativity. Gardner (1982) suggested that "The incidence of extreme creative behavior is so unusual that perhaps it can occur only under very special circumstances . . . that conjunction of genetic, familial, motivational and cultural factors which must all be present if the efforts of an Einstein, a Darwin, or a Beethoven are to come to fruition" (pp. 356–357).

The implication is that these geniuses do something different, although no one can prove it. What seems apparent is that their powers of concentration and memory are uniquely intertwined. These people have an organizing image or themata in their area of expertise, through which information and ideas constantly are sifted and rearranged. Their focus on this theme and the problems related to it is obsessive. Gardner (1982) found that

> the individual experiences a strong, almost primordial tie to the subjects of his curiosity. . . . The creative individual comes to live his work—indeed, cannot thrive without it. And the kind of pleasure he derives . . . can be compared in a non-facetious way with the kind of pleasure most individuals gain from sexual involvement with someone they love. (p. 355)

At the minimum, given the above, we all will have at least one baseline for discerning where we fit on the continuum from competence to creativity. Yet, the focus in this text has been on the transition area of the continuum, where the skills required partake of those noted above, but probably are qualitatively different.

This transition area is the home of the improviser. People can learn to be better improvisers. If our aspirations are greater, the skills and talents required to improvise are quite likely to be those most useful for attaining larger ambitions.

Gordon and Zemke's (1986) statement on creativity is striking: "There's no such thing as a best technique or a perfect approach to becoming more creative. What were you doing the last time you used something in a new way or made something new? How did you do it? Never mind someone else's formula: that's what works for you" (p. 40). The admonition here is to pay attention to oneself, to do a self-audit of "what works." Focusing on and building personal strengths probably is a more practical approach to getting better and more creative ideas than focusing on one's weaknesses. However, an awareness of these weaknesses also can prove useful.

First, creative areas, or zones, should be defined. Zones might be the generation of new ideas or inventions, showing or proving that ideas work, or getting others to try out new ideas and adopt them. Second, persons should determine the mix of talents, cognitive styles, values, processes, and motivations that come in play when they are most creative.

This should help to locate zones of cognitive, attitudinal, or motivational strengths.

After this self-audit, the next step is to focus on a professional problem that is both intriguing and that requires the use of one's creative strengths. Middleman and Goldberg (1986) suggested a way to begin:

> It is the central image, or pattern that enables the . . . worker to see the particular . . . situation as a "kind" of . . . situation, a special case of a more general type. . . .
>
> If a practitioner has only two images stored in memory, then that person will "understand" every situation as one or the other of these two types. But with more different images to try out, one's capacity for differential understanding is greatly increased . . . and thus, increased [is the] probability of a sophisticated response. (pp. 31, 33)

Monitoring and noticing anomalies in the fit of one's mental models or cognitive maps of problems with reality is crucial for generating novel ideas. Perkins (1981) described how and why this is done. He suggested that those who create build up their products, rather than pick them out. In his view, creating is selecting, through building up. Because there is no recipe, the creator does four things:

> [1] Planning: Instead of producing the work directly, the maker produces a plan for it, or for part of it. [2] Abstracting: instead of always working from general intent to particulars, the maker abstracts new ideas from the particulars of the work in progress or other sources. [3] Undoing: instead of getting everything right the first time, the maker undoes and redoes parts of the work. [4] Making means into ends: instead of always being preoccupied with the final product, the maker often addresses a means as an end in itself. (p. 276)

After noticing something unexpected that raises questions, creative people go on and get novel ideas by making surprising connections between ideas, sensations, or things. They then make unique choices about what to do next with these connections. Making choices and making connections are important aspects of creativity.

Making Connections

In building up to a unique or novel product, new ideas are important. There are a number of sources that should be tapped. Following are 13 guidelines for making novel connections among phenomena.

Knowledge and Experiential Determinants

A creative idea almost always is the result of seeing and making novel connections between events, objects, people, or ideas. These connections cannot be made if there is nothing to connect to.

1. Learn as much as possible about the way other groups and professions deal with similar problems.

Pelikan (1983) has pointed out that those who make great contributions to almost any profession or field are distinguished from their less creative colleagues by their preparation and knowledge of fields other than their field of specialization. These great contributors are aware of others' cognitive maps, which tell how others expect to reach their goals. These maps also imply specific competencies—task competencies, relationship competencies, context competencies, and self-competencies (Middleman & Rhodes, 1985). Matthew Arnold's (as cited in Ozick, 1987) advice to literary critics is appropriate for people trying to develop the range and sophistication of their maps: "Try and possess one great literature, at least, besides [your] own: and the more unlike [your] own, the better" (p. 51).

2. Experience problems from a variety of perspectives.

Experience is quite different from simple knowledge. Experience provides a range of sensory images and cues, perceptual as well as conceptual, that are extremely useful for making connections. These connections, as noted in previous chapters, often are the result of sensitivity to the unexpected—such as might result from client feedback or from experiences with self-help groups.

When a range of actual experiences about particular problems is not possible, imaging and visualization can be extremely useful. Former Supreme Court Justice Oliver Wendell Holmes is reported to have responded to a question on a college exam about the American and the Canadian positions on a fishing treaty by saying "Since I know nothing about the American position and less about the Canadian position, I shall respond in terms of the position of the fish."

To use experience creatively, a mix of traits and abilities is required. Some of these traits and abilities are not intrinsically creative—such as memory, association, or recognition (Perkins, 1981). As noted earlier, highly creative people have analogical themata or images which organize their work experiences in their memories (for example, Darwin's tree of life or Freud's iceberg). These images of wide scope "serve as a kind of conceptual and aesthetic focus for a person's developing inquiries" (Perkins, p. 24).

To be more creative in dealing with particular problems, an important step is to develop both logical cognitive maps and analogical frames or images to retain experiences or ideas about the problems. These themata make it possible to practice making connections without having to start again each time one has an idea.

Creativity is related to possessing fruitful themata and using them. Studies of great improvisers in various professions show that they constantly practice or play around with the maps and themes of their field. Gardner (1982, p. 368) deduced that there is a suggestive tie between invention and repetition.[3]

Cognitive Determinants

Creative capacity is affected by *cognition*, or the process of knowing. One factor in this process is the pattern of beliefs and rules of action that guide a person's thinking. These often are encapsulated in metaphors and stories.

3. Practitioners should examine their operating values and beliefs and consider how these affect their cognitive maps or guides for action.

Morgan (1986) pointed out the close relationship between the way people think and act. Such a viewpoint encourages people to accept responsibility for the part they plan in shaping situations and opens up the possibility of framing problems differently. For example, many managers use the metaphor of a machine for their organizations. Yet, according to Morgan,

> Organizations can be many things at one and the same time. A machinelike organization designed to achieve specific goals can simultaneously be: a species of organization that is able to survive in certain environments but not others; an information-processing system that is skilled in certain kinds of learning but not in others; a cultural milieu characterized by distinctive values, beliefs, and social practices; a political system where people jostle to further their own ends . . . an instrument used by one group of people to exploit and dominate others; and so on. Though managers and organization theorists often attempt to override this complexity by assuming that

---

[3]However, Perkins (1981) warned that people often end up practicing and entrenching their mistakes. He suggested that "they should think about, criticize, revise and devise the ways they do . . . some activity they usually undertake" (p. 218).

organizations are ultimately rational phenomena that must be understood with reference to their goals or objectives, this assumption often gets in the way of realistic analysis. (p. 322)

Every metaphor raises a different set of questions. Awareness of how a dominant metaphor guides thinking in a particular situation can counter premature closure in searching for solutions, and open the possibility of creative insights. Embedded in the metaphors are "injunctions for action" (Morgan, 1986, p. 331). The political metaphor leads to the search for power, the machine metaphor to control and "getting organized," and so forth.

These metaphors are what Schön (1987) has called "theories in use" (pp. 255–256). "Our images or metaphors are theories or conceptual frameworks. Practice is never theory free, for it is always guided by an image of what one is trying to do" (Morgan, 1986, p. 236). Certainly, creative ideas are less likely to emerge in an individual held in thrall by all-powerful and unquestioned metaphors. Combined, these metaphors represent our perspective, or *frame of reference*—our attitudes, values, feelings, knowledge, and ideas about life. Middleman (1983) found that "one's frames of reference determine what has meaning and value, how much openness and difference one can entertain, and what must be ignored or transformed because it doesn't fit with one's expectations and systems of belief" (p. 232). In a sense, people's frames of reference determine what they can see and what they will do. People's metaphors program their thought processes and affect the choices they make. Yet, creativity is enhanced when unbiased comparisons are made between competing approaches to problems or situations.

In this sense, creativity begins with dissatisfaction. From the active choice of a goal come energy, commitment, access to the unconscious and the preconscious, and the road to intuition and insight. Logic is a precise algorithm for choosing. Synthesis and judgment involve choice where the rules of choice are imprecise. In such situations, knowing how personal choices are made when the rules are not clear is important. Choosing the path of least resistance because it is less risky or more familiar is a serious block to creativity. If there is no dilemma, there is no challenge, and no creativity.

4. Practitioners should identify their preferred style of choosing. The more flexible the patterns of choice, the more likely creative choices will be made.

Fritz (1984) suggested that the way choices are made molds perception and focuses concentration.

> Choice by limitation is choosing only what seems reasonable. . . . Choice by indirectness means choosing a process rather than a result. . . . Choice by escalation . . . is choosing the lesser of two evils. . . . Choice by default is the "choice" not to make a choice. . . . Conditional choice . . . imposes certain conditions or circumstances on the result. Choice by reaction is . . . choice merely to reduce discomfort. Choice by consensus . . . choice by adverse possession . . . lies in some unknown part of you and therefore beyond your reach [and choice]. (pp. 87–91)

Inflexible choice using only one technique or method limits improvisation. As much clarity as possible about how choices are made is needed, because the ability to be open to possibilities, both actively and passively, is crucial to creative potential.

Skilled improvisers use their intuition and ability to choose in reworking and remolding cognitive maps or plans. Those who aspire to skilled improvisation (or invention) must ask to what extent they can summon up the courage and will to see things differently. To what extent can they educate their intuition—for example, to "smell trouble" or to have a "sixth sense"? Skilled improvisers use these abilities to solve problems with little information and to perceive situations holistically when only a few elements are recognizable. To learn how to do this, two different types of knowledge are required: (1) knowledge of one's personality and motivation and (2) cognitive skills, or know-how. Middleman and Goldberg (1986) provided a sense of what is required:

> Invention . . . requires knowing the general rules, procedures, algorithms, axioms, techniques, history, and precedents of a knowledge domain, and then daring to leap beyond these known "ways." Invention requires know-how but also vision, flexibility, a disciplined use of the imagination, self-confidence, and courage. (p. 30)[4]

In a similar vein, new ideas depend on getting new information. If information merely slides into familiar contexts, it is unlikely that creative thought will be produced. It is important to throw a "glitch" into the usual process of perceiving and thinking to develop a "sixth sense."

5. The road to creativity should be paved with consciously constructed glitches to keep thoughts out of familiar ruts.

---

[4]For a discussion of how computers may affect the capacity to get new ideas, see Mutschler (1989).

One simple glitch is wariness about words. The words people use are traps. At best, words are maps that guide but do not represent the totality of reality. The words id, ego, equity, justice, empowerment, artistry, and creativity never can convey the complete reality of what they describe. Reasoning on the basis of incomplete meanings is necessary in life. Not knowing that one is doing this or being unaware of the limitations of this reasoning is dangerous. For example, creating programs to empower clients without fully understanding the dynamics of empowerment could be counterproductive. A good glitch for social workers is to assume that all such concepts are understood incompletely unless proven otherwise.

Seeing only the expected, imposing false limits, not using all of one's senses, the inability to see a problem from various viewpoints, and the inability to construct "glitches" to prevent falling into these traps limit the ability to perceive problems and solutions.

6. Flexibility in problem finding and problem solving is enhanced by the knowledge of different problem solving, associational, and think-ing techniques.

Knowing how to use these techniques—brainstorming, hill climbing, synectics, forced-fit, and so on—provides a means of looking at problems from different perspectives. By offering a fresh approach, even if insights are not provided, these new approaches can help to overcome frustration and the sense that one is at a dead end.

Orientational Determinants

Jung (as cited in Haber, 1980) suggested that people orient themselves to the world in four basic ways: (1) sensation, (2) thinking, (3) feeling, and (4) intuition:

> Sensation includes all perceptions of the sense organs; thinking is concerned with the function of cognition; feelings modus operandi is through subjective valuation; and intuition is the perception of unconscious contents. . . . Sensation establishes what is actually present, thinking enables us to recognize its meaning, feeling tells us its value and intuition points to its possibilities. (p. 114)

These orientations probably differ in dominance or development with the individual. Each person has an individual preference, or style of using these capacities in processing information.

The virtue of knowing one's cognitive style or how one processes information (perceives, thinks, remembers, and solves problems), is that some styles may be better suited for certain situations than others.

Middleman (1983) offered this example of *descriptive, relational,* and *inferential or categorical* styles:

> I shall illustrate these dimensions with a simple example of arranging spices in one's kitchen. Person A arranges them alphabetically (allspice to whole pepper); this approach is descriptive. Person B prefers those used most frequently in front (salt, pepper) and those least used behind (tarragon, cayenne); this approach is relational. Person C makes arrangements related to different cooking requirements (Italian seasonings, Indian seasonings); this approach is inferential-categorical. (p. 246)

Other people might organize the spices by color or smell. Still other people might not organize them at all, preferring to improvise with whatever is on hand at a particular moment.

Knowing one's cognitive style can be useful. For example, one could team up with people who have different strengths to increase the likelihood of creative responses. This is a more feasible approach than trying to change a basic orientation to the world.[5]

7. Ask for advice from people who approach the world in a different manner.

As noted earlier, many theories of creativity stress determinants based on character: access to "primary process," use of archaic logic, regression in the service of the ego, and so forth. Other theories deal with personality differences between creative and non-creative people—their flexibility, persistence, need to conform, ability to risk and so on.

The usual prescription is to diagnose what blocks the creative process. Unfortunately, diagnosis is easier than treatment. However, this self-knowledge is useful, if only so that one can surround oneself with people who do not share the same blocks.

Motivational Determinants

Rogers (as cited in Gelfand, 1988) pointed out that the creative person is guided by an internal locus of evaluation. The focus is on self-judgment and self-satisfaction, rather than external praise or criticism. De Bono (1977) commented that the need to be correct and be rewarded externally is a major impediment to getting new ideas.

Rapoport (1968) suggested that the need to bring order to disorder is an important motivation for creativity. Siporin (1988) suggested striving

---

[5]Robert Quinn (1988) provided an interesting case example of this approach (pp. 123–124).

for an aesthetic experience as a major motivator. Still others have noted the need to see, explore, understand and experience—to go beyond what is already known. However, the extent to which people can change, or even know, their own characters is debatable.

What is possible is to try to change or rearrange the external factors that push people in the direction of creativity—whether it be order, beauty, or praise. Motivation is related to situational, or external, pushes and to psychological, or internal, pulls. Just as the R-mode and L-mode vary in dominance or converge during different phases of the creative process, it may be that similarly different motivations are preeminent or converge during different phases.

Playful Determinants

Necessity is an important situational or external motivator. Csikszentmihalyi (1975) gave an example of an important internal motivator—the desire for pleasure or enjoyment:

Slowly it became obvious that something in the activity of painting itself kept them going. The process of making their products was so enjoyable that they were ready to sacrifice a great deal for the chance of continuing to do so. There was something about the physical activities of stretching canvas on wooden frames, of squeezing tubes of paint or kneading clay, of splashing colors on a blank surface; the cognitive activity of choosing a problem to work on, of defining a subject, of experimenting with new combinations of form, color, light, and space; the emotional impact of recognizing one's past, present, and future concerns in the emerging work. All these aspects of the artistic process added up to a structured experience which was almost addictive in its fascination. (p. xii)

8. The creative person is able to structure experience to maximize pleasure.

Csikszentmihalyi (1975) operationalizes this process of creating. One factor is intrinsic motivation. "The basic issue is whether a person feels that he himself has originated an act, or whether he feels forced to do it because of external constraints. In the former case, he will enjoy the activity; in the latter, he will experience it as drudgery" (p. 25).

Another factor related to the pleasure in a task is the sense of challenge. Those who are fascinated by their work appear to find in it a challenge to explore the limits of their abilities. They also enjoy the opportunity to make full use of their skills and to get feedback as the task progresses.

Creativity necessitates a centering of attention and an obliviousness to extraneous stimuli. Creativity also can be seen as a form of play. When asked to describe their creative experiences,

> The composers and dancers in our sample described their feelings in ways that did not differ substantially from the descriptions of climbers or chess players. Surgeons involved in medical research and mathematicians working on the frontiers of their field answered the interviews in terms that were almost interchangeable with those used by players. Almost any description of the creative experience includes experiential accounts that are in important respects analogous to those obtained from people at play. (Csikszentmihalyi, 1975, p. 37)

It appears that a specific type of play is related to professional creativity—serious play. It depends on a structure that allows the centering of attention, the control of one's own actions, the blocking out of extraneous stimuli, the loss of self-consciousness, the challenge of skills, and the reception of clear feedback. "These structural characteristics produce a sense of elation, a feeling of creative achievement which, although typical of games, can be provided in any structured activity, including work" (Csikszentmihalyi, 1975, p. 140).

Huizinga (1955) defined play as "an activity which proceeds within certain limits of time and space, in a visible order, according to rules freely accepted, and outside the sphere of necessity or material utility. The play mood is one of rapture and enthusiasm" (p. 132). Although work is necessary and useful, Margolin (1967) suggested that the play spirit encourages the willingness to pursue a task, which affects energy level; the willingness to withhold judgment of one's performance, which affects learning; and involvement in self-selected activities, which encourages a willingness to experiment, to become deeply engrossed in an activity, and to relax the need for praise. Margolin saw work and play as intertwined activities. To saturate oneself with work requires play.

A hypothesis worth testing is that creative people are able to structure their work life to simulate serious play and thereby saturate themselves with a problem. As Csikszentmihalyi (1975) pointed out, the ability to pattern experience in this way could be the most simple and most basic manifestation of the creative process.

Gruber (1983) has drawn the implications of this hypothesis for one's career—the ability to develop supportive work structures. For example, an insight or illumination usually needs expansion and reworking. Many great ideas have been lost because the person who had them did not or could not work them out—they lacked the discipline to do it. A disciplined approach requires a structure of time, place, and task. As Gruber (1980) put it,

> A creative moment is part of a longer creative process, which in turn is part of a creative life. How are such lives lived? How can I express this peculiar idea that such an individual must be a self-regenerating system. . . . The system regulates the activity and the creative act regenerates the system. *The creative life happens in a being who can continue to work.* (p. 269)

Creative people seem to have a network of enterprises. As Perkins (1981) found, one problem or pursuit leads to another in the context of their general goals or aspirations. "Typically, several somewhat related enterprises will be pursued; one may spin off to another; an enterprise may be dropped, now one and now another will receive emphasis . . ." (p. 242).

Patience, energy, and commitment are required to work out ideas. Even more important is the need for discipline—the ability to stick with an idea or task and apply one's skills. Yet discipline alone is not sufficient. To sustain themselves over time and be more creative, social workers have to consider certain basic aspects of their work. Are their skills challenged? Can they center their attention on the problem at hand and lose self-consciousness? Does their work provide a flow of feedback that gives clear signals or directions? Do they feel in control of their actions?[6]

Rather than to try to be creative, the admonition is to try and enjoy one's work in the specific ways noted above. Admittedly, this is difficult given the tasks social workers often are called on to do. Yet, not trying to seriously play at work dooms them to more drudgery than necessary and may limit their creative potential. Enjoyment sustains creative effort.

One of the important factors in structuring enjoyment is the ability to structure time to support creativity. No one knows how much time it will take to incubate any particular idea. Yet the ability to use time, rather than be controlled by it, plays a part in the incubation and saturation phases of creativity. Theories of the processes of creativity suggest that after saturation, a problem should be set aside to let the solution incubate. But setting problems aside is no easy matter, as Wilson (1986) pointed out:

---

[6]Perkins (1981) pointed out that the accidents that carry creative work along, because the maker encounters an opportunity in the work so far or in another experience altogether, are not mere accidents. The opportunity never would have been recognized had the maker not been saturated in the subject. So, he said, accidents are reflections of the teleology of the maker and the making.

Why is the time trap antithetical to play and creative processes? Primarily, I should say, because our bondage to a short-range future that is implicit in a heightened sense of time and an anxiety about its passage makes us basically unfree to be players. An individual's adjustment to the demands of time keeping constricts play by rendering it arbitrarily interruptible, by erecting cut-off points that intervene no matter in what valuable direction play might be leading him. (pp. 158–159)

Each person needs to know how he or she relates to time. Time is one of the major variables that affect creativity.

9. The creative person can manipulate time in many more ways than the uncreative person, by expanding its horizon, losing consciousness of it, managing it, or ignoring it.

Situational Determinants

Although creativity resides in the individual, it is socially patterned. Creativity cannot flower fully in an environment that throws up impediments and devalues anything new and different. Adversity is not always detrimental to creativity, yet the question is one of degree. In fact, tension often plays a part in innovation. For example, the manager, the bureaucrat, and the businessperson generally are posed as the natural enemy of the innovator. Television is a "wasteland" because of monetary pressure and ratings wars. Architecture is homogenized to ensure the maximum return per square foot.

This view of how limits are put on creativity is partly a myth. It contains elements of truth, yet its mythic function is to handle reality tensions. In this case the tension results from the fact that creative ideas do not exist in a vacuum. They have to be accepted, or at least appreciated, by others if they are to become innovations.

Moses may have gone up to Mount Sinai, but when he came down with the Ten Commandments, there was trouble. How is the creative person to overcome rejection? One way is to believe that the "Philistines" or, in the case of social work, "administrators," are the cause of rejection.

Another method is to recognize that although there are administrators who reject anything new or who have no appreciation for innovation that cannot be measured monetarily, there also are a great many false prophets and fads in art, science, and social work. Resistance is not always self-serving. Resistance to innovation also can be based on the desire to preserve important individual, professional, and organizational values.

Innovators must deal with the environment in which they work, whether it is resistant or supportive. The professional, cultural, social, organizational, and political milieus must be recognized if creative ideas are to become innovations accepted by others. Sometimes, gaining this acceptance requires an idea manager, whose creative skills need to be at least equal in complexity to that of the idea generator.

10. Social and political skills are as important as cognitive skills for an innovator.

Social and political skills offer insight into others' motivations; a sense of how others will respond to situations and events; and a capacity to strike bargains, create alliances, and defuse opposition. In addition, as Bromberg noted in her chapter, innovators also need a keen sense of timing and of organizational and social change.

> A number of elements bear on the birth of a program innovation. These include the attack and rejection of traditional formulations which produce discontinuity, shifts in values which result in new constellations of possibilities, situations of conflict wherein arise contrasting systems of expectations, and the recombination of elements in ways which are recognized as new and different. In addition when the perception that there is a need for change is distributed throughout the community, the chances increase that innovation will result. (p. 248)

There are a range of talents that are useful for innovation. Some professionals are not especially talented at generating their own ideas, but are excellent at encouraging others. Case studies of creative managers show them as able to act in ways that give subordinates elbow room, to imply by their actions that mistakes can be useful for learning, to see the possibilities in half-baked ideas, to be good listeners, to respond in useful ways, and to be unafraid to stretch policy when the situation demands it (Stein, 1983).

To a certain extent a self-audit of one's organizational persona is needed. If social workers do not foster each other's creativity, they also may be limiting their own creative potential by helping to create an environment unconducive to innovation. The Golden Rule applies.

Only individuals can think, yet when individuals are organized in a collectivity their thinking affects each other. In this sense, organizations think. The concern must be not only for building in organizational supports for individual creativity, but also adding supports for organizational innovation (Zaltman, 1983).

Play on the job usually has been relegated to the informal organization, and often has been viewed only as a tension-reducing mechanism. This is a limited view. Play also helps both individuals and organizations adapt to their environments by providing opportunities for the exploration of novel or unusual connections or adaptations. Play allows experimentation with different ways of attaining goals. Most important, play helps to soften rigid boundaries between people and ideas. It helps to open new lines of organizational communication and to expand the quantity and quality of available rewards. Innovators must seize these possibilities.

Jones, Moore, and Snyder (1988) suggested that the connection between work, play, and creativity can best be understood through the use of the concept "working":

> A vital component of working—as a process—is playing. Limited attention span and the fatigue of intense concentration require relief, routine spawns monotony, continuation of tasks requires breaks with carryover of interest, cordiality among people compels joking and socializing, coping with stress demands fantasizing and projection, success stimulates celebration, and pleasant ambience encourages festive events. (p. 240)

There are a number of different forms and purposes of play. As Laird and Hartman pointed out in their chapter, rituals, ceremonies, and celebrations can support creativity and innovation by symbolizing their importance. The creation of such playful roles or structures as an organizational jester or special departments where playfulness and relaxation of rules is sanctioned can open an organization to the need to adopt new ideas. Likewise, "galumphing," such as purposefully not following procedures for a day, can open individuals to making new connections.

Similarly, forms of play evolve or emerge out of the nature of the work, which not only relieve tension, but also foster new perspectives.[7] First impressions of such activities often are misleading. Conversations appear childish, physical actions look like horseplay, things appear nonsensical. Over time, these interactions take on structure, form, and meaning for work and for transcending old ideas and perspectives (Jones, Moore, & Snyder, 1988).

There also are individual forms of play. People improvise, tinker, or adapt both for instrumental and for expressive reasons. They compete with others. They set goals or standards for themselves and enjoy meeting them. They "lose themselves" in their work, their attention is centered, and they derive great satisfaction from the process of what they are doing.

---

[7]For an interesting discussion on humor at work, see Paulson (1989) and Durant and Miller (1988).

They are playing while working. In doing so, they make new connections and produce novel ideas.

March and Olsen (1979) have discussed the dangers of depending only on a rationality that dismisses intuition and favors analysis that reveres work and denigrates play. A strict insistence on purpose, consistency, and rationality limits one's ability to think creatively (Margolin, 1967). Professional playfulness involves the temporary relaxation of rules of practice to explore the possibility of alternative rules. Too much consistency and too much memory can be the enemies of creativity, as March and Olsen (1979) noted.

A certain amount of flexibility or play must be introduced into a system. Yet, most agency work is, of necessity, routine. As important as a systemic structured playfulness is, the question of how individuals are asked (or made to) handle routine is of crucial importance. Routine operations drive out creative operations. The only counter to this tendency is to construct routines that can support creativity.

11. The more challenge presented in the routine operation of an agency, the more enjoyment its workers will have, and the more innovation will be produced.

People must know what keeps them from using their skills and capacities in a challenging way, what keeps them from enjoying their work, what makes them feel out of control, and what could be done to help them center their attention and receive the kind of feedback that would encourage experimentation and a focus on the challenge of their tasks.

Organizational hierarchies tend to stifle debate and risk taking. Managers interested in promoting learning and innovation thus have to find new ways of structuring relations to promote the creative process, especially through the values defining agency culture. The ability to foster an appropriate culture will become increasingly important, especially one permeated by attitudes that encourage openness, self-questioning, a proactive entrepreneurial approach, an appreciation for the importance of "adding value," and a general optimism and orientation toward learning and change that energizes people to rise to challenges (Morgan, 1988, p. 8).

An agency profile is needed. Does an agency's structure inhibit serious play? How? Is it the way roles are defined, a reward system that sustains mediocrity, the accountability system, the layers of hierarchy, an oligarchy that must maintain control? Is creativity stifled by a rigid supervisory structure? Do workers get enough information to be able to make intelligent judgments about larger work issues than the details of their jobs?

Do procedures limit enjoyment? Are the agency's staff meetings designed to "cast out sinners and sin" in the form of unacceptable ideas and people, or are these meetings more like brainstorming sessions? Not every procedure can or even should be enjoyable. However, if there is an interest in innovation, the question that should always be asked is, "Is this procedure going to make people tired, angry, and uninterested or centered, challenged, and in control?" Is the technology adequate to the goals or is there a vague technology? If the methods must be developed as the work is done, then room for improvisation is required.

In a similar vein, an agency profile must include an analysis of an executive director's capacity to promote flexibility, or play, in the system. A rigid executive director will tend to nullify a structure that has flexibility built into it.

Executives have a tremendous effect on the process of innovation. As Morgan (1988) pointed out, innovation involves risk, balancing creativity and discipline, timing, and most important, infusing the organization with a sense of mission that helps overcome doubt and uncertainty. To embrace variety, innovative managers need special skills in negotiation, consensus building, and conflict management. They also need a philosophy that encourages people to deal with issues rather than bury them. And they must be skilled in designing an organization for innovation.

12. The greatest spurs to innovation are the legitimization and institutionalization of criticism by organizations.

To achieve this institutionalization, methods of finding errors, such as feedback systems and program evaluation, are needed, as well as designs that allow for comparisons among alternative programs, adversary plans, and other established benchmarks. Playful approaches to criticism also are needed. An organizational "day of atonement" could be held. Whatever is done should be done in a spirit of discovery rather than one of blame.

Those designing organizations for innovation must consider how flexibility, openness, and an experimental attitude are affected by the flow of information, the role of organizational elites in controlling the acceptability of ideas, the location and circulation of people, and the institutionalized procedures for appealing leadership decisions, among other things.

In creating such designs, good executives often also create the conditions for serious play, a crucial variable that affects saturation with problems and emergence of creativity and innovation.

13. Employees should avoid working for employers who cannot stimulate their thinking.

Those interested in promoting their creative capacity should take an active role in the selection of all executives for whom they will work and pay attention to the capacity of these people to promote innovation. Do they have the social and cognitive requisites? Nobel laureates tend to inspire more Nobel laureates.

Creativity and the Social Work Profession

Social workers should take an active role in their profession, especially in its organized entities—associations, credentialing bodies, policy-making groups, and schools. The need for innovative leadership, the promotion of professional flexibility, and the need to create a playful atmosphere for learning apply equally to these professional groups.

Other suggestions for an agenda to promote creativity in the profession have been made in preceding chapters. There is a need for openness to the ideas and perspectives of nonprofessionals; for the avoidance of a self-serving professionalism and a narrow scientism; for setting a flexible professional agenda of programs and concepts for exploration and verification; for the openness of journals to nonacademic authors; for novel and playful uses of professional meetings; for a professional structure for the diffusion of ideas; and for a means of salvaging the best out of ill-formed ideas, such as deinstitutionalization.

Even students who look forward to a creative career need to take an active role in promoting creativity and innovation in schools of social work. The essential issue schools face is how to provide students with a beginning sense of mastery, while encouraging questioning, flexibility, and openness to nontraditional ideas. As Garrison (1986) suggested,

> New learners in any situation are anxious and thus vulnerable to adopting the perspectives and attitudes of their teachers. The emphasis on self-awareness in social work education enhances this vulnerability. How these teachers model behavior is crucial for what happens to such students' creative potential. (pp. 112–113)

According to Stuart (see chapter in Part Four), the capacity for creative modeling of teachers is affected by the structure of the schools in what

273

they teach. He suggested such structural innovations as school–agency mergers, similar to the merger of medical schools with hospitals; placing practitioners-in-residence in schools of social work; and providing faculty members with academic leaves in social agencies.

The studies of the effects of graduate education on students' creative capacity are inconclusive. One study confirmed the idea that through their graduate career, master of social work students become more prolific in generating ideas, but the ideas are narrower in range and less innovative and original in nature (Garrison, 1986). Another study showed that when students were taught techniques of creativity as part of a casework course, they increased their flexibility, expressional and ideational fluency, and originality in at least one of three measures (Wheeler, 1978).

The problem of adequately preparing students, yet not stifling them, is related to the issue of telling versus teaching. Students require a certain amount of knowledge, and given time constraints, some of it has to be told. Yet the teacher must have larger goals, such as imparting the need for specificity, showing the differing sides of arguments to develop a critical approach, and so forth. In many ways it is the same tension mentioned in other contexts—between logic and intuition, discipline and creativity, chaos and control. As such, students interested in a creative career should ask their educators how they handle such tensions.

Some methods to promote creativity could be introduced in courses on social work practice. These courses, according to Wheeler (1978, p. 123), could include

- the skill of exploring alternatives with clients while withholding judgments, such as in brainstorming techniques
- proper timing for evaluating alternatives
- problem essence analysis from synectics
- sensitivity to clients' conflicts and learning the "art" of identifying "compressed conflicts" from synectics theory
- the skill of making connections as in [question lists]

Necessity for Creativity

Ultimately, it is as important for clients to be creative as it is for social workers. Clients are the ones who are best able to come up with creative solutions to their problems. Social workers can help teach them how to tap into their own potential.

Competence is the bedrock on which creativity rests. Any competent person has the potential to be creative under certain conditions. Since creative ideas come most frequently to the prepared mind, there is no better justification of the need for professionalism.

Knowledge, skills, and values are necessary but not sufficient preparation. Individual and structural capacities and supports also are needed to help question assumptions, defer judgment, reframe problems, listen to different perspectives, perceive anomalies in cognitive maps, and relax the stranglehold of logic on intuition. To learn to be creative, social workers need to learn how to occasionally slip their cognitive moorings.

Maier (1979) found that play "sanctions risking beyond the bounds of what has been already tried and found safe; it offers personal pleasure in mastery as well as pleasure in experimentations. In popular terms, play is a process of 'trying out for size' " (p. 1). In an organization, a playful spirit complements the mix of talents and traits that determine creative capacity. It ensures that the prepared mind does not develop a trained incapacity for change.

Creativity is a state of mind. Social workers see what they want—or what they are prepared—to see. The challenge is how to expand and deepen their vision. The best hope for this deepened vision, in the context of an innovative career, lies in working toward a mesh between individual creative talents or style, and professional and organizational requisites and style in one's workplace.[8]

Finding or making the correct mesh is a long-term task. However, it suggests a strategy to follow. This book contains a set of tactics to use in operationalizing the strategy, from learning how other groups and professions approach problems, to avoiding work with unstimulating employers, to promoting intuition and imagination.

The students in Wheeler's (1978) creative practice class put it this way:

> The art of social work has to do with mobilizing the creative within the social worker (and the agency) in an effort to foster the creative in the client. Creativity is both a learning process (making connections) and an innovative process (breaking connections) and creative social workers . . . act as catalysts in the process for clients. . . . (p. 111)

The preponderance of expert opinion is that the psychological and cognitive aspects of creativity are to a considerable extent set in childhood rather than at birth.

> The developing brain can be likened to a highway system that evolves with use: less traveled roads may be abandoned, popular roads broadened, and

---

[8]The editor/senior author is indebted to Harold Lewis for suggesting this concept to him. Herrmann (1988) offers a set of tests for individual cognitive style.

new ones added where they are needed. . . . Even though the basic organization of the brain does not change after birth, details of its structure and function remain plastic for some time. . . . (Aoki & Siekevitz, 1988, p. 57)

Although opinions are divided over the evenness and extent of development over various domains in childhood, experts tend to agree that most people have a "zone of potential" for artistry or creativity in some aspect of life. The task is to realize our potential even though (or thankfully) it is not completely ascertainable before the fact.

Social workers are most likely to attain their creative potential if they determine the types of tasks and activities that bring out their inventiveness and originality. Social workers then need to focus on a problem or concern that intrigues them and that uses their specific skills and capacities. Heus and Pincus (1986, p. 69) described this activity as an alignment of skills, logic, imagination, [knowledge,] and energy. Social workers usually will need to persist, and may do this by working on a number of loosely related activities and interests, rather than one specific focus, thereby creating a network of enterprises that can enrich each other. Another way is to develop an aesthetic of work. Einstein's highest praise for a good piece of work was not that it was correct but that it was beautiful (Whitrow, 1973, p. 17). The quest for beauty and originality is a powerful motivator.

> Elegant solutions have simplicity, poise, grace. They offer the most impact for the least expenditure of energy. In a multiproblem situation an elegant solution solves not only the immediate crisis but connects and has positive effects on all sorts of related problems. . . . The elegance can be found in this economy of motion and powerful resolution, like poetry. (Heus and Pincus, 1986, p. 122)

Practitioners will help themselves if they consider a number of general issues related to creativity and innovation. Making new and elegant connections requires a mix of traits, such as perseverance and curiosity, and capacities, such as openness to differing perspectives and a sense of how to use them. Logic and intuition, purpose and process play a part as do knowledge, expertise, and competence, as well as such ordinary skills as noticing, remembering, and choosing. These capacities can be improved best by practice, not only through the use of association techniques that aid in shifting perspectives and challenging assumptions, but also in the context of improvising on cognitive maps and visual images of problems and potential solutions. Creative results are built through planned repetition and practice.

Social workers will be aided immeasurably in making creative connections if they work in an agency and professional context that enables them to center their attention, receive clear feedback, challenge their skills, lose self-consciousness, and get pleasure from what they do. This kind of serious play or playing while working is a basic ingredient for simultaneously avoiding sterile conformity and promoting an openness to the new and better.

Erikson (1988, pp. 130–145) offers the intriguing hypothesis that with every effort to do something new and better one relives or renews in sequence one's life struggles—between trust and mistrust to maintain hope, between initiative and guilt to develop purpose, between industry and inadequacy to be competent, between intimacy and isolation for love. An attempt to solve a substantive problem creatively may also be an attempt at resolving anew a set of developmental problems.

Yet, such attempts occur in a professional context. And there are unique factors in social work that can both promote and retard creative efforts.

The high degree of commitment engendered in social workers for helping those in need promotes purpose and perseverance, indisputable requisites for creativity. On the other hand, this commitment can slide into passionate adherence to narrow social or therapeutic ideologies that simplify and blur distinctions, retard the capacity to ask critical questions, and ultimately constrict the inner and outer space from which creative ideas are drawn.

When these constraints are added to the ordinary organizational pressures "to go along to get along," an individual social worker may be up against a powerful set of retardants on creativity. Nevertheless, the profession provides counterbalancing supports.

If anything, social work is process oriented. This training for process provides social workers a unique appreciation of the fact that creativity cannot be forced, that ideas need time to incubate, that resistance is to be expected and can, if understood, lead to new insights.

Finally, the greatest asset of the profession is the varied experiences that social workers have in their careers. Few social workers work at only one job or with one type of client. Varied experience makes for the capacity to make novel connections.

Social work may be the "Lewis and Clark" of the professions—creating and exploring new fields of practice, responding to changing social conditions, incorporating bits and pieces of wisdom from many places

277

and experiences, forever on the move and never complacent. Not a bad recipe for creativity.

References

Aoki, C., & Siekevitz, P. (1988). Plasticity in brain development. *Scientific American 259*(6), 56–64.

Bell, H. (1984). Making art work. *Western Folklore, 43*(3), 211–221.

Csikszentmihalyi, M. (1975). *Beyond boredom and anxiety.* San Francisco: Jossey-Bass.

Davis, S. (1988). Soft versus hard social work. *Social Work, 23,* 373–374.

de Bono, E. (1977). *Lateral thinking: A textbook of creativity.* Middlesex, England: Penguin Books.

Durant, J., & Miller, J. (1988). *Laughing matters: A serious look at humor.* New York: John Wiley & Sons.

Edwards, B. (1987). *Drawing on the artist within: A guide to innovation, imagination, and creativity* (Fireside ed.). New York: Simon & Schuster.

England, H. (1986). *Social work as art.* London, England: George Allen & Unwin.

Erikson, J. (1988). *Wisdom and the senses: The way of creativity.* New York: W. W. Norton.

Fritz, R. (1984). *The path of least resistance.* Salem, MA: DMA Inc.

Gardner, H. (1982). Art, mind and brain. New York: Basic Books.

Garrison, R. (1986). The effects of social work education on student creative thinking skills. *Journal of Applied Social Sciences, 10,* 103–118.

Gelfand, B. (1988). *The creative practitioner.* New York: Haworth Press.

Goleman, D. (1988, April 5). New intelligence scales rank talent for life. *New York Times,* p. C11.

Gordon, J., & Zemke, R. (1986). Making them more creative. *Training, 23,* 30–34, 39–45.

Gruber, H. (1980). The evolving systems approach to creativity. In C. Modgil & S. Modgil (Eds.), *Towards a theory of psychological development.* Windsor, England: NFER.

Gruber, H. (1983). History and creative work: From the most ordinary to the most exalted. *Journal of the History of the Behavioral Sciences, 19,* 4–14.

Haber, R. A. (1980). Different strokes for different folks: Jung's typology and structural experiences. *Group Organizational Studies, 5,* 113–122.

Herrmann, N. (1988). *The creative brain.* Lake Lure, NC: Brain Books.

Heus, M., & Pincus, A. (1986). *The creative generalist: A guide to social work practice.* Barneveld, WI: Micamar.

Huizinga, J. (1955). *Homo ludens.* Boston: Beacon Press.

Jones, M., Moore, M., & Snyder, R. (1988). *Inside organizations: Understanding the human dimension.* Beverly Hills, CA: Sage Publications.

Maier, H. (1979, March). *Play in the university classroom.* Paper presented at the Annual Program Meeting of the Council on Social Work Education, Boston.

March, J., & Olsen, J. (1979). *Ambiguity and choice in organizations.* Bergen, Norway: Universitetsforlaget.

Margolin, E. (1967). Work and play: Are they really opposites? *Elementary School Journal, 67*(7), 343–353.

Middleman, R. (1983). Role of perception and cognition in change. In A. Rosenblatt & D. Waldfogel (Eds.), *Handbook of clinical social work* (pp. 229–251). San Francisco: Jossey-Bass.

Middleman, R., & Goldberg, G. (1986). Maybe it's a priest or a lady with a tree on it, or is it a bumble bee?: Teaching group workers to see. In M. Parnes (Ed.), *Innovations in social group work* (pp. 29–41). New York: Haworth Press.

Middleman, R., & Rhodes, G. (1985). *Competent supervision.* Englewood Cliffs, NJ: Prentice-Hall.

Morgan, G. (1986). *Images of organization.* Beverly Hills, CA: Sage Publications.

Morgan, G. (1988). *Riding the waves of change.* San Francisco: Jossey-Bass.

Mutschler, E. (1989, May). *Computers in agency settings.* Paper presented at the Boysville Conference on Research Utilization, Wayne State University, School of Social Work, Detroit, MI.

Nagel, J. (1988). Can there be a unified theory for social work practice? *Social Work 33*, 369–370.

Ozick, C. (1987, September 27). God's work and ours. *New York Times Book Review*, p. 51.

Paulson, T. (1989). *Making humor work.* Los Altos, CA: Crisp Publications.

Pelikan, J. (1983). *Scholarship and its survival.* Princeton, NJ: Carnegie Foundation for the Advancement of Teaching.

Perkins, D. N. (1981). *The mind's best work.* Cambridge, MA: Harvard University Press.

Quinn, R. (1988). *Beyond rational management.* San Francisco: Jossey–Bass.

Rapoport, L. (1968). Creativity in social work. *Smith College Studies in Social Work, 38*, 139–161.

Rittel, H., & Webber, M. (1977). Dilemmas in a general theory of planning. In N. Gilbert & H. Specht (Eds.), *Planning for social welfare* (pp. 133–145). Englewood Cliffs, NJ: Prentice-Hall.

Schön, D. (1987). *Educating the reflective practitioner: Toward a new design for teaching and learning in the professions.* San Francisco: Jossey-Bass.

Siporin, M. (1988, March). Clinical social work as an art form. *Social Casework, 69*, 177–183.

Stein, M. (1983). Man as the creative transformer. [Audiotape.] Available from the Center for Creative Leadership, Greensboro, NC.

Thayer, B. (1988). Social work as a behaviorist views it: A reply to Nagel. *Social Work, 33*, 371–372.

Wheeler, B. (1978). *Creativity in social work: An educational experiment.* Unpublished doctoral dissertation, University of Utah.

Whitrow, G. T. (1973). *Einstein: The man and his achievement.* New York: Dover Publications.

Wilson, R. (1986). *Experiencing creativity.* New Brunswick, Canada: Transaction Books.

Zaltman, G. (1983). Knowledge disavowal in organizations. In T. Kilmann, K. Thomas, D. Slevin, R. Nath, & S. Jerrell (Eds.), *Producing useful knowledge for organizations* (pp. 373–394). New York: Praeger.

Index

Contributors

Editor/Senior Author

Harold H. Weissman, DSW, is Executive Officer of the Doctor of Social Welfare Program, Hunter College School of Social Work, City University of New York. He is the author or editor of eight other books on social welfare.

Authors

Gary R. Anderson, PhD, is Associate Professor, Hunter College School of Social Work, City University in New York. He is a child welfare consultant for the Catholic Guardian Society in Brooklyn. He is the author of the book *Children and AIDS: Challenge for Child Welfare* and coauthor of the book *Health Care Ethics: A Guide for Decision Makers.*

Frank Ayala, Jr., MA, MEd, is Acting Vice President for Student Affairs and Dean of Student Development at Incarnate Word College, San Antonio, Texas. He also is completing a doctorate in Higher Education with a curricular emphasis in social work at the University of California at Los Angeles.

Eleanor Mallach Bromberg, DSW, is Associate Professor, Hunter College School of Social Work, City University of New York, and Director of its post-master's program in advanced clinical social work. She is Director of the Intensive Case Management Project in New York, Chairperson of the New York State Task Force on Case Management, and has served for 6 years as Chair of the New York State Mental Health Services Council. She is coeditor of the books *Mental Health and Aging* and *Mental Health and Long-Term Physical Illness.*

Kay W. Davidson, DSW, CSW, is Associate Professor, Hunter College School of Social Work, City University of New York. She has been a practitioner and administrator of hospital social work services. She recently coedited the book *Social Work in Health Care: A Handbook for Practice.*

Irwin Epstein, PhD, is Professor, Hunter College of Social Work, City University of New York, and an evaluation research consultant to Boysville of Michigan, Clinton, and several other social agencies. He is coauthor of the books *Research Techniques for Program Planning, Monitoring and Evaluation* and *Research Techniques for Clinical Social Workers.*

285

Michael Fabricant, PhD, is Professor, Hunter College School of Social Work, City University of New York, and specializes in the areas of delinquency and homelessness. He is now at work on his fourth book.

Daniel J. Finnegan, PhD, is Assistant Professor, School of Social Welfare, Nelson A. Rockefeller College of Public Affairs and Policy, State University of New York at Albany. His teaching and research interests focus on the use of fiscal and programmatic data to affect the decision processes that determine the delivery of mental health and related social services.

Anthony J. Grasso, DSW, is Director of the Research and Training Institute, Boysville of Michigan, Clinton. He also is an instructor, School of Social Work, Wayne State University, Detroit. He has published several papers and currently is coediting a book on research utilization.

Burton Gummer, PhD, is Chair, Management Concentration, School of Social Welfare, Nelson A. Rockefeller College of Public Affairs and Policy, State University of New York at Albany. He has written a number of papers on the administration of social service organizations and is at work on a book on the politics of social administration. He is a regular contributor to the journal *Administration in Social Work.*

Ann Hartman, DSW, is Dean and Elizabeth Marting Treuhaft Professor, Smith College School for Social Work, Northampton, Massachusetts. Before assuming the deanship, she was on the faculty of the School of Social Work at the University of Michigan, where she taught in the areas of practice, policy, and human behavior. She also was the faculty director of the National Child Welfare Training Center. She was a founder and, for 10 years, a staff member of the Ann Arbor Center for the Family. Her publications include *Family-Centered Social Work Practice, A Handbook of Child Welfare,* and *Helping Families Beyond Placement.* She has remained in practice throughout her career and has worked in the fields of child welfare, family service, and community mental health.

Roberta Wells Imre, PhD, is Associate Professor, Social Work Department, Seton Hall University, South Orange, New Jersey. She also is Coordinator, Study Group for Philosophical Issues in Social Work. The group is sponsored by the School of Social Welfare, University of Kansas, Lawrence, and the Smith College School for Social Work, Northampton, Massachusetts.

Toba Schwaber Kerson, PhD, is Professor, Graduate School of Social Work and Social Research, Bryn Mawr College, Bryn Mawr, Pennsylvania. Her books include *Medical Social Work: The Pre-Professional Paradox* and *Social Work in Health Settings: Practice in Context.* She also is editor of a column in the NASW journal *Health and Social Work.*

Joan Laird, MS, is Associate Professor, Smith College School for Social Work, Northampton, Massachusetts, where she teaches family theory and practice. She taught at Eastern Michigan University, Ypsilanti, for 12 years and is a founder of the Ann Arbor Center for the Family. Currently interested in family myth, story, and ritual, she is coauthor of *Family-Centered Social Work Practice* and *A Handbook of Child Welfare.*

Mildred D. Mailick, DSW, is Professor, Hunter College School of Social Work, City University of New York. She has published several books and many articles on clinical and service delivery issues in health care.

Anthony N. Maluccio, DSW, is Professor, School of Social Work, The University of Connecticut, West Hartford. He has authored or coauthored a number of books on social work and child welfare, including most recently *No More Partings: An Examination of Children in Long-Term Foster Care.*

Jack Rothman, PhD, is Professor, School of Social Welfare, University of California at Los Angeles, and Director of the Research & Development Program, Center for Child & Family Policy Studies. He is the author of numerous books, including *Social R & D: Research and Development in the Human Services* and *Marketing Human Service Innovations.*

Rose Starr, DSW, is Associate Professor, Hunter College School of Social Work, City University of New York. As a member of the NASW New York City Chapter board of directors, she chairs an advisory committee on social work in the New York City Public Schools. She is coauthor of the book *Designing a Work-study Program: Where Social Service Employment Meets Professional Education.*

Paul H. Stuart, PhD, ACSW, is Associate Professor and Chair, Bachelor of Social Work Program, School of Social Work, University of Alabama, Tuscaloosa. He is the author of several books and papers on social welfare history and is a former president of the Social Welfare History Group.

Francis J. Turner, DSW, is on sabbatical leave as Visiting Researcher, Mandel School of Applied Social Sciences, Case Western Reserve University, Cleveland, Ohio. He is Chairman, School of Social Work, York University, Toronto. His most recent book is *Child Psychopathology.*

Dennis R. Young, PhD, is Director, Mandel Center for Nonprofit Oranizations, and Mandel Professor of Nonprofit Management at Case Western Reserve University, Cleveland, Ohio. His books on management and nonprofit organizations include, among others, *If Not For Profit, For What? A Behavioral Theory of the Nonprofit Sector Based on Entrepreneurship* and *Casebook of Management for Nonprofit Organizations.*